A Lifetime of Serving

By

H.T. Johnson

TABLE OF CONTENTS

	Page
Prologue	1
Childhood	5
Clemson	23
Air Force Academy	27
Early Years in the Air Force	43
Combat	59
After Combat	77
CENTCOM and Joint Staff	101
TRANSCOM	115
Civilian Life	147
Department of the Navy	167
Civilian Life Second Round	197
Life's Lessons	209
Epilogue	213
Closing	219
Appendix: Awards and Citations	221

PROLOGUE

This is a story about a blessed journey of a little boy from a farm in South Carolina and how he was able to serve his country and so many others throughout his life.

Life is filled with many opportunities to make a positive difference. Along Life's Journey, we are touched by many and do not always understand their impact on us and our impact on them. It is always reassuring to learn much later in our lives of our positive impacts on others. I was invited to visit with a group in my hometown of Aiken, SC. The resulting article shown below discusses the biases that many have about senior military officers – and then reveals the very positive compliments that reflect the true spirit of serving others.

    Augusta Chronicle
    Sunday, May 19, 1991
    Marty Jackson
    123 Pendleton

I was ready to be unimpressed.

Sure, Hansford T. Johnson is a local boy who has done well, done very well indeed.

And yes, he played a major role as the commander of the military organization that designed and executed an extraordinarily successful campaign in the Middle East.

He also was smart enough to marry an Augusta woman by the name of Linda Ann Whittle.

But I have dealt with the military before and I have just as many anecdotes about incompetence, arrogance, and egotism as I have impressive feats of heroism.

Our office received one fax after another about Gen. H. T. Johnson. I was, interested in our doing a story, mostly because of his Aiken ties. From a newspaper standpoint, any time you can show your readers how they are connected to what's happening, you jump at the opportunity.

I assigned a reporter to do the story, then went along on the assignment mostly out of curiosity.

We walked into the Houndslake Country Club lobby and there he was -- four stars lined up on each shoulder, row after row of ribbons mounted on his chest, not to mention an impressive assortment of metal adornments.

I was braced for an interview filled with military jargon, over rehearsed military public relations patter and military bovine scatology.

Gen. Johnson did not come through, however.

Instead, we were received by a gracious man who was proud and continues to be proud of his organization's contribution to the U.S.'s effort in the Middle East.

His organization, or organizations, as the case may be, is the U.S. Air Force's Military Airlift Command and the U.S. Transportation Command, the latter having been in operation only since October 1988.

The war with Iraq was its first major test and it passed with flying colors.

This is a man who was given the responsibility of getting every man and woman (more than half million) and everything they needed to do what had to be done (more than a billion pounds worth) in the Middle East over there and back.

Try as I might to lighten it, I wound up being impressed.

It wasn't just his success with the command. It's the way he tells the story. There was not an "I" in his description. It was all "We." And his eyes danced like a school boy's as he related the accomplishments.

His pride was tempered with the knowledge that somehow they had managed to violate Murphy's Law.

It is no fluke that Gen. Johnson wound up in this position.

After graduating from Aiken High School, he went to Clemson, then the U.S. Air Force Academy, Stanford University, University of Colorado and Dartmouth College, in addition to the Army Command and General Staff and National War Colleges.

Along the way he studied and/or earned degrees in thermodynamics, aerodynamics, aeronautics, business and management. He volunteered for duty in the Vietnam War, flying 423 combat missions. He relaxes by working with a home computer.

Very often in the military, as in many businesses, the Peter Principle determines who winds up in charge. In Gen. Hansford T. Johnson's case, however, it is the cream that rose to the top.

Over the years, Linda and I received many high honors. Without degrading any of them, being the Honored Guest at the Marine Corps Evening Parade was perhaps most impressive of all. As the acting Secretary of the Navy and Marine Corps, we were the honored Guests at the last Evening Parade of 2003. We were treated with utmost respect and highest honors during the reception. The Evening Parade is held in the Marine Barracks with a most impressive brick structure in the background. As the Parade begins, the lights highlight two Marines playing the Herald Trumpets at the very top of the structure. The Marine Bulldog Mascot is announced and paraded across the parade ground. Then, Linda and I were announced, the only lights are focused on us, and we were the center of attention as we "marched" across the Parade Field. Uncharacteristically, Linda was on my left arm so I could salute.

It was an awesome "march" and evening. These types of ceremonies truly set the military apart from other parts of society. Our lives were greatly enriched by our military service.

This "Lifetime of Serving" tries to capture my opportunities to serve so many along my life's journey.

CHILDHOOD

A remarkable story of how a young farm boy learned to love life, fell in love with a wonderful lady, and tried to serve his Nation and every life he touched with great distinction. It tells of a life filled with adventures, dedication, and an attitude of believing in possibilities.

On January 3, 1936, my parents Wade Hansford and Julia Terrell Johnson welcomed me into the world. I was born in our home in Aiken County, SC. I assume someone came to help with my birth. I do not remember too many details. I was the middle child, and although I was named Hansford Tillman, I was called Tillman. My sister, Julia Claire, was born on June 3, 1934 and my brother, Denton Terrell, was born on April 19, 1937.

Tillman, Dent, and Claire

The Johnson family history is sketchy. As I understood it, our Great Grandfather, Jonathan Hansford Johnson came to Aiken, South Carolina from Vermont after the Civil War – making him a "Carpet Bagger!" He married a southern lady, Lavinia Toole. (Later, I found out that my Great-Great-Grandfather John L. Johnson was born in South Carolina in 1804 and married a native South Carolinian, Rebecca Heath in 1842, so the family probably moved to South Carolina in the 1700s which means I am not a "Carpet Bagger!")

My Grandfather was Arthur Tillman Johnson and was known as "Till." My father was Wade Hansford Johnson after his two grandfathers and called: "Bubba", W. H., or Hansford. My mother called him

Hansford, but he disliked both of his given names. Thus, I received the favorite names of my grandfather and father – Hansford Tillman. As a youngster and until I entered the Air Force Academy, I was called Tillman. I did not have any childhood nicknames, but my name changed over time to fit the situation, finally becoming HT to everyone except my family.

My mother was Julia Terrell. Her mother was Isabelle Stewart. Our great grandmother was Julia Stewart or Mama Julia. She lived with us for a few years when I was very young. Mother had one brother, Stewart Denton Terrell. My brother got Uncle Dent's name: Denton Terrell Johnson. My sister got Mama Julia's name: Julia Claire Johnson. "Claire" came from our grandfather Clarence Denton Terrell. The Terrell family tree is well documented from the King of Crimea in 443 B.C. The Stewart Family traces its roots back to Mary, Queen of Scots. However, I have never seen proof of this lineage. As you can see, most of the names in our family were handed down through generations.

Interestingly, when our children were named, my mother asked my wife, Linda, where we got Richard, Elizabeth, and David. Her reply was, "We liked them!"

Since he died before I was born, I never got to know my grandfather Terrell. Later, Grandmother Terrell married John Tryon and moved to San Antonio, Texas. I was able to spend some precious time with them in San Antonio. They invited each of their grandchildren to visit with them after graduating from high school. These visits were very exciting and we learned much. After her husband died, Grandmother Terrell built a home across the highway from my parents. When I visited my parents, it was always great to visit with her.

Grandfather Johnson died when I was four years old. I was his first grandson. I am told that he would pick me up and take me all over with him. I remember him most from stories that others told me. They had lived at Johnson Crossroads where Uncle James lived. He had several large farms which were divided between the two sons. We lived in the home where Grandmother Nettie Hankinson Johnson grew up. Shortly before his death, Grandfather Johnson moved to Augusta, Georgia. He did not want Grandmother Johnson to live alone and purchased a large home and had boarders. When we visited her, we would get to know the boarders. They all treated us as their children.

Our Mother and Father grew up during World War I and the Depression. Our Father was born in 1905 near where we lived. His father owned and operated large farms, a large store, the Talatha Hawthorne Post Office, the telephone exchange, and a cotton gin. When the depression hit, his father owned many bales of cotton and other farm products that could not be sold. Our Father was in a high school boarding school. Against his parents' desires, he insisted that he leave school and help his family. After the Depression, they recovered very well. Although he was very smart, he was never was able to complete high school. He spent all of his adult life running the family farms.

Mother and Daddy

Our Mother was from Covington, Ga. Her father was a City Manager in several cities in Georgia. He was the City Manager in Decatur when our Mother entered Agnes Scott. Later, her father moved to Athens, GA and she transferred to the University of Georgia. Our Father hauled oranges from Florida during the winter, and he would stop in Oak Park, Ga. The local store manager would let him sleep on the counter of his store. He met our Mother at this store when she was teaching in Oak Park. Apparently, they fell in love, and he brought her home to meet his family.

When they first married, they farmed the Horne Place in Beech Island on Storm Branch Road. Our sister Claire was born at the Horne Place. After Claire was born, they moved to the Hankinson Place where our Grandmother was born. Dent and I were also born there.

Our Father taught us many wonderful practical lessons. Our Mother was a full time mother, our academic teacher, a substitute teacher, and community leader. Together, they were most wonderful parents.

Our family attended Springs Methodist Church. It was an old church with only one room -- the sanctuary. My mother and others fashioned some draperies to separate the sanctuary into temporary Sunday school rooms. We attended church regularly and I was raised in a home with Christian values and beliefs. I was baptized when I was around 12 years old. The church was very typical of a rural church; each year the church would have revival meetings. The preacher did not live in the local area, but would come regularly on Sundays. The Ministers would preach at more than one church. Often the regular preacher or a visiting preacher would eat at our home on Sunday after church. My mother was a very gracious hostess.

Our mother was a very good cook. I liked almost everything she prepared – except liver. She liked liver and onions and would prepare it for the family, but when she served liver to the family, my father and I got steak. We had other differences in taste in the family, my mother and I drank hot tea; my father, brother, and sister drank coffee. I never developed a taste for coffee and still do not drink it.

Mother also made the most wonderful fried chicken. I once made the mistake of telling Linda that Mother's fried chicken was better than hers -- I did not get fried chicken very often after my faux pas. My Mother also made my favorite dish then (and now) – sweet potato soufflé. When she made it, I had a habit of taking a dip of it with my finger before it was served. This led to something that I will never forget.

During the World War II days, Mother made lye soap. One day, I saw a pan that was "cooling," thought it was caramel candy, and took a finger full. As soon as I got it in my mouth, I knew that I had made a grievous error. Mother washed my mouth out and assured me that I would not die – but I wasn't so sure. She used the piece that I had sampled last, and I had to keep looking at it! I was more careful about what I sampled after that mistake.

I grew up during World War II, but we did not experience all of the difficulties of urban families during the war. Since our father was a farmer, rationing and shortage of items never affected us. We were able to get all of the gasoline we needed "for the tractors." We had a good supply of vegetables and meat from the farm. We received sugar from "moon shine" stills that the Sheriff raided. I'm not sure how my father got the sugar. I guess the sheriff shared the confiscated sugar with the community. We were not wealthy, but we never lacked for money. I was never paid by my father but always had money. At the end of each summer, we were given money to shop for school clothes and supplies. I never received a paycheck until I became a cadet at the Air Force Academy – and never felt deprived of anything. My childhood is filled with many wonderful memories.

Although we did not feel the shortages of World War II, I vividly remember the drives to collect metal, rubber, and paper for recycling into war materials. Our school and each of us were always involved in helping collect things. We, like all of rural America, supported the war effort in any way we could.

When I was in the sixth grade, we got our first telephone. There were eight parties on the line. There were different rings for each; however, only one party could use the phone at a time and all could listen to the other calls. I never recall listening in except to see if the line was open. Before we got a telephone, our nearest neighbor had a phone that was used to report forest fires. It could also be used for other things like emergencies. Earlier, my grandfather Johnson's store had included a switchboard. I do not know why it was discontinued.

TVs became available when I was in high school; however, we never had one until after I went to college. We did not miss having a TV. We were always very busy with many activities and work. It was always exciting to go a movie theater.

Everyone in the community had a large role in our lives; some were very special in my life. Our nearest neighbor was Ethel Owens Yonce. She was also the best and most influential teacher in the Talatha-Hawthorne elementary school. She took a "family-like" interest in all of us. Mother would occasionally substitute at our school and knew everything that went on at Talatha-Hawthorne. I had to be especially careful when Mother was teaching. One day when Mother was teaching, I was disciplined for some offense and required to walk up and down the hall a number of times. Since the classroom doors had glass panels, I would turn around just prior to passing my mother's door. I suspect Mother knew everything that I did in school.

In high school, a confirmed bachelor, John Eubanks, was involved in every aspect of our school and the city. He was a great teacher and friend to everyone. He taught math and several other subjects. Mr. Eubanks inspired me to study math and other technical areas.

Mrs. Bobo taught English and I believe, was my "homeroom" teacher. I seemed to have her for several years. She took an interest in my studies and me. We had great mutual respect for each other and became friends.

I do not remember a first date. We would do things in groups. We would swim in a local creek, picnic, attend sporting events, and occasionally see a movie – sometimes at a drive-in movie. I believe that a "first date" was probably with a friend, Olene Redd.

Again, I do not remember a "first kiss." In the South, a normal greeting was a hug and a kiss on the cheek. I do not remember kissing a girl on the lips until I met "the love of my life," Linda. I certainly have never kissed anyone else passionately – until after Linda's death and I met the second love of my life and wife, Ann.

I do not remember many embarrassing events in my childhood. We had an old gas pump in our yard. The gas would be pumped into a ten-gallon glass container and then drained into a vehicle. One night, I was trying out a new bee-bee gun and accidentally shot a hole in the glass container. Of course, it was easy to discover. I carved a piece of wood and glued it in the hole. I am confident that my father knew what had happened; however, he never mentioned it to me. When necessary, I would re-glue the wooden peg!

One day, several workers and I were starting a tractor parked in a shed, which contain a loft full of hay. Somehow, the tractor caught on fire. We threw so much dirt on the tractor that we got a lot in the fuel tank.

Somehow we put out the fire. We were very scared. Again, we were never questioned about the incident.

As a very young boy, some of our farm workers and I carried a truck of watermelons to "market" in Columbia. For some reason, I had all the money. In the middle of the night, I crawled into the truck cab to take a nap. When the others tried to find me, I was not in the truck. They panicked and were about to make the dreaded call to my father when I walked up. Apparently, I had somehow moved down several trucks and went to sleep in another truck. They were very happy to see me and not have to call my father! Needless to say, I did not get into any trouble.

My best friend was my father. As I was growing up my playmates were most often African American children whose parents worked with us or lived nearby. We also had friends from school; however, the rural environment made it more difficult to get together. At a very early age, I was perhaps more comfortable in being with adults than children my own age. The farm life did not allow much time to become involved in sports and other activities away from home.

Tillman and Daddy

The closest neighbor who was my age was Tom Mixon who lived a mile from us. We went to elementary school together. When we were in the sixth grade, he lost his father and sister in an accident. He and his mother moved away. When I went to high school, my best and lifelong friend was Tommy Griffin. He lived in Aiken and is a brilliant man. He became a medical doctor and had a wonderful practice. Our families have maintained a close friendship over the years

Our immediate family was very small, but we had many in our extended family. My mother had one brother, Dent, and he had only one son. Uncle Dent attended Georgia Tech and flew for the Navy prior to World War II. During the war, he flew the Flying Catalina (passenger plane that landed on the water) for Pan American World Airways. He continued to fly for Pan Am until he retired. We did not see him often. He was a hero of mine, and I was always disappointed not to know him better. Much later in life, when I attended graduate school at Stanford, he and his wife came to visit us, and we spent some time together in Santa Cruz, California. It was great to visit with them and hear some of his stories first hand. We always heard our Mother talk about her brother

Our father had a brother and two sisters. Uncle James lived at our Grandfather's "home place" and ran the store and cotton gin at "Johnson Crossroads," which was one mile from our home. Uncle James had one daughter, Virginia. Her mother divorced Uncle James, and we saw Virginia infrequently. Uncle James was our closest family and treated us well. His oldest sister, Aunt Nellie Colough lived in Batesburg, South Carolina. Aunt Nellie and Uncle Buford had a daughter, Nellie Kathryn who was several years older than us. We always enjoyed visiting in Batesburg, and we would often spend some time alone with Aunt Nellie. Nellie Kathryn met a young Dent Graham, who was a boarder in Grandmother Johnson's home. He served in World War II. When he came home Nellie Kathryn had another "boyfriend," but very quickly fell in love with Dent and married him. We were always most impressed by Dent and Nellie Kathryn and enjoyed their stories. We did not know our Father's youngest sister, Aunt Kathleen, as well as Aunt Nellie. I do not remember much about her early life. Aunt Kathleen married Gene Forester of Sumter, South Carolina. When we were older, the family would visit Aunt Kathleen in Sumter. They seemed much more affluent than our family and it was nice to visit the city.

Cousin Randolph and Myrtle Johnson lived about a mile from us. He was our father's first cousin. We would visit with them and were always afraid of the "haunted room" at the top of the stairs. None of us ever had the courage to go up to the haunted room. I suspect it was not haunted and they said it was because they did not want us to go "upstairs."

I never knew the exact relationships, but we had many extended family members in our area. Our nearest neighbors, the Yonce, Hankinson, Smith and Green families were distant relatives and very close friends. They took very good care of us.

As I mentioned earlier, "Miss" Ethel Owens Yonce (in the South, we called all of the Ladies "Miss" out of great respect) was my teacher, closest neighbor, and mentor. She had two children --- Murray Owens and Carol Owens. Murray was much older, and we treated him as an adult. Carol was 3 – 4 years older and like a big sister. Miss Ethel's husband, Mr. Grady Yonce was in the forestry service. During World War II, he was in the Army in Italy. We were very pleased and most impressed when he came home after the war. We were in awe of his stories of fighting in Europe.

Uncle Edgar Hankinson was my grandmother's brother. He and Aunt Katie lived ¾ of a mile from us in a very large pecan grove. It was always a treat to visit with them. They seemed to "have everything," and we thought that Aunt Katie was very sophisticated.

"Aunt" Blanche Smith and her family attended our church. We always "understood" that there was a kinship between "Aunt" Blanche and our father, but I do not know exactly what it was. Regardless, she was our "Aunt," attended the Springs Methodist Church, and took a very special interest in us. She had three children: Jewel, Sara, and Joe. Jewel was much older and an adult to us. Sara was a little older and like a big sister. She was always full of life and enjoyed everything that she did. I had utmost respect but also a special closeness to Sara. Joe was Dent's age, and we played together.

Many years later, we became very close to Sara Smith Toomey's family when we all lived in Columbus, Ohio. We had moved to a new city with two children and Linda was about 7-8 month pregnant with David. Sara and her family adopted us and helped all of us through a difficult time. As always, I was traveling a great deal, and Linda was particularly grateful to Sara and Jim Toomey. Sara was the perfect, well-organized mother with ten children, eventually.

"Aunt" Daisy Owens Green lived near "Miss" Ethel and was again "related", I believe, through Aunt Katie Hankinson. She was a widow and had three children, Dave, Steve, and Peggy, who were all older than us. Her mother ran a small store, which was the closest place to buy things. Of course, I liked going to "the store." Once when I was very young (2-3) and my mother could not find me, she reportedly found me sparsely clothed sitting on the bench in front of "the store."

Tillman

When I was very young, immature, and naïve: Steve Green called one evening and pretended to be a girl asking me for a date. I was excited until I realized it was a hoax. I suspect that my father knew about it.

Outside our family, my mentor was "Uncle" Jerome Williams. He lived near us. Jerome was an African American and much older than our father. He had in fact also been a mentor and friend as our father was growing up. He taught me how to treat everyone with great respect. At that time, he taught me to call African Americans "colored" people. The words have changed over time; however, the teachings I received from "Uncle" Jerome have held me in good stead. While I am confident that he and our father talked, neither ever betrayed a confidence or shortfall on my part. Once, we were desperate to find some eggs to dye for Easter. We found a "nest egg." On the way home, we dropped and broke the egg – and found it was rotten! I suspect that the eggs were not really ours. Jerome found some good eggs and ensured that we had dyed eggs for Easter.

We lived in a beautiful and stately farm home that had been our ancestors' home at some point. Some parts of the hand hewed foundation wooden beams had been put together with "pegs" before nails were used. We were very much connected to the outside. We always had "outside" dogs, cats, chickens and farm animals. Once, I was given three rabbits. We soon had more than we could handle and got rid of them. We also had a flock of three geese that multiplied. They were very loud and destructive and were soon moved to our pond a long way from our home. Our life on the farm was very good, but like all families, we did have some difficulties to deal with that made our family stronger and changed our lives in some good ways.

When my younger brother, Dent, was 4 years old in December 1941 (the Friday before the attack on Pearl Harbor), we were shocked when he contracted polio.

Dent had been sick with a fever for 2 to 3 days. Mother had to go to Aiken, and he begged her to let him go with her. When they returned home, Dent could not get out of the car. Mother raced him to the Aiken Hospital, and he next remembers being in the Quarantine room. When he came home, he was in a body cast. Mother talked the doctor into cutting the cast in half so that she could take him out each day. Each morning, Mother would unwrap the cast, take Dent out, and wrap him in hot wool cloth strips. Then, she would massage his arms and legs. The Doctors always said that if she had not done this, Dent would have remained paralyzed from the neck down. Mother's love made a tremendous difference in Dent's life.

Our father was in Savannah, GA when Mother took Dent to the hospital. When he stopped at the crossroad store, our Uncle James told him about Dent, and he immediately came to the hospital. Mother always thought that Dent caught polio from some sick monkeys at the County Fair. She had taken us to the Fair and the lady that had the monkeys told her that the monkeys were sick and would not be out that day. We begged Mother to get her to let us go back and see the monkeys, and this is where Mother thought Dent caught polio. This still may not be the place.

I vividly remember when the health officials posted a Quarantine sign on our home. Despite Mother's and the doctors' best efforts, Dent would be paralyzed from the waist down for his entire life. He still wears braces on both legs and walks with crutches. Fortunately, with a "motorized chair," he gained much more mobility. The March of Dimes was very helpful. Dent spent a great deal of time at the Polio Treatment Center in

Warms Springs, Georgia. During one of his visit, he met with President Franklin Delano Roosevelt. Dent enjoys a very active life with a son and two grandchildren. Dent and I shared the same bed and had the same activities. Polio could just as easily have afflicted me. (Interestingly, much later, I served on the National March of Dimes Board with Anna Eleanor Roosevelt – the President's granddaughter.)

As the oldest son and because of Dent's polio, I was more active in our farming activities. We lived on a dairy farm, had a much larger beef cattle farm five miles away, and a smaller hay farm six miles in the opposite direction. We grew cotton, corn, peanuts, hay, grass, watermelons, cantaloupes, and a few other plants. All of us were quite involved. Our mother grew many vegetables, kept the books, was very active in the community, would always be ready to step in and teach or care for others, and actively taught and took care of us.

Daddy was always trying new things. Our dairy herd was primarily Jersey and Guernsey and the beef herd was Hereford cows – all were small. Daddy purchased a much larger Brown Swiss bull to breed to the smaller cows to increase the size and productivity of the calves. I am not sure that he also realized that the calves would be much larger (110 pounds versus the normal of 75 – 80 pounds). As the calves began arriving, the cows needed help in having the calves. I became a "midwife" to the cows. I would take a bucket of warm soapy water and a ratchet device. When we got the calves feet out and head straight, we would attach the ratchet to the feet and slowly help the cow have the calf. I do not recall ever losing a calf. Once they were born, they were larger and more productive.

Daddy was always bringing things home. Once, he and one of our workers, Jesse Widner, picked up two pretty kittens along the road. Mother told them that they were skunks, and of course, Daddy didn't believe her until she got a book and found a picture of baby skunks. After he was convinced, I was told to kill them – the first one died without a struggle; the second one was able eject its foul smelling liquid before he died. Everyone scrambled for fresh air. I was given the honor of carrying them off and burying them.

Growing up on the farm, we were always early risers. Beginning before sunrise, we would work for several hours before breakfast. The early morning chores involved feeding the livestock and getting everything ready for the workers to begin their day. Mother would have a big breakfast for us before school. The biggest meal for the day was always lunch or "dinner" as we called it. In the early days, the farm bell would be rung at noontime and everyone went home for lunch. "Supper" would be after work was over and a lighter meal – perhaps even leftovers. After we were married and Linda observed these work routines, she said that if I decided to live on the farm, she would live in the city. Although I enjoyed the farm life, neither of us ever desired to return to the farm life.

As I was growing up, I always enjoyed learning how "to operate" things. At a very young age (6-7), my father and I were at a field being plowed. He asked if I wanted to drive the tractor home, and he would drive the tractor driver to his home. I had never driven anything, but I was confident that I could drive the tractor. I assume our father shared my confidence. He and the driver departed. I climbed into the tractor seat, placed it in gear, engaged the clutch, and proudly drove it home. As I arrived home, I realized that I did not know how to stop the tractor. It had a hand clutch, and I had always seen others push in the clutch on vehicles to stop them. I almost broke the clutch handle pushing it forward. I began going around in circles near the dairy. A short time later, the Dairy Man came out and pulled back on the clutch, and I stopped! Needless to say, I learned very quickly to do many things – amazingly, I was never injured or caused any damage to the vehicles.

During World War II, many German POWs were brought to camps in the United States. There was a POW Camp near our home in Aiken. The POWs would be brought to our farm to work in the fields. We had little understanding of the war or their backgrounds. Our mother treated the POWs very well. She would often provide additional food. Being used to butter, we were amazed that the POWs liked "lard" on their bread, which we only used for cooking. When one of the POWs was injured (I believe a cut), I was pleased by how our mother took care of him as she did any of us. We were impressed by their manners and seeming joy of being able to work in the fields.

After the war, our parents adopted a "displaced family" from Latvia. They lived in our home and worked in the dairy until they found a permanent home.

I do not recall being a prankster. I certainly found ways to "get my way" but do not remember any pranks. At the dinner table, we (mother, father, sister, brother, and I) would discuss many things. Everyone always had an opinion. I would "give the facts" and not argue. Everyone would disagree. At the next meal, I would bring the book that proved my point. As you can imagine, I really upset the others.

Having never overtly known fear, I was a very brave little boy. As with all youngsters, I sometimes would "show off." When I was very young, our father built a "40 foot silo." One night, I finally got enough courage to climb to the top. I was very proud and "fearless." Later, my sister had a group of school girl friends visiting from the city. To show off, I very quickly climbed to top of the silo. As I triumphantly grasped the top rung, I put my hand in a wasp's nest. Despite being stung and totally embarrassed, I am proud that I did not jump. Lessons are sometimes hard to learn.

High School Football

We lived 13 miles from the high school and rode school buses both ways. It was difficult to participate in after school activities and sports. To ensure that we could play football, a group of Aiken businessmen offered to take my schoolmate, James Key, and me home after practice. It was a 25-mile trip for them. James was very good. I played guard, tackle, and end. James and I were most grateful for the civic support for us, and they took fatherly pride in us. One year, I ran track. Because of the strenuous nature of running, our father would never let me run track again. Mother and Daddy knew the value of Scouts. He talked to a business friend who was the leader of the Scout Troop in Aiken. He was advised that it would be difficult for me to participate in all of the Scout activities and I would learn more in doing my other activities. Dent and I did receive and study "Boys Life" very carefully. This was one of the few disappointments about living so far from town.

When I was in high school, the Atomic Energy Commission built the large Savannah River Nuclear Plant near us. As we boarded the school bus on the day it was announced, the driver told us that they were going to build a "Boom" plant nearby. The plant area included our hay farm. To support the huge influx of people, we operated two farms, a large store, a service station, a trailer court, apartments, etc. I soon learned how to do many things. I was able to handle electrical wiring, lay and care for sewer pipes, pump gasoline, and act as the "butcher" on Sundays. I received many electrical "shocks" but was never hurt. My father treated me as a brother and a full partner from age nine on. I was most fortunate to have parents who taught me so much about living and doing.

As a youngster, I had not yet articulated the Quality principles. Later, I realized I had practiced them since my very early days under my father's tutelage. As a very young boy, my father treated me as a full partner in his large operations, always asking me how I wanted to do a particular operation, then telling me how he would do it, but always insisting I do it my way. As the operation progressed, I would slowly transition to his way with no encouragement or critiques.

This approach was to hold me in good stead in war, peace, and business situations. The people actually performing the work know more about their jobs that I ever would. My job as a leader was to listen, set the objectives, facilitate initiatives, empower, ensure accountability, and acknowledge the expected fantastic results.

Early in our courtship, Linda joined our family for a dinner. She was very impressed when I volunteered to clear the table and serve desert. Linda had very lofty ideas about my being most helpful. I served dessert to everyone else. When Linda saw that I had well served myself, she understood why I was so eager to clear the table and serve dessert. I still enjoy serving dessert – and my generous serving!

I was extremely fortunate not to suffer many injuries. Once as a 4–5 year old, I was carrying some Coca-Colas in bottles and pulling a wagon across a field. I fell, broke a Coke bottle, and managed to severely cut my left forearm. This was too much for Mother to handle – so she had to take me to a doctor who placed three stitches in a two inch cut. I have had a big scar ever since.

Once, I hurt my leg in football. I was told to stay in bed for a while. After one half day in bed, I got up and used crutches for an hour or so. Then, I just handled the pain and returned to normal activities. This is the only time in my life that I have stayed in bed for an illness or hurt.

Tillman in High School

I do not remember very many fights. After he contacted polio and began walking with crutches, my brother Dent developed very strong arms. If we were tussling and he caught me with his arms, he was much stronger, and I was in trouble. Of course, I could stay outside the range of his crutches and be very safe. A playmate who was my age, "Son," and I tussled a great deal and were very good friends. When we were working together as teenagers in the field one evening, Son was very upset about something and grabbed me from behind with the intent to hurt me. I managed to break free. We never had the same relationship after that. It was as if we were "just friendly playmates" before; and then, we became adults and he worked for us. It was a strange, but very abrupt change. I suspect that his father gave some guidance. We seemed to go our separate directions.

In high school, I joined the band and tried to learn to play the trombone for a year. I was not very good. Our family made me practice on the front porch – out of everyone's way. At the end of the year, Mr. Slaughter, the band director, suggested that I go out for football. This was the end of my high school musical career. At Clemson, I volunteered to join the Glee Club. This adventure did not last long – I could not carry a tune.

I do not recall having many (or any) long-term goals as a youngster other than wanting to attend Clemson College and become an engineer. I wanted to do well in school and be involved in many different activities. I did very well in school but do not recall having to work very hard. I was not a good athlete, but I was strong and determined. There were always many activities and opportunities to learn in our home and on the farm. Unfortunately, it was not easy to become involved in many activities in the city.

CLEMSON

It was always understood that I would attend Clemson College in engineering rather than agriculture. Although it was never discussed, I never remember any thoughts from Mother, Daddy, or me that I would return to the farm. I enrolled in Mechanical Engineering and Air Force ROTC. I did well in academics and ROTC. My poorest grade was in Mechanical Drawing during the semester that concentrated on "lettering." I did well in the actual drawing; however, my lettering was horrible!

The Clemson Methodist Church was very much a part of my life at Clemson. I ran track my freshman year. I was elected as the Vice President of our freshman and sophomore classes.

Until the spring semester of 1955, Clemson was an all men's school. During my last semester at Clemson, the first six ladies were admitted and lived off campus. I never saw any of these ladies. My social life was limited. I occasionally dated a high school classmate, Gail Sloan, at Furman in Greenville, SC. She came for a weekend and dance at Clemson. One evening at Furman, we saw Frank Selby shoot 100 points in a basketball game. Through the various church and other activities, I met several ladies but never dated them seriously.

One weekend, we visited Winthrop College for a church retreat. I had dated two ladies at Winthrop, Carolyn Corley, and Harriet Poore, but did not make any arrangements with either of them. My sister, Claire, was also a student at Winthrop and had warned me to decide which one I wanted to see. Of course, she was right! I managed to upset both of them.

In those days, Clemson was a military school and all freshmen and sophomores had to be a part of Army or Air Force ROTC. As soon as the class pictures were taken at the beginning of school, we all had our hair clipped off. This freshman picture is the last time that I remember having a full head of hair. Being in ROTC changed my career choice and my life.

Initially, I was a category "C" Air Force ROTC student and would be an engineer in the Air Force. As I began to be noticed in ROTC, an instructor asked if I still "walked in my sleep." I responded, "No!" I had checked the block on the pre-college physical profile which indicated that I had walked in my sleep. Apparently "walking in your sleep" was disqualifying for the military. The instructor said, "We have lost your physical profile. Please complete a new one that correctly reflects that you do not sleepwalk." I did so.

Tillman at Clemson

Later, I was asked to select an Air Force ROTC "flying option." We were taken to Donaldson Air Force Base in Greenville, SC, and I was given my first flight in an Air Force aircraft. It was in a C-119. Later, I got to fly in a T-33 jet trainer. I did not realize that I was under very strong consideration to be selected as the outstanding sophomore in Air Force ROTC and would only be selected if I were in the "flying options."

As I was going to Clemson, I told my father that I wanted to go to West Point. His political friends assured him that I would receive an appointment to West Point the next year. Nothing happened. The second year, the "friends" became more active on my behalf, and I received an appointment to Annapolis, and Senator Olin D. Johnston made a highly competitive nomination to the first class at the Air Force Academy. The Annapolis requirements allowed no missing teeth. When I reported that I had some teeth replaced, they responded that they would "waiver" that requirement. When I advised that I could not take the required Naval Academy test, they replied that since I was doing well in college the tests were not required.

To be selected for the Air Force Academy, one had to pass a flying physical. (This requirement was dropped after the first three classes.) I was sent to Shaw AFB in Sumter, SC for my flight physical. As I was taking my EKG, the operator was having a difficult time getting the system to work properly. In those days, there was also a big problem with body "static" interfering with the results. In a couple of weeks, I was notified that my EKG results were not proper and I should retake the test. Of course, the medical center could easily have decided not to call me back—and just disqualify me. I passed the test with no abnormalities.

As we were waiting to hear from the Air Force, my parents visited Clemson for the Mother's Day Parade. They and I were pleased that I was selected as the outstanding sophomore cadet in Air Force ROTC – the only sophomore recognized. Daddy suggested that I was doing very well at Clemson and probably should not accept an appointment to an academy. The following day, I received a telegram advising me that I had been selected to attend the Air Force Academy and had 48 hours to accept. When I called home, Mother was extremely happy, but I could not talk with my father. The next day, I still missed Daddy, but Mother told me he was bragging to everyone that I was going to the Academy – and was obviously supportive. My engineering advisor lamented, "You could have been a good engineer!" The ROTC advisor would not even discuss the decision saying, "You have no choice. This is a phenomenal opportunity!" When I wrote the Naval Academy that I had accepted an appointment at the Air Force Academy, they did not reply.

After I accepted the appointment to the Academy, I was offered a rather good Milliken Scholarship at Clemson. As I was leaving Clemson, I was told that I had been selected to be the Sergeant Major of the Clemson Cadet Corps –the highest position a junior could hold.

Under the "Rat" system at Clemson, each freshman was assigned to an upperclassman room. I was assigned to three juniors. We were required to clean the room, take laundry to the cleaners, return and fold laundry, lay out books for next day's classes from their schedules, and run errands. I was very fortunate to have three outstanding upperclassmen (Duffie Taylor, Clyde Poovey, and Bill Cockrell) that became mentors and close friends. The system instilled discipline and accountability. I never considered it "hazing" – but rather a game. I often smiled when "they" were most serious about correcting me! However, it prepared me well for the Air Force Academy. We were also required to learn many "facts" called "Freshmen Knowledge."

AIR FORCE ACADEMY

Once I accepted the Air Force Academy appointment, things moved very quickly. We reported for duty on July 11, 1955, so I only had a very short time to prepare for this new adventure.

It was awesome to arrive at Lowry Air Force Base in Denver, Colorado and become one of the initial 305 to enter the Air Force Academy. With no history, traditions, or baggage, the Academy leadership, faculty, staff, Air Training Officers (ATOs), and cadets very quickly built a tremendous institution. The initial 35 ATOs were our "upper-classmen," mentors, leaders and <u>became</u> our lifelong friends. With some encouragement, we very quickly developed the Honor Code: "We will not lie, cheat, or steal nor tolerate among us those who do" -- a simple but powerful code to live by. The obvious Air Force Academy mascot, the Falcon, had a lot of competition from the Tiger. The ATOs were all rated as pilots or navigators and came from all parts of the Air Force – approximately 1/3 were West Point, 1/3 Annapolis, and 1/3 ROTC graduates. They ensured that our Fourth Class year was most memorable.

General Harmon

LtGen Hubert Harmon played the leading role in establishing the Air Force Academy and became the Superintendent for the first year.

In his biography, "Hubert R. Harmon, Airman, Officer, Father of the Air Force Academy," Dr. Phillip S. Meilinger captures General Harmon's advice to us in his final talk with us:

"He offered advice based on his own long experience in uniform. He emphasized to his cadets the absolute importance of 'complete integrity, both internal and external. In this connection, I can think of no better advice than that of Shakespeare's Polonius to his son: "**This above all: to thine own self be true, and it must follow as night the day, thou canst not then be false to any man.**' Harmon stresses the important of loyalty, but cautioned that this was a two-way street. Too many thought that it only extended upwards, to superiors, but he emphasized that it must also flow downwards, to subordinates. A commander must take care of his personnel. If he did so, they would take care of him. He stressed the need to ensure an attention to detail in all work. As officers, they must always remember to take their duties seriously, but never themselves: 'Your reputation will be the sum total of what others think of you.' He concluded by advising his young men to choose very carefully whom they marry: 'A loyal wife with interests similar to her husband's can contribute enormously to success in life; the wrong wife can be a tremendous handicap.'"

General Harmon set the tone for the Academy and our lives!

General Harmon was a member of the famous 1915 class at West Point with General Dwight D. Eisenhower. President Eisenhower was unable to attend the Dedication on July 11, 1955. In September 1955, the President did visit the Academy. I vividly remember his visit and sitting behind him in the Cadet Chapel.

Wonderful Compliment

One ATO, Lt. John Englehart, was most concerned that when I smiled, I seemed to be "smirking" at him. He offered to get me kicked out of the Academy! I obviously bit my lip when I was around him. Today, when John Englehart sees me, he takes immense pride in his "Cadet Johnson." Later when I was selected as an Air Force Academy Distinguished Graduate in 2006, he sent a wonderful congratulatory letter:

March 8, 2006
San Antonio

Dear Sir:

Congratulations!

Today, the Superintendent's Formal Invitation arrived for the Annual Founder's Day Dinner & presentation of the Distinguished Graduate Award citing you as a recipient of this year's award.

As one of the few remaining, original 'greeters' on your first day at Lowry, I still see you in my mind's eye, dressed in blue coveralls, double timing here and there, and, as many of your classmates, looking for your misplaced Contrails. Now you must honestly recall that you did not start off well – being dubbed 'the old man' by your classmates (when really I believe that title should have gone to Mister Dean Wood), and significantly, when all the 59ers thought you were still carrying the Clemson Guide-On -- but you slowly, and carefully, wore down those pesky ATOs.

It is truly a shame that Linda could not have seen you in those days when you truly excelled and were on top of your game ... at the end of the mess table acting as the water corporal, reciting plebe knowledge so hesitatingly, and at inspections in ranks, caught with unshined and dusty shoes. Those were the days when you truly excelled in getting the attention of Caudell, Frederick, Sanders, Strain, Pedjoe, Cole, O'Malley & Englehart. It is quite obvious that Linda has done what the countless ATOs could not do!

Some of us, more than others, know how far you have come, and how successfully you 'have stayed the course' reflecting on those classmates who left active duty, even the service for civilian life. Looking in the rear view mirror, we ATOS might have done better and that is regretful. Yet, you with four stars mitigate that sadness greatly. When you take the D.G.A. in your hands the evening of April 7th, please know that your old upper class is truly happy for the splendid way you have represented the Academy, the USAF, yourself and your family in your career.

Ellen & I will not be in attendance physically, but we will be there in spirit. In that far off back corner of the O'Club, if you listen carefully, you may hear my resounding voice, "Mr. H. T. Johnson, Front and Center, Congratulations from ALL of your ATOs!"

Sincerely,
John R. Englehart
Major, USAF, Retired

One never knows when someone is trying to help. His concern with "what I was thinking when I was smiling" has confounded many people along the way. I guess it is unusual to consistently smile.

Having completed two years of engineering at Clemson, I did fairly well at the Academy. Many in our class had some previous college and all were very competitive. Many of us took accelerated and advanced courses. We would often complete the full normal academic course in six weeks and go on to higher levels. We could also take additional courses. Having studied Thermodynamics at Clemson, I asked to take an exam to validate the first Thermodynamic course. I became the first cadet to validate a course. With the accelerated and advanced courses, a very small number were able to qualify for a BS in Engineering Science. We were the only ones who graduated with majors.

As all of America, we were totally confident from our study of aeronautics and astronautics of our nation's technological superiority. We knew no other nation could come close to us in technology. We were totally shocked when the Soviets launched "Sputnik!" This changed our Nation's focus.

Again, I was not an athlete. I ran track as a freshman and participated in intramural sports. I am right handed, but I swing a bat left handed. I had never thought much about it until I was in a boxing class. On the first exam, we were required to only use our lead hand. Assuming, I was right handed, I used my left hand as lead. I received a 69 – the only failing grade that I ever received at the Academy. Later, I realized that I was a "south paw" and could "fight" either way. My equally inept opponents were confused when I would change stances throughout the matches. Later, I was "runner up" wing champion twice in my weight class. The instructor who gave me the "69" was a lifelong mentor. I could fly equally well with either hand. I played racket games with the racket in right hand; however, my back-hand (or left hand swing) was better.

Skiing was very popular at the Academy, and I skied a little during the first two years. I did not enjoy skiing and never got hooked. For a while, I dated Candy Taylor who came from a family of skiers. Her father had been a founding member of the "Ski Patrol" before World War II and became a part the Army Ski division. They had a cabin near the ski slopes. I would visit with them. When it was time to ski, we went in different directions – they to the expert slopes and I to the beginners slope! They were wonderful family who treated me as a member of the family.

During one of our first visits to Colorado Springs, we attended a football game with Colorado College. Since we had the evening free in Colorado Springs, I called a lady that I had met at Colorado College to ask for a date. She was not available but introduced me to a friend who agreed to bring a friend and meet us downtown. Roger Counts and I stood near the appointed corner. When the four of us saw each other, we were all most impressed. Roger's "date" was a beautiful cheerleader named Margaret Day and later became Mrs. Margaret Counts! We had a wonderful evening.

There was a very active social life at the Academy. The "First Ladies" of Denver brought their daughters out to be interviewed to be a part of our dancing classes and other social activities. The results were well guarded. We most wanted to know "if they had a car!" I dated a few ladies. During our sophomore summer, I met a young lady, Edie Lawrence, during a class trip to Kansas City. We dated infrequently for a couple of years.

Later that summer, I came home for the first time. After Mother met me at the airport, we stopped to see my sister, Claire, at the Augusta Library. While we were there, I met Linda, the First Lady of my life. Since the final uniforms were not available, we wore uniforms adapted from the Air Force. Shoulder boards and stripes were added to the "silver tans" to make a dashing summer uniform. Linda thought that I was a Navy Ensign and a "good catch." Little did she know that I was not available for another three years. A couple of days later, we had our first date. We saw the "Bus Stop" movie and later went to a "drive in." Linda's favorite was a milk shake, but since I only ordered lemonade, she also ordered lemonade. She claimed surprise when I kissed her on this first date. After the second date, she told her aunt that she was going to marry me; she did not tell me for several years. We began a courtship by mail. I understand that my letters were often ambiguous.

Young Linda Whittle

In the first read, they brought great excitement and later, on rereading, created some doubt. (I am sure that was unintentional on my part.) We dated anytime I was at home. Linda was either fearless or eager to please me. One night, I took her to an old graveyard at the church I had attended. It was back in the woods. We parked along the fence, climbed the fence, and went to a viewable grave. Many times, I had slid the marble top back and viewed the body from the 1920s, which was within two feet of the top. I must admit that it was a little eerie in the dark of night as we peered into the tomb with a flashlight. If Linda was afraid, she did not show it.

"Blurting out" the candid truth is not always wise. During the first Christmas that I dated Linda, I planned to leave two days after Christmas. She was very upset that the Academy required me to return so quickly. Being totally honest and candid, I told Linda that I was going to Kansas City to visit Edie Lawrence and would return to the Academy after the New Year. I am confident that she would have found out anyway – my blurting out the truth did not help!

During our visit to Maxwell Air Force Base during our junior summer, I had my first mixed drink at the Elite Café in Montgomery, Alabama.

Unfortunately, I did not come home during the junior or senior summers. The first summer, we were allowed to go to Europe and the next, the Far East -- in lieu of summer vacation. Prior to our trip to Europe, I wrote Kate Roosevelt, granddaughter of President Roosevelt and stepdaughter of Jock Whitney, US Ambassador to Great Britain, and asked to see her during our visit. She wrote a most gracious note saying that she would not be in London during our visit. (Many years later, I told this story to her half-sister and a fellow member of the National March of Dimes Board, Anna Eleanor Roosevelt. Anna said that Kate had never told her that she turned me down!) We dated the daughter of the First Secretary of the US Embassy and a college friend of hers. I dated the friend. We had a delightful time – but missed the more organized visits to the Parliament, etc. Many years later, "my date" attended an Air Force Academy event in Washington and reintroduced herself. Linda was eager to meet her. Of course, we had a delightful visit.

Berlin was divided into East and West Berlin, but the wall had not been constructed. We visited a most impressive cemetery in East Berlin. One evening, we visited the "Resi" a luxurious dance-hall in Berlin. Each of the 200 tables had a number, a telephone, and pneumatic tube encouraging communication among the visitors. There was a very large dance floor, an orchestra and "dancing water" shows. For the first time, I met my Senator, Strom Thurmond, who had moved to Aiken, our hometown. It was an exciting evening.

In Madrid during the trip to Europe, we met Hopalong Cassidy (William Boyd) and his wife at our hotel. Later, three of us attended the Matinee at the La Florida at 11:00 PM. Hopalong and his wife were there. I asked her to dance, and she graciously declined. Later, a young lady sang American songs with a southern accent. I asked her to join us for a drink. She was from the South of England and spent every break at our table. We discovered a "light" punch called Sangria! When we stood up, we realized that it was not really punch. It was a long night with an early departure for Paris. Needless to say, we had a most rewarding and educational trip to Europe.

During our senior summer, we were offered a three week tour of the Far East. We flew in a C-121 for a total of 91 hours stopping at Fairchild AFB in Washington, Eielson and Fairbanks in Alaska, Shemya in the

Aleutian Island, Tokyo and Okinawa in Japan, Taiwan, Hong Kong, Philippines, Guam, Wake Island, and Hawaii, It was a most exciting and quick tour. We were still very naive. When I followed the directions to the "men's room" in a Tokyo club, I walked into the "ladies' room." I quickly retreated and asked again – to be told to walk through the "ladies' room" to get to the "men's room." In Taiwan, I sat at the head table and every other table had to toast us. We were drinking rice wine in small shot glasses. "Kanpai" or "toast for health," which meant "bottoms up." We soon learned "swei bien" or "with ease and comfort," which meant "small sip." In the Philippines, we did some exotic cane dancing. In addition to the social activities, we learned much about our Air Forces in the Pacific area.

Sometime during my junior year, my love for Linda became overpowering, and I knew that she was to be the Lady of my life.

Linda finished high school a year after me -- and college a year before me. (I had gone to Clemson two years and then four years at the Academy.) After college, she asked if there were any job opportunities in Colorado Springs, I responded that I had not looked. Later, I asked if she would like to come to Colorado. She responded that she had agreed to run a branch library and could not leave. I suspect that her parents would not have let her come to Colorado anyway.

As the senior year progressed, we began thinking of graduation and marriage. I wrote Linda a long letter asking: "If someone proposed and were to give you a ring, what type would you like?" I provided a long description of the miniatures of our class rings and a little bit about a five-pronged solitary diamond. She replied, "If someone were to offer and should I decide to accept, I would like a miniature." Linda proudly wore the Air Force Academy miniature throughout her life.

At Christmas time, Mother, Dent, and Linda met me in Greenville, SC where I had gotten "space available" military flight. Linda and I sat in the back seat. As we embraced, she could feel the ring box in my "watch pocket." Neither of us mentioned it until we got home. On the longest night of the year, December 21, 1958, I then got down on my knee in front a fire in the living room and proposed to her. She very graciously accepted. The next morning when Mother woke her, Linda extended her hand to show my mother her ring. Mother said, "I have already seen it!" Linda was devastated. Mother was a little insensitive. We decided that she would come to Colorado for my graduation, and we would be married on the shortest night of the year, June 21, 1959, in her church in Augusta. Later, I showed her the china that I had purchased for her the previous summer in Hong Kong. I think Mother was disappointed that she liked it – and Mother would not get it. It is still our favorite china.

During our senior year, Lou Kingsland and I designed a commercial canard aircraft with the horizontal control surfaces up front and the engines on the rear fuselage. It was designed to carry 162 passengers on a range of 5,500 miles. The first aircraft, the "Wright Flyer"

Canard Aircraft designed by Lou Kingsland and HT Johnson; modeled by Roger Counts

had the horizontal stabilizer up front, but it was later considered unstable. At that time, the French Caravelle was the only aircraft with the engines mounted on the rear fuselage. Since the normal stability equations were for aircraft with the horizontal surfaces in the rear, we had to derive the proper equations. We did not yet have computers and had to perform the calculations with slide rules and hand calculators. I well remember that when the extensive "weight and balance" calculations were the same twice, we assumed them accurate. Roger Counts most graciously built a model from balsa wood. The Canard jet transport was featured in the May 13, 1959, Air Force Times.

The senior year went very quickly. Jerry Elsbernd and I rotated as the cadet commander of the Ninth Squadron. Our Air Officer

Commanding was Army Major Bill Patch. As graduation approached, we began to think about weddings, assignments, and social activities. Many of the Academy officer families volunteered to host young ladies during the graduation activities. We were most fortunate that Colonel and Mrs. Wilson invited Linda to stay with them for two weeks. They also invited Mother to join them for her one-week visit. Colonel Wilson was head of the Electrical Engineering Department – and later the Engineering Sciences Division. As the final days approached, some of us were taking an advanced course in supersonic aerodynamics. We were offered an oral exam to gain an exemption from the written final. I guess I did not do too well, and the instructor suggested that he would have to think about whether I needed to take the written final. About this time, we began getting invitations to participate in a practice for the graduation awards ceremony. I was most surprised when I was invited to participate. They did not tell us the recognition that we were to receive. I knew that I did not have the highest grades in any area. Later, I found out that I was selected as the Outstanding Graduate in Aeronautics and also Thermodynamics. When I told Mother, she said, "I already knew." (Since I had already been selected as the Outstanding Graduate in Aerodynamics, the supersonic aero instructor wisely did not require me take the written final!)

Cadet Hansford T. Johnson

The Academy life was competitive; however, the current measures of performance were not well established. When examining my "Cadet Records" many years later, I found that I had done better than I had realized in overall class standing.

Without any sense of music or timing and having a soft voice, I had difficulty "marching in step" with everyone else and did not have a strong "command voice." I suspect my military standings were not very high.

My overall, class standings were:
4th Class Year: 26/248 – 10.5%
3rd Class Year: 19/237 – 8.0%
2nd Class Year: 7/212 -- 3.3%
1st Class Year: 11/207 -- 5.3%
Overall Graduation Standing: 12/207 - 5.8%

During our time at the Academy, an Outstanding Cadet had to be in the top 5%. Now, it is the top 10%.

As we were about to become seniors at the Air Force Academy, Milton Caniff, the author of the favorite Steve Canyon comic strip sent the following words to our class:

GO AHEAD FIVE-NINE

It's good to have that sense of winning…of
Being first in something – ahead of everyone.
The pioneers who broke the hard land and saw
First green of plants that meant continued life – they knew it!
It was in the Air at Yorktown when British fifes played
The world turned upside down' – and liberty was born.
No mere winter wind brought such tingling of the
Spine to brothers Wright the fateful day at Kitty Hawk
Doolittle's people felt the forward drive into
History as their wheels cleared the Hornet's soggy deck.
Whatever travails lies ahead, there is a point of
Departure when past trails dim before the looming victory.

So it is with this star-marked group --- "Blazoned for
All time as the first class to scale the torture heights.
Eighteen six for the Army; forty-nine for Navy and
Fifty-nine for Air will always be numerals of beginnings.
You're not yet on the platform; bars fixed; commission
Gained, but you're locked on target --- with fuel gauge high.
No American will ever forget you… oddly assorted
Bodies that first day in 1955 --- Now forged into proud unity
Your last Academy review will be yet another starting
Point – because the air arm of tomorrow will be of your making.
This nation will lean upon your strength and vigor. It
Trained you well – Now willingly puts life into your hands…

Steve Canyon and Milton Caniff
First Dining-In
March 16, 1958

I trust we have been able to live up to Steve Canyon's expectations.

Love of My Life

I tell people that Linda and I had our honeymoon on the way from home from the Academy. My mother was with us and she was a very good chaperone. We did have a wonderful drive home. We stopped in San Antonio to visit my grandmother. Since we were spending an evening in New Orleans, I arranged for a tour of the nightspots. A newlywed couple accompanied us. The driver told dirty jokes, but no one could laugh and acknowledge knowing what he was talking about. We managed to hit all types of entertainment from New Orleans music, to girls dancing with barely any clothes, to cross dressing entertainers, and the most famous U.S. stripper, Lily St. Cyr. It was a memorable evening – especially since none of us had seen such shows before and we were all uncomfortable.

Johnson Wedding Party

All of the arrangements for the wedding were in place and we were married in the afternoon on June 21, 1959. Linda's father escorted her to the altar and presented her to me. My father was my Best Man. It was a wonderful wedding and reception with many relatives and friends attending. We were most proud as we departed to begin our wonderful lives together.

Linda and Tillman with Parents

Lt. and Mrs. Johnson beginning their life together

The first night of our honeymoon was in Greenwood, SC. Linda and I had a delightful honeymoon in the mountains of North Carolina in Cherokee and Gatlinburg. We saw a Cherokee play, "Unto These Hills," and just spent time together. We had a marvelous time getting to better know each other and begin our married life. On return, we stopped to visit one of Linda's friends in Athens, Georgia. She invited us to swim and told us where Linda could change. Fortunately I asked in a soft voice that the friend could not hear, "Where do you want me to change?" As soon as I said it, I realized that now that were married, we could change in the same room.

When we returned to Augusta on Saturday afternoon, we stayed in my sister, Claire's apartment. Linda suggested that we would go to church on Sunday and accept an invitation to lunch. I suggested that it would be neat to fix our first meal together. We went shopping for fresh vegetables, etc. On Sunday morning, we began cooking the lunch while we got ready for church. As we smelled a "sweet" odor, we realized that we had 'burned the string beans!' Since preparing our first lunch did not go well, we accepted an invitation to lunch. Linda became an outstanding gourmet cook.

We were soon off to pilot training in Bartow Air Base in Florida as young newlyweds.

EARLY YEARS IN THE AIR FORCE

During my early days, I always worked hard to properly prepare. I was a "good listener" and often would cut through the considerations and suggested the solution -- which turned out to be the "best" approach. Over time, I learned to lead others to these solutions rather than pronouncing them. I have always enjoyed life even during the "difficult moments." I tried to treat difficulties as a "game" to find good outcomes. This has always held me in good stead, but I must admit it sometimes bothers others who become very excited and wonder why I am smiling or at least not emotionally engaged.

Flying as a Forward Air Controller in the northern-most province of South Vietnam and in Laos, I learned much about myself in coming face to face with great danger and how to survive and flourish in the most hostile environments. I provided strong support for the troops, protected our attacking forces, was well decorated for my heroism, and was selected for early promotion on return to the U.S.

In leadership positions, I try to provide counsel through the other person's perspective. Only in the most stressful and time-sensitive situations would I show emotion. Most often, I share the "offender's" disappointment. It is a long lasting and very positive experience when I can lead someone to inwardly see the errors and understand the need to change without making it a "personal," degrading encounter.

In a very stressful command position, I had to personally "fire" six people individually and was surprised but pleased to receive "thank you" notes from four of them. Most people understand their shortcomings but can become very defensive when being criticized. However, when they reach the conclusions and solutions on their own, everyone maintains self-respect.

Married life

Linda and I began our phenomenal journey together in Winter Haven, Florida as I attended pilot training at nearby Bartow Air Base. We lived in a two-room apartment that was adjacent to a grapefruit grove. We had a large bedroom and a large room that included the kitchen, dining, and living areas. Not knowing any better, we thought we had a spacious living area. It was certainly bigger than our previous dorm rooms. The neighbors were very good to us.

One evening, we thought we heard someone outside one of the windows. As I went out the front door, the prowler ran into the grapefruit orchard. We were pleased that I had not gone out the back door and confronted the prowler. We never had any other problems.

One night soon after we were married, I woke Linda up and told her to "sit up!" I then directed her to put her back against the head of the bed. After wondering what kind of guy she had married, she squirmed to put her back against the head of the bed. She then asked, "Why do you want me to do this?" I quickly responded, "So you will not fall out of bed!" Before she could ask any more questions, she heard me snoring.

During Basic Pilot Training in Laredo Texas, I had recurring dreams of "backing up" in a car and not being able to see. One afternoon as I was taking a quick nap on the bed, this dream came. Since I could not see behind me, I rolled over to clear the rear window. I hit the wooden Venetian blinds and broke several slats. Hearing the loud noise, Linda ran in and asked what happened. I nonchalantly replied, "I was backing up and could not see!" I know Linda was pleased not to have been in the bed when "I cleared the rear window."

I do not recall any other such dramatic dreams. However, I have been told that I talk in my sleep.

During our primary pilot training at Bartow, the Base Doctor would have lunch with us and often tell us which wife had been to visit him and was expecting. It sometimes destroyed the bride's telling us when we came home. It also ensured that there were no secrets. Many of the young brides became pregnant at the Primary Training Base and gave birth at the Basic Pilot Training Base. We were fortunate to be at Bartow and then Laredo with Joanne and Jerry Elsbernd. Linda and Joanne were very close in their pregnancies and were of great help to each other. After Joanne delivered Curt, the doctors said, "Why don't you walk back to your room!" and she did. Linda was not so brave when Richard arrived. As our "first borns" arrived in Laredo, no mother or family member came to help. Their responsibilities were re-doubled when the doctors would tell the wives that if they did not get up and give us a good breakfast, we might "crash and burn." The new mothers learned "the old fashioned way" – by doing it. All of them were magnificent.

France

Enroute to our first operational assignment, I attended Survival School at Stead AFB in Reno, Nevada. During a night evasion exercise, we had to cross the Little Truckee River. As we entered the water along a fence line, we met another group which included Bill Posey. In our brief discussion, we found that he was a 1959 graduate of the Naval Academy, and we were going to the same 41st Squadron at Evreux, France. We became instant friends. The next evening, we joined each other at a Reno night club to meet his favorite singer, Ann Margaret. I was most impressed when she came to visit us at our table. (Many years later as the acting Secretary of the Navy, I attended the Correspondent's Ball along with President Bush and a thousand or so others. During the ball, Ann Margaret was honored for her tremendous contributions to the USO. I visited with her and "reminded" her of our earlier meeting. She also most graciously "remembered" our earlier meeting. We had our picture taken, and Bill Posey was most grateful to receive a copy.) It is indeed a small world.

Bill and Virginia Posey were among our best friends. Our children arrived near the same times, and our families are still very close.

We were scheduled to fly from McGuire AFB, NJ to Orly Field in Paris on an Air Force C-118. We decided to travel from South Carolina to Trenton, NJ by train. Being very sophisticated, we checked our baggage to Trenton, NJ. On arrival the evening before our departure, we inquired about our baggage and received the reply, "Oh, the baggage car stops in

Washington, DC. Your baggage will arrive early tomorrow!" The next day, I hurried to the train station, found the bags, and we had plenty of time to board the plane. The crew was very kind to give us an extra seat and a cardboard box bassinette for Richard. It was a long flight. We were most pleased to be met at Orly Field by a future neighbor and friends, Lee and Joanne Pratt.

Being totally naïve, we had assumed that government quarters in France would be furnished. As we were on leave waiting to fly to France, we found that not only were the quarters not furnished but it was difficult to find affordable furniture in France. We received permission for a second "shipment" from Augusta, Georgia, and we purchased the minimum furniture. Knowing that Europe used 220 volt electricity rather than the 110 volts in the United States, we purchased a 220 volt washer/dryer. Unfortunately, I did not realize the difference in European 220 and US 220 volts. US 220 has three wires: two 110 volts and a ground. European has two wires a 220 volt and a ground. After many headaches, we were able to connect our 220 volt washer/dryer to European 220 through two transformers. This worked OK – except when we plugged the transformer in backwards. Then, a short occurred. With plenty of "fuse wire," I could just rewire the "fuse!"

We were fortunate to visit Copenhagen, Denmark and select some beautiful teak furniture that we still proudly use.

Unfortunately, we had a three week wait for quarters. We were assigned a room in the Normandy Hotel, which had the very best restaurant in Evreux. The rooms were very cold and not very good. Linda and Richard had a difficult introduction to France. The hotel turned the heat on for a couple of hours each evening -- when it was needed all day. We were fortunate to buy and pick up a new car in Paris. Linda was not too impressed by Paris traffic. She and the other ladies would drive to the outskirts and ride the Metro all over Paris. I do not believe she ever drove in Paris – except when the Metro was on strike.

Evreux, France

My mother's family tree is traced back to 443 BC and the King of Crimea. (Antenor, King of Cimmerians, inhabiting the shores of the Azof, now known as the Crimea, lived in 443 BC). One of the ancestors was Fulk de Tirel, Seigneur of Guernanville, Dean of Evreux, France who married Orieda, daughter of Richard I, third Duke of Normandy in the 900s. Our daughter, Beth, was born in Evreux in 1962 and brought the family tree back to Evreux. Soon after Beth's arrival, my mother and father came to visit us.

All of us enjoyed living in France and traveling around Europe. My father had never flown; however, when his first granddaughter arrived, he and Mother flew over for a most memorable visit. The four of us were able to visit, France, Germany, Holland, Belgium, and England. Mother and Daddy learned much on their first visit outside of America.

Richard and Beth became very close to the other children young children in our neighborhood. They were especially close to our next door neighbors, Linda and Lida Foncerada, and the Pratt children. They also visited with Lisa and Emilee Posey. Richard began French school when he was three years old. He did not talk about his school activities.

Linda and I enjoyed living in France and traveling around Europe. Our weekly cleaning lady and her husband would move in to keep the children when we were traveling. We knew the kids enjoyed her when they would cry when we returned and their hostess left.

Operations

Our unit provided the only C-130s stationed in Europe and supported all of Europe, Africa, and East to India. We flew a wide range of missions from carrying and dropping cargo and paratroopers. We also provided a wide variety of support missions to the military and other activities in our area. When we needed additional support, other C-130s would come from the US.

The Belgian Congo achieved Independence on the Fourth of July 1960. There were many resulting conflicts, and our C-130 units at Evreux, France were very busy supporting the UN Forces. When we arrived in October 1960, most of the conflicts in the Congo were over, but we still provided many support flights.

As an eager young aircraft commander on a flight to the Congo, I was impatient to get our aircraft refueled quickly during a stop in Kano, Nigeria. When the refueling truck ran out of fuel, we still needed more. To encourage a quick trip to the fuel farm and return, I asked to ride with the driver. As we drove far outside of town, the driver developed a fascination with my Air Force Academy ring. Even I fanaticized that he could easily chop off my finger, take the ring, and leave me along the roadside to be devoured. I am not sure that I was ever so insecure. I quickly established that he knew of the Sears Catalog and suggested that he could order a similar ring from Sears. The driver filled his truck, returned, and refueled our aircraft. I was most relieved to safely return and depart Kano. I was never so brave again.

My most interesting flight to the Congo involved carrying Indian Gurkha troops from Cairo, Egypt to Kamina Air Base in the Congo. As we refueled in Khartoum, Sudan, we were told that the US government had not been paying our fuel bills, and we would be detained until they were paid. They put us up in the best hotel and hosted us on some very exciting tours. The next day, we were allowed to leave and continue to Kamina.

We were required to stay at Kamina for a couple of days while the US State Department decided how we should best return to France. We were hosted by the Indian Officers who commanded the Gurkha troops. These Indian Officers knew more American military history than we did. They also gave us a helicopter flight deep into the jungle to visit the most beautiful waterfall that I have ever seen. As we arrived, I was most taken by seeing a small Gurkha soldier standing guard on top of giant ant hill much taller than the soldier. Our visit was soon ended with the decision to return through Nigeria.

On a subsequent return from the Congo, we were given an emergency night flight from Lagos, Nigeria to Mogadishu, Somalia with a refueling stop in Entebbe, Uganda. We were assured that the flight was properly cleared and approved. I had flown through Entebbe before and was quite comfortable. As we approached Entebbe around midnight, we were unable to contact the flight controller in the tower. Finally, the young man charged with spending the night in the tower responded and told us the field was closed. We had no other good alternatives. By the time we arrived, the field was open, and we were allowed to refuel and go on – after a good lecture from the air field bosses. We flew on to Mogadishu, circled the tower, and landed uneventfully on a strip lighted by kerosene flares. After our "crew rest," we came back to the field and realized that the "tall" tower that we had circled the night before was really a small building on top of a high hill! This was indeed an exciting and dangerous flight.

Soon after joining the 41st Troop Carrier Squadron, I was asked to be the Ground Training Officer. Many of my friends recommended against taking the position. A short time later, I became the Squadron Administrative Officer working directly for the Commander. In this position, I learned and contributed enormously to the Squadron. I was told that I could have a crew as soon as I could find a copilot that I out ranked. Many friends soon saw the value of stepping forwarding and serving.

Early, I learned to make and accept consequences of decisions. As a young Lt., I was serving as the Airdrome Officer when an aircraft blew a tire on the runway. Another aircraft needed to depart down-wind on the remaining runway. I approved the departure. A short time later the "big" Major who was in charge of the airdrome came running in to the control area and demanded. "Who authorized the departure?" I quickly responded "I did!" We had a nice discussion without any criticism. This "take charge" experience has served me well of over the years

During the support of Iran during an earthquake, I was not picked to support the mission. When I asked why, the Commander told me I could not go to Iran as long as Linda was in the hospital with pneumonia. I called her doctor, and he indicated she would be released shortly. I went directly to the hospital, picked her up, "farmed" out the children, and went to support the Iranians. It was probably best that I left – I was not very popular at home!

During 1961, our squadron supported Pakistan in resupplying the outposts in "their" part of Kashmir. We flew from Peshawar, Pakistan near the famous Khyber Pass into Afghanistan. We initially stayed in the Dean Hotel in Peshawar. This is the hotel that Gary Powers stayed the night prior to his ill-fated U-2 flight over the Soviet Union when he was shot down. It was so hot that we could not sleep. The only cool air came from the overhead fans. Someone suggested that we would be cooler if we went to bed naked with a wet towel over us. This worked well until all of the dampness evaporated. It was decided that we could not get the proper rest and fly while staying in the Dean Hotel. We were moved to an air conditioned gymnasium at a security site nearby.

The Kashmir terrain was very rugged and dangerous. We had to plan our turns very carefully. Rather than turning around in a boxed canyon, Captain Jack Schmidt decided that he would climb a little and fly through a saddle back. He did not know the height of the saddleback and the climb rate of the aircraft. Reportedly as he approached the saddleback, the African American engineer sitting between the pilots turned "white" as they barely cleared the ground. Needless to say, we learned a lot very quickly.

Ironically during the next year as we were supporting the Indians in "their" part of Kashmir against the Chinese, one day there were twice the proper numbers of aircraft call signs on the Division radio frequency. We quickly realized a sister squadron was supporting Pakistan in "their" part of Kashmir! The group in Pakistan got off the frequency very quickly!

<u>Indian Airlift</u>

In the fall of 1962, the Chinese attacked India. The 317th Trooper Carrier Wing was sent to India to provide airlift support to India. Our squadron was sent in December, and all except one crew were in New Delhi, India at Christmas. As units began to go to India, I was on a mission in the Middle East. When I returned to Evreux, I was told we would go to India immediately. Each day, I had a different departure date for Linda. She searched downtown Evreux to find a Christmas tree. We continued to delay our early celebration of Christmas. Finally, we had our early Christmas, and I departed a few days later. On Christmas Day, the one remaining crew and all of the families tried to have the best possible Christmas. The rest of us who were in India visited Agra and the Taj Mahal on Christmas Day. Our Christmas was better than our families' Christmas.

Our missions were flown into Leh, Ladak in Kashmir. The Leh airfield was made of the same Pierced Steel Planking (PSP) used in World War II, had tremendous slope, and was at 11,000 feet elevation. We always landed uphill and departed downhill. A friend tried to land downhill once. As fast as he descended, the runway was lower – he never touched down. This area was very much like Tibet. On the Fourth of July, we flew Ambassador and Mrs. Kenneth Galbraith to Leh. We spent much of the day with them visiting the City, temples, and our operations. That evening, we joined them at the Fourth of July party at the Embassy in New Dehli.

Lieutenant Colonel Ralph Bullock, our squadron commander, had some scary times while flying as an Instructor Pilot observer on two flights. One crew was testing some Indian cargo parachutes in the Leh area by dropping bags of flour. Through a variety of malfunctions, the bags of flour landed off the drop zone and hit some Russian-made Indian helicopters. A day or so later, Ralph was on board the first aircraft to land at the Leh airfield. Approximately 1,000 feet down the runway there was a 5 to 10 inch transition in the surface. There was a concrete ramp to smooth the transition. As this aircraft approached the "transition," the nose wheel strut was fully depressed. There was nothing to cushion the sudden jolt. Consequently, the nose wheel strut broke and hit the bottom of aircraft. It could not be moved. Indian troops were loaded and moved towards the rear until the nose wheel came off the ground; then, a tractor towed the aircraft from the runway. Other aircraft could now land.

The operations continued, and several days later, the incident aircraft was repaired. As Ralph was departing on another aircraft on the same day, the second aircraft "over rotated" and crushed the ramp. The aircraft had a load of troops and could not be pressurized. The navigator decided to follow the Indus River through the mountains at a lower level. Somehow the crew missed a turn in the Indus River and flew into a box canyon. Faced with this challenge, the crew had no alternative except to climb to 28,000 feet and go over the mountains. The crew had supplemental oxygen; however, the troops did not. Fortunately, most of the Indian troops had been operating at extremely high altitudes in the passes to China. Only one person "passed out" and no one was hurt. The day after these last two incidents, it was announced that Ralph had been promoted to Colonel. This was an interesting week for Ralph and all of us.

As a newly qualified Instructor Pilot, I had my copilot flying the aircraft on an almost catastrophic airdrop mission near Leh, Ladak in Kashmir. The aircraft was configured with rollers on the floor, bundles with parachutes, and a nylon gate, which held the bundles. The procedure was to lower the aircraft nose so the load would move slightly forward. The loadmasters would pull two ropes which would release the gate. The pilot would raise the nose slightly to start the load out of the aircraft. The pilot must then lower the nose to counteract the center of gravity changes as the load leaves the aircraft. This worked well. On this day, the copilot was flying and was out of synchronization. As the load began to leave the aircraft, he pulled the nose up. We very quickly got into a most dangerous nose high condition. We pushed forward on the yoke and recovered. The two loadmasters were thrown around in the cargo compartment. One was thrown to the opposite side and grabbed on to the side. The other was actually on the roller rapidly following the load out of the aircraft. Fortunately, he was able to grab the rollers and stop. This was a very scary flight for me -- and even worse for the loadmasters. Fortunately, we avoided a catastrophe.

On another mission some distance from Leh, Ladak in Kashmir, we were dropping (free fall) fence posts on a drop zone at 14,000 feet elevation. We were flying at around 16,000 feet. (Oxygen is a must above 13,000.) As the load began to leave the aircraft, some fence posts lodged on the side of the aircraft and the load could not exit the aircraft. Also, we could not close the ramp. We could not return home with the ramp open. Other pilots in area suggested that we land the aircraft at the Leh airfield with the ramp down. Finally, I decided to go into the back of the aircraft and help the loadmasters -- with no oxygen. Our adrenaline strength allowed us to throw some of posts over the ramp and get the door closed. After the crisis was over, we realized that we did not have a full servicing of oxygen and probably had not done everything exactly right, but our actions were most heroic. We (I) could have been decorated or disciplined! The return was uneventful. The Commander, Colonel Richardson, met us. He and I discussed the mission, and he put his arm around me, gave me a hug, and said, "Glad to have you back!" I was pleased not to be disciplined or decorated.

We had three 30-day tours in India. During the first tour, we stayed in a downtown New Delhi hotel. During, the next two tours, we stayed in the Maharajah of Kotah House in New Delhi, a government guesthouse. We decided that we wanted to have a party. To serve alcohol, we had to obtain an Indian alcohol license. I visited the agency that gave the licenses. It was very hot and overhead fans provided the only circulation. The agency used very thin paper and joined them together with straight pins. As I patiently waited to get our license, I watched the papers move around the table. The fans were "re-filing everything." We obtained our alcohol license and had a great party. It was always an experience to deal with the Indian agencies.

Leaving France

President DeGaulle requested that all of the US troops leave France. Our units moved to Lockbourne AFB in Columbus, Ohio in 1964. Since Linda was expecting our son, David in April, we came home early to be part of the advanced party. The move went well. David arrived on time. My "cousin", Sara Toomey, was like a Mother to Linda and a Grandmother to our children. We prepared for the arrival of the remainder of the wing. Before the wing arrived, I needed to fly four hours a month to earn my monthly flight pay. Somehow, I arranged to fly with a B-47 unit at Lockbourne. For the B-47 crew of four, there are four seats. There is also room for an instructor to stand between the pilots. For twelve hours, I stood or laid in the alley between the crew. It was an exciting flight. I was pleased to return to the C-130.

Our unit including me, rotated back to Evreux on temporary duty for a year or more. My 60 day rotation was not bad at all until we were delayed a few very long days at the end. You can always prepare for the expected; however, extensions are very difficult. Many years later as Commander of Military Airlift Command, I would learn much about the bad parts of extension as some reserve units were told they would be released at a certain time during Desert Shield only to be extended by a local commander. Remembering my experience, I reversed some of these extensions.

The next year, I attended Squadron Officers School at Maxwell AFB, AL enroute to graduate school.

Stanford

After graduating from the Academy, two departments offered me opportunities to return to graduate school -- first, in Psychology and then in English. I did not particularly want to study either area and showed no interest. The Aerodynamic and Thermodynamic Departments had been merged into the Aeronautics Department. Having been the outstanding graduate in Aerodynamic and Thermodynamics, I thought I would be a natural to study these areas and join the Aero Department. My letters to the Aeronautics Department went unanswered. "There were plenty of well qualified engineers in the Air Force, and they saw no need to send anyone to graduate school."

By this time, Colonel James Wilson, Linda's host at graduation, was head of all of the Engineering Sciences. After writing Colonel Wilson, the Aeronautics Department most graciously asked to send me to graduate school and become a part of the Department. They suggested that I consider attending, California Institute of Technology, Michigan, Massachusetts Institute of Technology, and Princeton. I responded that I would like to attend Stanford. Everyone agreed, and we were off to California.

Being young and proud, I knew that "I could do anything!" The challenges of attending the "best school in the Nation" after not being in an academic environment for eight years would make me work very hard. I did well in everything except differential equations. "Kidding" me the Aero Graduate School Secretary, said, "We let you in because Colonel Bullock said you were a good pilot!" I suspect that they were eager to look at a graduate of the Air Force Academy. They treated me very well.

During this 1965 - 1966 time period, there were a lot of anti-Vietnam protests around the country. Our friends from the University of California at Berkeley would come to Stanford on the weekend to get away from the protesst there. While we were there, we did not have many protests at Stanford. I recall a scheduled protest that Stokeley Carmichael was supposed to attend. He was detained by the New York draft board. The protest continued in a carnival like atmosphere. The most active area was a "come paint your friend" booth. The faces were most humorous. David Harris, the President of the student body, had long hair and a beard and became a hero when some students forcefully shaved his head and left his beard. David married Joan Baez who was quite an activist during that time period.

During some conversations with others, Linda overheard me talking about the need to go to Vietnam before going to the Air Force Academy. Her mother wrote a letter indicating that they understood why I would need to go to Vietnam. Although we had not discussed it, Linda had obviously written her mother. I told Linda "her mother told me to go." After the letter, we discussed it and agreed that I should go. The Academy gave me a one-year deferment in my report date. Since there was a great deal of training involved I asked Stanford to allow me to graduate two quarters (six months) early. I would have sufficient hours but would not have taken a couple of required courses. The Stanford Aeronautics and Astronautics Department waived the two required courses and let me graduate early. Stanford conferred an M.S. in Aeronautics and Astronautics in January 6, 1967.

<u>Rich and Beth schools</u>

All was set, and we would leave in December 1966. Linda and the children stayed in Augusta, GA while I was in Vietnam. Richard was in the first grade, was already reading, and liked his school in California. As a lure to move, Linda told him that he could get a library card in Augusta, Georgia. Beth had attended the Stanford Psychology Department Bing Pre-School and was ready to enter kindergarten. To ensure we had Christmas gifts for the children, we ordered our gifts from Sears in Atlanta to ensure delivery and were all ready to leave when Sears notified us that the order would be filled in Los Angeles. We were sure that the gifts would not arrive in time. When we arrived in Augusta, the Sears store most graciously allowed us to buy new gifts and return them if the shipment arrived. Of course, we had two sets of gifts and returned one set.

A short time before Linda was to come to Colorado for my graduation and our subsequent marriage, she developed symptoms that were diagnosed as "lupus." Initially, she had 'red splotches' on her face. I cannot imagine her pain and anxiety. To make things worse, she could not land in Colorado Springs due to weather and was bused down from Denver. Her lupus did not detract from our immense love for each other. Pregnancies have a depressing effect on Lupus. Linda became pregnant soon after we were married and all the symptoms went away.

As I was preparing to go to Vietnam, David was three years old. We left Stanford in mid-December 1966, drove to Augusta, Georgia, found a home, and celebrated Christmas. Linda developed bronchitis during all of the turmoil. I was gone most of the time for various training courses. When I left for Vietnam in April 1967, Linda was beginning to have increasing symptoms that the Lupus was returning with vengeance. She received care from Fort Gordon Army Hospital. Several times, they lost her charts. I suspect that the anxiety of having me in combat made everything more difficult. In December 1967, we had a wonderful R&R in Hawaii. When she returned, her father was diagnosed with lung cancer with little hope of survival. After losing her father in March 1968, her mother died 13 days later with a heart attack; it was the first night she had been alone after losing her husband. All of this stress was a tremendous drain on Linda's systems.

On the humorous side of living in Augusta, Richard walked to school. One day on the way home, Richard stopped by the "corner gas station/store" and bought a cigar. When questioned by the storekeeper, Richard said his grandfather smoked, and it was for him. Before Richard could walk home, the storekeeper called Linda. Richard showed off his cigar. His mother told him that he could smoke it but would have to smoke all of it. He proudly lit the cigar and continued smoking until he got sick. That experience seemed to cure any desire to smoke.

Later, she received extremely good care at the Air Force Academy Hospital. Tremendous stresses returned when David was diagnosed with diabetes. Her health was pretty good until I assumed command of the 22nd Bomb Wing at March Field, California. She had some kidney problems at March.

When we moved to San Antonio in 1992, she had some problems. I insensitively attributed them to the stress of the transition. The doctors finally did a kidney biopsy and found a buildup of "anti-bodies" in her kidneys which were causing her problems. The doctors decided she should have chemo for her kidneys. The date selected for the first Chemo was on Monday, the last scheduled day of hearings for the 1993 BRAC. All day on Sunday, the Chairman kept reminding everyone that we would complete our work by 4:00 PM. Finally, a reporter asked me why the Chairman was so insistent on finishing by 4:00 PM? I responded that Linda was scheduled for Chemo on Monday and my flight departed at 6:00 pm. She asked no more questions! The chemo did wonders. Although our medical coverage would allow her to go anywhere, she would not go anyplace other than Wilford Hall Air Force Medical Center. They certainly took very good care of her. We are always careful to place our families first. Sometimes, it takes a jolt to make us understand the really important parts of our lives.

COMBAT

Personal side of war

When we left Stanford in 1966, I was scheduled to go to school at Hurlburt Field, Florida to train to fly the AC-47 side firing gunships (Puff the Magic Dragon). While we were enroute, my orders were changed to attend training at Hurlburt to be a Forward Air Controller (FAC). I would be flying a single engine Cessna and directing air strikes and various artillery and naval gunfire.

David, Beth, Richard, 1967

Before going to Vietnam, I purchased an additional life insurance policy. During my time in Vietnam, I received very little pay with almost all of our pay being deposited in our joint bank account for Linda's use. One month, I was told that I would receive essentially no pay. When I checked, I was told that they had been not been taking the insurance premiums out of my pay. Before, I could respond, they said, "No problem, we found that we have not been paying the insurance company!" When I checked with the insurance company, they confirmed that they had not been paid, and I did not have coverage. I could get a new policy, which would not be effective until one month later. I initiated a new policy. As you can imagine, we were concerned, but I could not be very careful in hot combat. Fortunately, everything worked out!

Linda and I communicated through letters and small tapes. Once, I decided to call her using the MARS (Military Affiliate Radio System). Ham Radio Operators would connect us to a local telephone system. The speaker on each end would have to say, "Over," and the operators would switch to the other speaker. They are most interesting conversations: "I love you, Over!" "I love you too. Over!" It was great to hear each other's voice; however, it was not very romantic when all of the Ham radio operators were monitoring your conversation. In the next correspondence, Linda told me not to bother making MARS calls!

FORWARD AIR CONTROLLER (FAC):
With identification name of TRAIL 64 in Vietnam & COVEY 554 in Laos

The FACs flew a small aircraft as an observer and directed artillery and air strikes in support of ground forces. It could be very hazardous flying. Vietnam was divided into four military districts or Corps – I Corps being the most northern one. Later, Linda told me that she did not want me to go to I Corps. Of course, I was sent to the most northern portion of I Corps. My primary area was the extremely hostile De-Militarized Zone (DMZ).

As a Forward Air Controller in the northern most part of South Vietnam and in Laos, I learned much about myself in coming face-to-face with great danger and how to survive and flourish in the most hostile environments. We provided strong support for the troops and protected our attacking forces. I was well decorated for heroism and selected for early promotion on return to the U.S.

I do not ever remember being afraid of anything – not even in combat. However, during an early period in Vietnam, I was living in Quang Tri, an Army compound near the DMZ. In case of "incoming fire," I had been told to get under my bed. I had not checked this out. When we came under attack one night, I found that I did not fit under the bed. So I "coolly" decided to put on my flying suit. The rather heavy zipper "did not work"; so, I just ripped the zipper out. I am not sure how much force this required, but it was certainly more than I normally had. I might have thought that I was "cool"; however, my adrenalin was pumping, and I was scared. I am sure this was true in some rather scary combat situations; however, as long as I was busy, I was not scared.

La Vang Airfield, Dirt Runway

We flew the single engine O-1 from the very small La Vang 2,300 ft airfield in Quang Tri with three rolls of coiled barbed wire at each end. One day on takeoff, I was approaching the wires at one end without takeoff speed. I quickly realized the engine cowl doors were closed decreasing the cooling of the engine and its power. I opened them and became airborne over the wires.

On May 18, 1967 - one of my very first missions, we supported an "Agent Orange" Ranch Hand mission with 6 C-123 aircraft and 2 F-4Cs flying cover in the DMZ. I was so new that Captain Jim Lang from the Hue FAC unit flew up to help. The mission went very well until the very end when the formation came under intense ground fire -- with the Ranch

Hand aircraft taking a total of ten hits. I noted a lot of crashed aircraft around the area indicating it was very well defended site. The Ranch Hand aircraft and Jim departed. I stayed around, located the ground fire, and successfully directed fighter aircraft to destroy the three gun positions. The ground fire was so intense that the first three flights of fighters were hit. Only the last flight of fighters and I were not hit by ground fire. My fledgling performance was recognized with the award of a Distinguished Flying Cross (DFC) – when I hardly knew where I was or what I was doing. Combat matures one very quickly. Jim Lang and I would later teach Aeronautics together at the Air Force Academy and maintain a lifelong friendship.

O-1 Cessna FAC Aircraft

(The Distinguished Flying Cross Citation is in the Appendix.)

On July 2, 1967 while flying a visual reconnaissance mission near the Marine Base at Con Thien on the edge of the De-Militarized Zone (DMZ), I was asked to contact a USMC Company pinned down by fire from a trench and bunker complex. Although unable to see the enemy troops, I requested air support to bomb the trenches and bunkers. Increasing my area of search, I saw what appeared to be "trees crossing a road" approximately 500 meters east of the Marine Company. The "trees" were uniformed North Vietnam Army (NVA) troops with branches on their backs. When advised of the sightings, the Marine Company ground FAC confirmed that there were no Marines in the area wearing camouflage. Initially, I saw 40 NVA troops cross the road and continue south along a hedgerow. As I saw more troops crossing the road, we realized that they were an overwhelming North Vietnamese Army (NVA) force attempting to surround the Marine Company. I requested armed helicopters and fighters with napalm (liquid gel bomb which is most effective against troops) and 250 LB GP bombs, and asked that all available air support be diverted to this position. The Marine ground Forward Air Controller (FAC) and I were in constant contact.

When the first fighters arrived with 500 LB GP bombs, I directed the fighters against NVA in the open at the point where the NVA had crossed the road. This was 400 to 500 meters from the friendlies. As the strike continued, the drops were moved closer to the friendlies until the friendlies said not to come any closer. By this time the NVA troops were within 100 meters of the friendlies on the east and south. When the strike began, so did the ground fire directed at the fighters and me. When armed helicopters arrived, I directed them against the NVA in the open within 100 to 300 meters east of the friendlies. The helicopters were again worked nearer the friendlies, where the majority of the NVA were located. Throughout the helicopter strikes, the intense ground fire continued, and one of the helicopters gunners was hit.

After the helicopters expended their ordnance, another flight of fighters arrived with 500 LB GP bombs. By this time, the forces were in very close contact. Working closely with the Marine ground FAC, we brought the strikes dangerously close to the friendlies. The ordnance was placed as close as humanly possible to the friendly lines. It is a great tribute to these fighter pilots to be able to get so close to the friendlies with great accuracy. I realized the great risk involved, but I also saw many NVA troops about to overrun the greatly outnumbered Marine Company, and we were willing to take the great risk to save the company from complete annihilation and provide time for reinforcements to arrive.

By the time a flight of fighters had arrived with napalm and 250 LB GP bombs, I discussed hitting the gulley with the Marine ground FAC. Although it was only 75 to 100 meters away from some friendly troops, if the napalm could be placed in the gulley, it would wipe out the NVA in the gulley and the gulley walls would shield the friendlies. The Marines were unable to mark friendly positions since the enemy was only 120 meters away. I briefed the fighters in great detail on the location of the friendlies and the enemy concentration. I directed the fighters to place the napalm in the gulley or just north, but definitely not south. We decided to drop the first napalm just north of the gulley. The first fighter did a magnificent job of hitting the northern rim of the gulley. Unfortunately, the Marines on the ground advised that the fighters could not bring the napalm any further south into the gulley without injuring friendlies. We did an outstanding job of covering all NVA entrances to the gulley with napalm and 250 LB GP bombs. In this strike, one of the fighters took a hit attesting to the intense ground fire environment.

After this strike, I was out of marking devices and low on fuel and briefed an airborne Marine AO (Airborne Observer) on the ground situation and suggested future targets.

As I departed, three relief groups of Marines were approaching the area. The battle continued to increase in size. Before the day was over, five Marine Companies were committed against what turned out to be a well disciplined and well equipped NVA Regiment. The overall friendly losses were high and two fighters were lost. The friendly and enemy casualties were extremely high, and this was a most important battle. Reportedly, the initial B Company, 1st Battalion, 9th Marines suffered many casualties – only 27 of the 200 Marines were unhurt. In the 1st Battalion of the 9th Marines, 84 were killed in the battle.

I was most impressed by the strong, cool, accurate Marine ground FAC. I could not have asked for a better partner in coordinating the battle. Later, I learned the ground FAC had been killed almost immediately, and I was working with a Marine Corporal radio operator as the last standing person to serve as the Marine ground FAC. As we all do, the radio operator well met the demands placed on him!

I was so low on fuel that I had to land to refuel before I could get home. Later as I read about this action, I was scared and felt most fortunate to support the Marines and not to get hurt. I was recognized for my small role with the award of the Silver Star for Gallantry. (The Silver Star Citation and narratives are in Appendices, page i.)

When everything looks so good, BE CAREFUL! After being recommended for the Silver Star on July 2, 1967, I was involved in the "short round" incident two days later. The term "short round" comes from the field artillery community. When an artillery round lands short and hits friendly troops, it is called a "short round."

At approximately 11:00 am on 4 July 1967, I received a request to replace another FAC who was directing air strikes for a Marine Company near the DMZ. Between 12:15 and 2:00 pm, I directed six flights of fighters in support of the Marine Company. I was in radio communications with Company ground FAC during all strikes. The Company was located south of a road. They marked their position, and I was told that all friendlies were south of this road. We were conducting strikes with napalm and 2,000 lb and 500 lb GP bombs against this hedgerow. I directed in two flights of 2,000 lb GP bombs 400 to 500 meters north of the hedgerow. All targets were cleared by Company ground FAC. The bombs were going where the Company wanted them. Since I had run out of smoke grenades and rockets, the Company was marking the target with 60 mm white phosphorous rounds fired from a tank located at their position.

Another flight (two A-4s) checked in with eight D-2's. I asked them to hold until a strike east of my position was completed. In the meantime, I flew over the target area and found 10 to 15 NVA troops in a gulley covered by a hedgerow. After the earlier strike, the A-4s arrived on station. I pointed out Marine Company's position to the fighters and told them all friendlies were located south of the road. The Marine Company marked the target, and I described the target to fighters. I directed a 270 degree run-in heading and a left break to keep the fighters south of North Vietnam and east of artillery activity to the west. The fighters made four passes. The first three drops hit in the target area. On the fourth pass, the wingman dropped 800 meters short and 300 meters left of the target. After it impacted, I noted troops around the impact point. Very soon, I received a call from the Marines on the ground saying a bomb hit in the friendly lines of another USMC Company. The fighter had expended their ordnance, and I had them hold while I tried to determine the damage. The Marines on the ground said the bomb hitting in the lines of the other Marine Company was a dud and no damage was done.

After confirming the Company position and receiving clearance from Company ground FAC, I directed another set of fighters against the NVA position.

Later, we found that there were two bombs dropped on the Marines. One was a dud. The other wounded nine Marines. All survived but one Marine lost a leg. My boss went to the Hospital Ship to visit with the wounded.

Realizing that both pilots had initially hit the proper target, I still wonder what I could have done to avoid the short round.(The statement about the "Short Round" is in the Appendices on page vi.)

I was also flying as the FAC Advisor for the 1st ARVN (Army of Viet Nam) Regiment. The ground Advisor was a Marine Major. I always wanted to go on some ground patrols with the Regiment; however, the ground Advisor repeatedly found excuses that I should not go. In truth, he did not want to expose me to land mines, etc. One day, the ground Advisor flew in the back seat with me. We were directing Naval gunfire from ships, Vietnamese artillery, a Marine fighter strike, and a medical evacuation on the southern edge of the DMZ. Needless to say, I was very busy. As I rolled in to mark a target, the aircraft engine quit. Of course, I had forgotten to change the fuel tank. Without even stopping talking, I changed the fuel tank, pumped the throttle and the engine was running again. The Major was terrified and sure that we would not return alive. When we landed, he said, "Thanks for the flight; I will not let you go with us on the ground because we need you in the air; AND I will NEVER fly with you AGAIN!"

While stationed at Quang Tri, we would often spend the night along the DMZ at Dong Ha to be "on alert" for night flights in the DMZ or further south at Hue where it was considered more safe. At Hue, I got to know a couple of lifelong friends, Jim Lang and Bob Mikesh. Jim was my partner on one of my first missions as discussed earlier. Bob Mikesh and I became very close friends at Hue and would both move to Plieku. He was a little older and gave me very wise counsel. Later, Bob and Ramona Mikesh and Linda and I lived in the same neighborhood of Camp Springs, MD. Bob was the "Air" curator as the Smithsonian Air and Space Museum that was being developed in downtown Washington. Bob is a highly respected and world acclaimed Aviation Writer. Over the years, we have maintained a very close relationship.

It was most fortunate that I was sleeping at Hue when our Quang Tri Army compound and airfield came under heavy attack in the middle of the night. At approximately 2:20 am on 12 August 1967, I was advised that a sub-sector near Quang Tri was under attack and directed to fly to Quang Tri. The maintenance team and I drove four miles to the Hue Citadel airfield over unsecure roads for the night launch of the O-1. After arrival at the field, we quickly prepared for my departure. Although it was an extremely dark night, I felt the urgency of the mission would not allow time for putting temporary lights along the runway. I was off ground within twenty minutes of being notified.

Immediately after takeoff, I was in complete darkness and flew instruments while attempting to navigate using barely discernible objects on the ground. Approaching Quang Tri, I was advised that at least three ARVN compounds were under attack – Hai Lang sub-sector, 1st ARVN Regiment at La Vang Airfield, and Trieu Phong sub-sector. A Marine C-130 flare ship was on station, and an AC-47 gun ship was enroute to Quang Tri. The Marine aircraft dropping flares was directed to illuminate the Hai Lang sub-sector, but the crew was unable to locate Hai Lang. Through my familiarity with the area, I was able to locate Hai Lang and direct the Marine aircraft dropping flares.

On arrival at Quang Tri, I found a very confused situation. The command post was unsure of the ground situation and communications with the various compounds were either nonexistent or poor due the confusion of the attacks. With little information, I decided to survey all the compounds under attack, determine the best use of the available airpower, and evaluate the need for additional support. Despite intense fire – friendly outgoing and unfriendly incoming – I flew low enough over each area to get an accurate appraisal of the situations. There were two combined mortar and ground attacks at La Vang -- one against 1st ARVN Regiment, and one against the 7th ARVN Cavalry. By this time, the AC-47 was on station. I directed the AC-47 to keep the two La Vang compounds illuminated and watch for mortar flashes. The status at Thieu Phong was completely unknown since communications with the senior Australian advisor had been lost. I proceeded to the area and found that the sub-sector and the PRU (Provincial Reconnaissance Unit) compound were near shambles. I immediately directed the Marine flare ship to proceed from Hai Lang, where the attack had ceased, to Trieu Phong and illuminate the area. A more extensive survey of Trieu Phong indicated that many of the bunkers had been blown up and several buildings were on fire. I was able to establish radio contact with an advisor in the sub-sector but was unable to determine the conditions of the compound since the advisor was pinned down in a bunker. Later, a Vietnamese came up on the advisory radio in the PRU compound. We were able to determine that the PRU compound had been overrun and demolished and that all Americans had been killed or were missing. The Vietnamese PRU men were able to regroup and push the enemy out of the compound. It was obvious that Trieu Phong needed air support quickly. I directed the gunship to illuminate Trieu Phong and attempted to find enemy positions. The flare ship provided illumination for La Vang, and the 1st ARVN Regiment, and the 7th Cavalry were able to put out a large aggressive fire.

The gunship and I began to receive intense automatic weapons fire from three positions around Thieu Phong. We immediately cleared the gunship to return fire to an enemy position in an open field. The gunship tried to get clearance to fire on the other two positions near hamlets. The situation on the ground was so unclear that no one could authorize the fire into these positions. Finally, permission was received to return fire regardless of its point of origin. I requested an immediate air strike against the center of enemy activity, but ARVN sources were unable to approve the target due to unknown location of friendlies.

While the gunship fired into the enemy positions, the mortar attack on Trieu Phong stopped, but the attack would begin again when the gunship ceased firing. At this time a new crisis developed. The gunship expended its last flares. There was still a hour of darkness, and no replacement gunship was available. The gunship was ready to leave station when we decided to have the Marine flare ship drop flares over Trieu Phong while the gunship continued to fire into the enemy positions. This required a great deal of coordination but it was effective. We kept the La Vang compounds under surveillance while it was illuminated with artillery flares. When the compounds were not illuminated, both sides would fire incessantly. Through judicious use of illumination flares, the compounds were kept lighted until first light.

Although low on fuel, I remained over Trieu Phong to help coordinate medical evacuation of the wounded at day break.

This was an extremely dangerous morning. Since I was very busy, I was not afraid. I must admit that I was a little startled when the pilot of the "side-firing" AC-47 gunship aircraft (Puff the Magic Dragon), called and said, "Trail, are you still there?" After assuring him that I was all right, the pilot said, "You were in my 'sights' when I fired!" Later, we determined that the Marine "flare" aircraft was above me, and the other pilot saw my shadow! "Whew!!" At day break after flying for more than four hours, I was nearly out of gas and landed at the Quang Tri La Vang airfield – unsure of who owned it after the night fight. All was well, and I was a hero in my Quang Tri compound.

This was a most interesting and exciting evening. Later in the day, I was able to visit some of the areas where the NVA had attacked and see some of the enemy casualties. It looked much different after the fight! (Narrative in the Appendix.)

H.T. and the O-1

In flying in and near the DMZ, I was only hit once and did not know it. Then, we were flying the "push – pull" Cessna Sky Masters with an engine in front and one in the rear. After landing the crew chief checked the oil and could not get the dipstick to go back into the engine. Upon further investigation, he found a bullet had hit the rear engine, rattled around the engine area, and impacted on the dipstick tube. I was very fortunate that the bullet did not damage the engine and cause major problems or a crash.

On October 20, 1967, I was flying a mission with a reporter on board when a battle evolved. I responded to an urgent call from an ARVN advisor for air support. I quickly diverted to the area of the ARVN units. Two ARVN battalions and an armored cavalry unit had an enemy main force surrounded on three sides with the forth side being a natural barrier reinforced by ARVN artillery barrages. Being familiar with the battle plans, I flew low over the area to determine the friendly and enemy disposition of troops. There were intense incoming mortar fire and several anti-aircraft positions firing. The enemy forces were desperate and furiously pounding the cavalry unit with mortars, recoilless rifles, and automatic weapons in an effort to break out of the cordon set up by the ARVN units. The cavalry unit was in an extremely vulnerable position, unable to maneuver into a more favorable position, and was receiving heavy casualties.

The immediate problems were to silence the guns firing on the cavalry unit and to provide medical evacuation for the critically wounded. Despite marginal air support flying conditions of 2,500 feet of broken overcast clouds, I called for medical evacuation helicopters, armed helicopter, and fighter support. When the medical evacuation helicopters arrived, the landing zone was not secure. In an effort to get the wounded out as quickly as possible, I directed the fighters against the gun positions and had the medical evacuation of the wounded follow immediately. To successfully direct the fighters against the enemy, we had to stop the friendly artillery, clear all helicopters from the area, contend with low weather ceilings, fly through intense automatic weapons fire to mark, and direct the ordnance extremely close to the cavalry unit. After briefing all units on two different radio frequencies, I directed the fighters against the enemy gun positions and held over the nearest friendly units to provide a visual foul line for the fighters, as the fighters pulled off of their last pass, I cleared the medical evacuation helicopter into the landing zone while directing the armed helicopters to make rocket and machine gun passes on the known and suspected gun positions. The risks involved in sending the medical evacuation helicopters into a vulnerable, insecure landing zones were high, but it was critical to get the critically wounded out so the cavalry unit could move and to save human life. Through detailed planning and extremely close direction of the operation, the medical evacuation was successful and the cavalry unit was able to redeploy to a less vulnerable position.

It was becoming more apparent that a large enemy force was trapped by the ARVN units and was desperately trying to fight their way out. We were able to closely coordinate the ARVN artillery and armed helicopters to keep the enemy under continuous fire between air strikes which were extremely close to the ARVN forces. Knowing the key role played by the Forward Air Controller, the heavily armed hostile force desperately tried to shoot us down. The strikes were delivered with great precision and the enemy positions were devastated with resulting cessation of fire from these areas.

By this time, I was low on fuel and relieved by another Forward Air Controller. When the battle was over, there were 195 enemy killed by body count, versus 16 ARVN killed, and an enemy main force unit was essentially wiped out as a fighting unit. This was a large one sided victory for the ARVN forces, but more importantly, it gave them renewed confidence as a fighting unit at a time when they were sorely in need of a victory.

Our activities impressed the South Vietnamese military so much, that "they" awarded me a "Vietnamese Cross of Gallantry with a Silver Star." (Unfortunately, it was never presented or entered into my records.) A news reporter was flying with me as an observer. During the flight, the reporter became physically sick. After we landed, he asked, "How did you know where the artillery was coming from and its trajectory?" He was afraid that each round of artillery was going to hit our aircraft. He was "scared to death!" We were well under the arc for the artillery rounds and would only be endangered near the guns or the impact area. Again, when one is engaged, fear is minimal. Observers have nothing to do but be afraid.(The mission narrative is in the Appendix.)

The time working out of Quang Tri and Hue was both exciting and dangerous for me and many others. It is always inspiring to talk to some partners from the FAC days. David Sciacchitano was an aircraft mechanic at Quang Tri. He flew some missions with us. In retrospect, I can imagine his excitement and fear in flying with us on combat missions.

From his recollections, David and I were flying from Quang Tri to Hue. He was in the back seat enjoying the flight in a disconnected way. Suddenly, I needed to get a long look through binoculars at some sort of enemy activity down below. I asked David to release the back seat rudder pedals, put the stick in and hold the plane steady while I got a steadier, better look. (Normally, the back seat rudder pedals were disengaged and the "stick" was removed.) David was afraid and excited as I entrusted our lives to the sweaty nervous hands of a young man who had no idea whatsoever about how to fly an airplane. David only "flew" for a few minutes but it seemed like hours to him, and it is one of those Vietnam memories that will stay with him forever.

Later when David was flying to Hue with Ken Furbush, Ken asked him if he wanted "to see where HT is always catching VC out in the open" or something to that effect. And of course David excitedly said, "Yes." So they flew southwest of the route to Hue to the area, and Ken provided a running commentary, when he suddenly stopped talking for a second and then with an expletive of some sort said, "Look, there they are." Of course, David couldn't make out a thing at first, but Ken gave him the binoculars and he managed to make out four individuals along a jungle path. David said, "I see four of them," and Ken replied, "There are a hundred of them." There was something like a large company or two that had been walking along the road, and had stopped and squatted down when they came over, trying to avoid notice. Ken was delighted to have found such a prize, but also got very serious as he felt they were on their way to a night attack or ambush, and he spent a frustrating couple of hours trying to call in artillery and air, none of which was available, since all of it in the area was pre-assigned to those automatic free fire zone interdiction fire missions. Ken even tried to raise ARVN artillery in the area to no avail. They finally got a flight out of Danang (F-100s or Phantoms), but it was almost dark by then, and Ken had trouble marking the target with the rockets. The jets had even more problems sighting in, and while they dropped most or their entire ordinance (napalm and some 500 or 750 lbs bombs), it was obvious a lot of it went wide. When they flew over the area the next morning to assess damage, it seemed pretty clear that most or all of the ordnance had missed the target.

The Quang Tri and Hue FACs shared stories. One day as Hue FAC, Captain Bob Faloon, was working strikes in the very dangerous A Shau Valley, he saw a stream of bullets coming his way. Instinctively, he pulled his legs back just as a bullet ripped through the aircraft and literally cut the "zipper" out of his boot! Otherwise, he was untouched and did not qualify for the "Purple Heart." Bob still has the boot and is most proud that he pulled his leg back so swiftly.

Move to Pleiku

In late October of 1967, I was selected to join a small group of Covey FACs to be stationed at Pleiku in the Central Highlands and fly into Southern Laos – primarily at night. I flew as COVEY 654. We had no navigational equipment. At night, we flew with two pilots. One would use a night-vision "starlight" scope to locate and attack movement along the Ho Chi Minh Trail. We worked with fighters and side firing AC-130 gunships.

We had many exciting nights along the trail. On occasion, it felt as if you could "walk" on the anti-aircraft fire. We watched the larger shells climb to their maximum ordinate and fall back. It is always most difficult to see and evade the round that "hits you!" Of course, we were higher than the lethal range – we thought!

One night while flying with my boss, we found some North Vietnamese guns that were firing along the trail. When we got fighters ready to strike the guns, they stopped firing. Not wanting to give up, I turned on our aircraft landing lights to encourage them to fire. My boss was not impressed! He told me that he was going to "ground me" before my last flight to ensure that I did not do anything stupid.

During our activities over southern Laos, there were many challenges and opportunities as we flew mostly in the dark of night with no navigation aids except a map, our eyes, and a night vision "Starlight Scope." On a very cloudy day flight, I found a target and requested fighters. I was able to tell them how to find the area; however, I got lost in the clouds. When they arrived on station, the fighters gave me a DF (Direction Finding) steer back to the area. We found each other, I marked the target, and they attacked it very successful. As I reflected on my location, I was probably lost over Cambodia. It was OK because no one else could find me!

One evening on January 19, 1968, Captain Henry Salcido and I were flying over an active truck park along the trail. We had always suspected the activity but never able to find it. We were working as a team with Capt Salcido flying the aircraft and I was using the starlight scope to reconnoiter the road. The night was extremely dark and because of a thick layer, we could only see the road from directly above. Dragon 09 was flying with the FACs as the killer portion of the 'hunter-killer" team. When no trucks were found, we decided to expend Dragon 09 on a truck park. Capt Salcido marked the truck park and dropped an illumination flare. As Dragon 09 made his pass on the truck park, several anti-aircraft guns began firing. The hostile fire was too accurate to continue the attack on the truck park. Using the starlight scope, I was able to spot the area where the majority of the anti-aircraft fire was coming. Despite the heavy concentration of guns firing at the fragile O-2 aircraft, I dove down the barrels of the actively firing guns to deliver a marking rocket for Dragon 09. Dragon 09 made one pass on the gun position, but by now there were at least five guns (including 23 mm and 37 mm guns) firing at the FACs and the fighters from all angles. Then, we became convinced that a large group of hostile guns had intentionally been set up to protect this section of the road and a great deal of hostile traffic.

We decided it was imperative to attempt to silence the guns so that the other FACs and Dragons would be able to safely operate in the area later in the evening. We decided to wait until a second Dragon arrived in the area to continue the attack. When Dragon 10 arrived, we briefed both fighters on the anti-aircraft situation and the plan of attack. Dragon 10 was to hold high while Dragon 09 made a pass on the gun positions. If the guns fired at Dragon 09, Dragon 10 would immediately roll in and bomb the active position. We were unable to determine if any of the guns were destroyed, but the bombs hit very near the guns and the aircraft were able to operate in the area later in the evening without being fired upon. We held Dragon 10 high while we searched the road for traffic. A short time later, using the starlight scope, we found seven trucks moving along the section of the road lined with guns. With full knowledge that all of the guns were probably not destroyed, we held over the truck until the trucks moved out of range of the guns. By now, we had at least five of the trucks under surveillance at a ford. Dragon 10 was dangerously low on fuel, and the FACs had to get him on target as quickly as possible. Although we could only see the target with the starlight scope, we were able to place the marking rocket on the target. The flare ship illuminated the target areas and the two Dragons covered the entire area with CBU (Cluster Bomb Unit) and bombs. Their accurate strike resulted in at least four trucks destroyed and three large secondary fires. Needless to say it was a most exciting evening. Our efforts were recognized with the awarding of two Distinguished Flying Crosses. (DFC Citation and narrative are in the Appendix.)

In late January of 1968 during the Tet Offensive, I was invited (directed) to fly out of Danang in support of Khe Sahn. We would fly a four to five hour mission, rest for eight hours, and fly again -- around the clock. I flew in the DMZ, Laos, and North Vietnam. It was an exciting but very dangerous time.

Khe Sahn was under constant attack. I had flown many missions around Khe Sahn but had not landed there. One day, I landed at Khe Sahn to pick someone up. I was only on the ground for a short time; however, I could see the gun fire just off the runway, and it was scarier than being in the air – and getting shot at!

On a very foggy day, the US friendly Montagnard troops led by a leader with a call sign of "Elephant" came under attack just inside Laos near Khe Sahn. I established contact and tried to provide air support. We could not see the terrain and had no visual cues to use in directing the attacks. We were finally able to get some radar controlled air strikes, which were helpful but not decisive. Finally, the last call I received was, "Elephant run now!" I was never able to determine if they survived.

Towards the end of my scheduled tour, I was flying alone in the afternoon along a river in Laos. A North Vietnamese ZPU-23 very rapid firing 23 mm Gatling gun began shooting at me. I could feel the bullets going by and turned the little aircraft every way imaginable. Somehow all of the bullets missed me. When I arrived home, even before knowing about the attack, the commander met me and told me that I was grounded, and it was time to go home! I reflected a moment and AGREED!

A few minutes later, the Red Cross asked me to call to check on the loss of an "in-law." I told them that I knew that my father-in-law had died two weeks before. When I finally got through, I found that Linda's mother had died 13 days after her father. I was immediately sent home using the priorities of "emergency leave." It was a long trip; however, I never waited more than two hours at any en route stop. When I arrived at the San Francisco airport, there were no seats; however, the airline put me in First Class and took very good care of me. I gained immense respect for how military people are treated when they are traveling on "emergency leave." The funeral had been held by the time I arrived. Linda was most pleased to have me home after losing both parents within two weeks. It was a joyous but most difficult reunion.

AFTER COMBAT

U. S. Air Force Academy

I enjoyed three years as an Assistant Professor of Aeronautics at the Air Force Academy. I found teaching a very enjoyable and rewarding experience. I learned much about the subjects I taught but also how to motivate young people. I was quite busy. In addition to teaching a full load, I was the academic advisor to the 19th Cadet Squadron which was the best Squadron academically one year and the best overall the next; flew navigation training flights; completed an MBA; and became licensed as a Professional Engineer. In 1970, I was selected as an Outstanding Young Man of America by the Junior Chamber of Commerce.

Amazingly, I was presented the Silver Star from my Vietnam days at the first Cadet Parade after I arrived at the Academy. I became well known to the cadets. Many cadets sought my advice and counsel on a wide range of subjects. It was exciting to work with the outstanding young cadets. Our family and I enjoyed meeting cadets, the academic environment, and Colorado.

In preparing for our classes, I gained more than the cadets. Our respect for each other was mutual. Over the three years, I only received one negative comment, which was very helpful. "As you complete the derivation of every equation, you always say 'and it turns out …'" I became more careful not to use such comments. I have also been brave enough to tell others when they continually overuse a phrase. Much later in life when I was acting Secretary of the Navy, a person who had been in several audiences approached me and said, "I won my bet when you, as normal, ended your comments with 'God Bless America and our President!'" Of course, he and I were pleased that I had such a reputation.

One always thinks that things would have been different if she or he were the leader. During my time as an instructor at the Air Force Academy, several instructors bought a refrigerator in a nearby town and picked it up in a pickup truck. During the drive back, the refrigerator fell out of the truck and was destroyed. I was originally going with them but did not for some unknown reason. A Mechanics Instructor left a message on my blackboard, "Refrigerators are not supposed to fly, and Aeronautics professors cannot make them!" I told the Head of the Aeronautics Department, Colonel Dan Daley, that I had planned to go with them and was sorry about the loss. He responded, "If you had gone, it would not have happened. I do not know how you would have prevented the accident, but you would have!" Dan Daley gave me a phenomenal compliment. I am sure that fates are not predetermined and each of us can have an impact.

Colonel Daley wrote an awesome recommendation for the Meritorious Service Medal (Appendix). I was amazed and most impressed by his description of my activities and leadership as being so valuable to the cadets and the Academy – while I was humbly doing my duties. (Recommend reading the recommendations for decorations in the Appendix – I could not say the most complimentary things about myself!)

Many years later when I was selected as a Distinguished Graduate, I thanked Colonel Daley for being my mentor. He most graciously responded, "I was a Colonel and you were a Captain, and you were my mentor!" He went on to outline some things I had told him that changed his approaches. I remembered our discussion but did not know the impact.

During the first summer at the Air Force Academy, I was fortunate to be able to work at the Air Defense Command in Colorado Springs. I was able to gain a better understanding of the Air Force issues, how to contribute on a staff, and gain from others.

The next summer, I worked in the Directorate of Plans on the Air Staff in the Pentagon. It was thrilling and most rewarding to work on the Air Staff and learn so much more about the Air Force and the interactions in the Pentagon. I became a contributing partner and prepared and coordinated many papers. Being totally naive, I would coordinate a paper according to the "coordination list" and consequently would climb up and down seven flights stairs! I soon learned to more efficiently plan my travels from the basement to the fifth floor. I soon learned that nothing is impossible as long as you listen and work with others. This summer well prepared me for four subsequent tours in the Pentagon.

During that summer, Linda and the children were able to visit our parents in South Carolina and Georgia and me in DC for a short time.

During the summer, I found and gave Linda a gold pendant that well captures my love for her: in French, "**Je t'aime plus qu'hier et moins que demain**" -- interpreted as "I love you more than yesterday and less than tomorrow!"

Army Command and Staff College

When the Air Force selected me to attend the Army Command and General Staff College (CGSC) at Fort Leavenworth, Kansas, I was allowed to leave the Academy a year early. For the first time in my life, I was a minority. There were 1,200 Army, 113 from other countries, 8 Navy/Marine and 14 Air Force officers. This Intermediate Service School proved to be a very interesting year. I saw a much different approach to life and leadership from the Army officers. We enjoyed meeting and working with many officers from other countries and the US Army.

Over time, these officers from other countries rose to high positions in their countries. Reportedly, each time there is a coup around the world, the staff checked their graduates to see which side the Leavenworth graduate was on. It was exciting to work with and get to know many of these officers. I was fortunate to spend a lot of time in classes with Lieutenant Colonel David Jemibewon from Nigeria. Linda and I got to know him and his family. Prior to coming to CGSC in 1967-1970, David was an army leader as a Brigadier General in the Biafran Nigerian conflict. After returning to Nigeria, David was the governor of a couple states, served as the Adjutant General of the Nigerian Army, and later entered private business. During one of the many coups, he was governor of a Nigerian State near the capital in Lagos. He formed an army and began their march to Lagos to put down the coup. Fortunately, prior to his arrival, the coup was over turned. I corresponded with him several times but lost contact.

One of the students was the Crown Prince of Bahrain. He chose to be a Major at Leavenworth. We would meet again when I was acting Secretary of the Navy, and he was the King.

Air Force Plans

In 1972, I was fortunate to be an Action Officer assigned to Headquarters Air Force, stationed in the Pentagon, working in the office of Air Force Plans. Initially, I was in Airlift Forces under the tutelage of Colonel Bob Milstead. I was fortunate to work with my former roommate, Dennie See and 41st Squadron mate, Bill Posey. In this office, I learned much about how business gets done at the higher levels.

Later, I moved to the Analysis Office under Colonel (and later General) Harry Bendorf. I was head of the Strategy part of this office. We had an interesting blend of academic, policy-savvy, and operational talented officers to include, Charlie Stebbins, Barry Horton, Mike Wheeler, Wayne Jefferson, Lou Moses, Sam Westbrook, and Gary Saban. We were given the most demanding issues in Plans and became the favorite of the Director of Plans, General Dick Lawson. Nothing was impossible for this group. If a task were not initially assigned to us, we would help the primary office, and the most important issues were soon reassigned to us. Our early morning and late at night commutes were almost traffic free. There was much all-night work. One night Charlie worked all night, and his wife Sarah drove their RV to the parking lot for Charlie to clean up and change clothes for his early morning briefing. After the presentation, Charlie asked me if I had seen him "go to sleep at the podium?" Of course, "it" had been momentary and noticed by no one except Charlie. The talented officers inspired confidence and many were promoted to general officer and other competitive assignment such as the National Security Council.

National War College

I was most privileged to be a member of the Class of 1976 "Great Americans" National War College class. Each time the Commandant, Major General Jim Murphy, introduced us, he called us "Great Americans." And we believed him! It was a great year and created some extremely strong friendships and relationships.

During Desert Storm, our class was very well represented. Our classmates included: Lieutenant General Chuck Horner, Commander of the Central Command Air Forces; Lieutenant General John Yeosock,

Commander of the Ground Forces; General Jack Dailey, Assistant Commandant of the Marine Corps; Lieutenant General Mike Nelson, Air Force operations chief; General Colin Powell, Chairman of the Joint Chiefs of Staff; and me, CINC TRANSCOM. Near our thirtieth anniversary of our graduation, Colin Powell was asked to speak at the National War College. He told the story of calling the Commander of Transportation Command to discuss the plan for Desert Storm and added, "He was the Commander but he was also 'my classmate, HT Johnson'." The closeness of the "Great Americans" continues.

Castle Air Force Base

During the National War College, there was a healthy debate about where I would go after National War College. There was some interest in sending me to the Military Airlift Command in maintenance or the Strategic Air Command in operations. General Dick Lawson convinced General Russ Dougherty to send me to the fastest learning environment in SAC. In the summer of 1976, I arrived at Castle AFB as a 15 year Colonel to be the Assistant Deputy Commander for Operations. Never having been in SAC, I was closely watched. After a year as the ADO, I was sent to Base Commanders' School to gain a better understanding of leading an installation. Rather than being assigned to command the base, I was sent to be the Assistant Deputy Commander for Maintenance. This was a phenomenal opportunity to round out my training and give me a very healthy understanding and respect for the Non-Commissioned Officers and the tremendous support structure required for success. It also taught me how various groups are treated with more or less respect. Many must have assumed that I was in "trouble" and started treating me with much less respect. The maintenance Team gave me a model aircraft built from parts with a most respectful Plaque: "Where Others Have to Demand, He Only Has to Ask." After five months, it was announced that I would return as the DO. Several operations "friends" actually apologized for treating me with less respect. I learned that one is most often treated according to where he sits rather than what he is!

Family at Castle AFB, 1977

Leadership guidance as Castle DO (December 1977)

I was fortunate to find the notes from my initial discussion when I became the Deputy Commander for Operations. The views expressed then reflected my openness and approach in all positions.

> My Assistant has full authority to speak for me. When you speak to him, it is the same as speaking to me, and he will keep me up to date. Staff work should be a coordinated, finished product with a brief overview to explain what the paper is about and how it fits into our activities. I believe in recording agreement in writing.
>
> I want to be fully informed, I don't want to encourage rumors, but want to be totally aware of what is going on. I certainly do not have a corner on intelligence. I want to be informed prior, but if I misstate a fact of significance in a meeting, please correct me.

Many of you know that when I make a request, I want quick and effective action. When I ask you to do something, I want to be able to forget about it with the full assurance that it will be done in a timely effective manner unless you request additional guidance or assistance. I do not believe in status quo. When a new idea is presented, I will want to know advantages and disadvantages and how it can be implemented and consequences (positive approach).

I encourage maximum interaction with higher headquarters, but I must be informed of significant conversations and want to be involved.

We must always be prepared to provide highly professional briefings to visitors. We will normally give the "battle staff briefing." We will want to be candid and responsive to requests. I will want to be pre-briefed on any changes to the normal briefings.

I fully realize commanders can and should go directly to the Wing Commander in certain cases. I desire to be informed either going up or coming down. I also desire to accompany (or talk to prior) individuals meeting the wing commander for disciplinary reasons i.e., DUIs (Driving Under the Influence of alcohol).

In Operations, we depend heavily on Maintenance and other supporting groups. We will support Maintenance to the maximum extent possible; however, we will not be hassled on the flight line. Please work closely with Maintenance. When problems arise, call the operations center, and the appropriate people will assist in resolving the problem

Protocol is very important. Spouses have no rank. Obviously because of the military person's position, the spouse will ask other spouses to do certain things. Hopefully, everyone will all cooperate. All of us, including spouses, will sometimes be asked to do things that we are not totally enthusiastic about. In such situations, it is better to relax and gain max enjoyment rather than fight the problem. Linda and I are both most easily approachable and require no special treatment – rather, we hope you will accept and respect us for what we are. All of us will be better off if we aren't too critical of others. I and most of you will tend to unconsciously ask certain people or organizations to do things more often than others. Hopefully, my requests will reflect performance. I will discuss any subject with anyone – we need to keep problems in house.

I must be kept informed -- going up or coming down. But never slow down trying to find me.

Linda as Wing First Lady

After a short time as DO, I became the Vice Commander and rounded out my preparation for command. As the Vice Commander and Inspector General (IG), there were many opportunities to learn about the concerns of others. In addition to my lifelong commitment to honesty and candor, I learned that it is sometimes better not to offer unnecessary information and to be most discrete in sharing information about others. In a discussion with a Congressional Staffer about an IG complaint, I was doing very well in showing how we had properly handled the actions in question. I had become so open with the Staffer that I discussed another action unrelated activity about the individual. The Staffer became very upset and accused us of finding additional unrelated activities to imbue the individual. I became much more sensitive to sticking to the issues at hand!

I also learned my roles at home! During our move from Castle, I came home and offered to help the mover pack. Very quickly, Linda asked, "Don't you have something to do at the office?" My service was obviously not needed or desired! On another move, Dennie See and I unpacked the kitchen boxes. We placed everything in the obviously proper locations. It took Linda several months to find everything. I lost another job.

Wing Commander

In 1979, I became the Commander of the 22nd Bomb Wing at March Field, CA. Although I had been "trained," nothing is more demanding than to be placed in command. As the Commander and First Lady of the Wing, we very quickly learned through experience. Linda's role was often more demanding than mine. I could direct action. Linda had to ask and convince. We were fortunate to have General and Mrs. Jim (Barbara) Mullins as the 15th Air Force Commander at March. They were our mentors and became lifelong friends. We gained immensely from Jim and Barbara Mullins.

The 22nd Bomb Wing was not known to be one of the best units in SAC. In a very short time, my senior leaders and I had transformed the 22nd into one of the better wings. As I arrived, Colonel John Fairfield became the Deputy Commander for Operations and Colonel Dick Sneary became Deputy Commander for Maintenance. Previously, the two deputies had not cooperated very well. They and the entire wing became close partners. During the first readiness inspection, I was most impressed when I saw Dick and John riding in the same vehicle on the flight line to coordinate our activities. I would wander around the wing at all hours. One night shortly after midnight, I visited a maintenance activity. They were most surprised and wanted to know what they had done wrong to bring me out. I responded, "I just wanted to visit with you!" It is indeed amazing when you show trust and respect for others – they rise to meet in challenge! The results were phenomenal.

During the first large exercise, I decided to go to the Nuclear Weapons storage area, observe the break out of weapons, and accompany them back to the flight line. As the first trailer loaded with nuclear weapons approached the gate, we noticed the brakes were smoking, and it was unsafe to move them further. With great fear, I patiently watched the transfer of the nuclear weapons to another trailer. After the move was completed, I had a better understanding of the many challenges our people face.

The Weapons Storage area was some distance from the main base. In the middle of the night, I received a phone call, "There is a fire around a vehicle in the Weapons Storage Area and a weapon is onboard!" I was instantly wide awake, scared to death, and soon on my way to the area. Of course when I arrived, the fire had been extinguished. While a Security Police vehicle was driving outside the fence, it became stuck in the sand and the catalytic converter set the grass on fire. The "weapon on board" was a rifle. I was obviously most relieved!

In June of 1980, we were directed to launch the Nuclear Alert Force! Everything was most serious, and we directed the B-52's on Alert to prepare to launch. A short time later prior to a single take off, the launch was cancelled. Later, we found out that unknown to anyone a "war game" tape was played inadvertently at NORAD (North American Aerospace Defense Command), and the controller properly reacted to the indication that 220 Soviet missiles had been launched and were headed for the US. Fortunately, before the President could be notified, the error was discovered. We were ready to do our part in responding.

During our time at Castle AFB and March Field, our family began going in different directions. Richard attended the University of California at Berkeley. Beth began college in Riverside and would graduate from California State Polytechnic University in Pomona as an accountant. David would skip his senior year in high school and gain a degree from California State University in San Diego in three years and earn his law degree from George Washington University.

Richard as Midshipman at Berkeley

Beth and David at Farewell Dinner at March Field

We were honored to host the Non Commissioned Officers presentation of the "Order of the Sword" to General Curtis LeMay. It was a most dramatic evening. During the second break, I was surprised that the SAC Generals had a private meeting, and I was the only officer with General LeMay. I later found that this was the evening of the Nuclear Armed Titan II ICBM fire in Arkansas and the others wanted an update!

HT and General LeMay

Wing First Lady

Probably the most difficult position is to be the spouse of a wing commander. The wing spouses brought issues to Linda that would not otherwise have been discussed with me. Of course, we had some good discussion, and Linda was most respected by the other spouses.

Our children were also treated a little differently. Beth worked as a delivery girl for the base florist. Once, a young Airman asked to give a post-dated check. Beth readily accepted and then told him that her father was the wing commander. The check was paid very quickly! She was most respectful and would always bring "excess food" from her work at various places to the security police at the base gates. Needless to say, "they" watched over her very well.

Strategic Air Command

In early 1981, I was selected for promotion to Brigadier General and reassigned to SAC Headquarters at Offutt AFB in Omaha, Nebraska.

Since SAC was required to have a general officer airborne at all times, I was very quickly "frocked" (had all of the privileges of the rank but was not paid until the normal promotion sequence). I was invited to Offutt, trained in the morning to fly the airborne "Looking Glass," promoted around lunch time, and flew my first "Looking Glass" mission at 3:00 PM. Since we would be moving to Offutt shortly, Linda was not present for my promotion, and I asked Peg Ellis the wife of CINC SAC to pin the star that the spouse normally pins.

When I returned to March Field, I was most impressed that the Wing had encased the flag that flew over March Field when I was promoted and presented it to me. I still proudly display this flag. Linda, David, and I packed and drove to Omaha.

At SAC, I was the Assistant Deputy Chief of Staff for Plans. I learned much about Planning and Programming. After a couple of years, I was asked to escort Lieutenant General Larry Welch on a visit to SAC. He was the Air Force Deputy of of Staff for Programs. It was a privilege to meet and escort General Welch, and a week later, he selected me to join him as the Assistant Director of Programs. I suspect my "escort" duties were really an informal interview. One never knows the impact of opportunities. General Welch became a very strong mentor and friend.

Air Force Programs

When we returned to the Pentagon in November 1982, David had just completed his undergraduate degree at San Diego State and began Law School at George Washington University. It was great to have him with us. During his free time, he worked as maître'd at the Bolling Officers Club. He learned much about interacting with senior people.

Linda chaired the Air Force Officers Wives Club Charity Ball. It was a great and most successful evening.

During a three-year period of downsizing (1982-1985), I was charged with refining all the Air Force Programs to stay within the constantly changing $100 Billion annual budget. Working hard at consensus building, I was able to gain support from all competing areas to develop a balanced program within the required constraints. "I" really represented the hard work of the "engine room" that developed alternatives that I could use in the meetings. This same group had the tasks of preparing "plastic" slides for the presentations. The main Air Force briefing room had four projectors. Normally, we would use the two lower projectors; however, when "backup" slides were needed, I would call for a slide number to be shown on the top left or right screen. Since "they" never knew what backups would be needed, we could hear them running up and down the ladders to ensure the requested slide was on the proper screen. I

David, Mom, and HT at Charity Ball

Linda and HT

would normally review the final slides before going home on the evening before the briefings.

On one occasion, I made some additional changes the morning of the briefing. As I approached Air Force Secretary Vern Orr's briefing room, I was told the briefing slides were not yet in the area. I asked how they were going to handle the situation. "We have suggested that Secretary Orr stop by the bathroom." As he entered the bathroom, I saw the officer carrying the slides literally running down the hall. When Secretary Orr entered, it looked like we had been waiting for a long time. The briefing went so flawlessly that as we neared the end of the briefing, no one had changed a single recommendation. Then, Secretary Orr asked about a funding cut for an Air Force Reserve security project. I responded, "You have been so good so far; we can restore that cut." (Many years later, a member of the "engine room" was telling this story and added information that I never knew. Apparently, we began the briefing without all of the slides – we only had 6 slides! As new slides were completed, they were raced into the projection room! When I called for a slide, it was always available!)

Each time we had to confront major changes -- most often reductions, "we" would carefully scope the size of the 'problem,' establish the objectives, and outline some possible solutions. Then, we would assemble the proper people responsible for developing the solution. Long discussions would ensue. As long as everyone accepted the objective, we were always able to jointly develop a solution -- I must admit my potential solutions got much better in the process. In my three year of balancing the Air Force Program in these groups, we never had to take a vote but always achieved a consensus.

In Programs, we touched virtually every part of our Air Force. Many years later at the Falcons Landing AF Ball on Sept 18, 2009, the Chief of Staff of the Air Force, Norton Schwartz, told an interesting story. "As a young Major on the Air Staff, I had a brilliant idea about how to save a lot of money without much cost to the Air Force. I took my idea to then Major General HT Johnson, AF/PRP, and exclaimed, 'Sir, I know how to save the Air Force a lot of money.' After I explained my wisdom of reducing the number of musical bands, he looked me in the eye and said, 'Major, if you are so fortunate to become a general officer, you will find that there are generals with bands and generals without bands. The Air Force bands make a tremendous difference to everyone in our Air Force.' I chose not to pursue my great idea as a Major! Now, I fully understand the wisdom --- I like our bands!"

As a Programmer, I was very fortunate to work for some most impressive leaders. Initially, I chaired the Force Structure Committee and worked for Major General Chuck Cunningham and Lieutenant General Larry Welch. Later, we all moved up one position and one rank. I chaired the Air Staff Board and worked for Lieutenant General Cunningham. The

Air Staff Board reported to the Air Force Council, chaired by the Vice Chief of Staff, General Larry Welch. Later, Lieutenant General Tony McPeak replaced General Cunningham as AF/PR. Normally, I would pre-brief General Welch prior to briefing the Air Force Council. General McPeak asked to join us for the discussion. As always, I had the many changes on a 5x8 card. In 15 minutes, General Welch and I restructured the Air Force. As we walked back to our offices, General McPeak was most impressed by our discussion and said, "General Welch touched each program and made it better. I would have had to make each one 'the best' before moving on to the next. That is the difference between General Welch and me!"

During these years as a Programmer, I learned more about the Air Force and how to make a positive difference than in any other position. I also developed many lifelong friendships. John Shaud was my counterpart in Plans on the Air Staff. We were able to transform plans into programs to best serve our Air Force and are still close friends.

SAC Operations

General Welch became the Commander-in-Chief of the Strategic Air Command Operations. Later in October 1985, I joined him as the Deputy Chief of Staff for Operations at SAC (SAC/DO).

During this timeframe, the Strategic Air Command was beginning its transformation to the new realities in the world that would become even more stark four years later as the "walls of communism would come tumbling down" in 1989.

I orchestrated and directed the tanker and SR-71 reconnaissance support for the difficult and extremely successful El Dorado Canyon attack on Libya in 1985. Although the Secretary of Defense chose not to send any additional forces to Europe, we were able to ensure through "normal" activities (retention of tankers in theater) that there were enough KC-10s in England to support the mission, which required tanker escort from England through the Strait of Gibraltar to off the coast of Libya and return. No fighter ever lacked escort or fuel. The SR-71 reconnaissance missions were also flown from England with the same required support.

Unfortunately, a FB-111 crew was lost. Prior to giving his national speech about the raid, President Reagan wanted to call the parents of the two crew members. General Rogers, the European Commander refused to give the President the names before the notification process was complete. Fortunately, someone on the Joint Staff had the names and got them to the President. General Rogers also refused to share the SR-71 reconnaissance pictures with the President until after "he" had reviewed them. We considered returning the next SR-71 flight to Andrews AFB to avoid the pride of ownership problems.

As the SAC/DO, I was fortunate to fly the U-2 and the SR-71. On both flights, I piloted the aircraft from the front seat with all of the primary controls. During both flights, we cruised at 82,000 feet -- wearing full space suits. It was interesting to talk to the air traffic controller; we would only report that we were above Flight Level 600 (60,000 feet). We had to say no more. No one else was anywhere close to us, and everyone hearing our calls "wished they were with us!" The U-2 is like a large glider with an engine. It climbs at such a rapid rate that the crew has to "pre-breath" oxygen for 45 minutes prior to departure. I had decided to wear my glasses rather than the normal contact lenses. Since the space suits have a seal around the face, the arms of the glasses were removed, and the frame was mounted on a bracket at the center. Each time I moved my head, the glasses moved. As we passed through 5,000 feet, I opened the faceplate and removed the glasses. I could see well without any lens. When I told the instructor, he asked if I had held my breath while the face plate was open; otherwise, we would have to return because I had broken the "breathing cycle!" I assured him that the faceplate was opened only a very short time and that I had not broken the breathing cycle. In the SR-71, I wore my contacts with no discomfort (the case of the old contacts still says "we went Mach 3.2.")

The world is very beautiful above most of the atmosphere. You can see a long way. Some say that you can even see the curvature of the earth – I was too excited to notice.

Flying the U-2 is wondrous and beautiful. Landing is a bit of a challenge. As the U-2 taxies to the runway, it has four wheels and handles like most aircraft. As the U-2 lifts off the ground, the two out rigger wheels drop to the runway. On landing, it is like a bicycle with 100-foot wings. The front tire is fairly large (three feet) and the back tire is quite small. To avoid bouncing, the rear tire needs to touch first. To assist the pilot in landing, a crew chases the U-2 down the runway at over 100 miles per hour in a car and advises how high the rear wheel is from the runway. Linda was extremely excited and proud to be asked to ride in the chase vehicle. I had the normal difficulties in landing the U-2. We made four landings; however, when they sent the video of my landings, there were only three included. One must have looked too bad!

In the SR-71, we performed an aerial refueling and accelerated to over Mach 3+ (three times the speed of sound) or over 2,000 miles per hour. When an aircraft with jet engines is operating faster than the speed of sound, the airflow must be reduced to sub-sonic speed before it goes through the engine. As an aeronautics instructor, I had described the intricate system of "inlet ramps and spikes" required to ensure that there were a series of "oblique" shock waves. When the "oblique" shock waves are lost, the pressure drop with a "normal" shock is so great that the engine losses power, and it is called an "unstart!" Early in the aircraft test program, one engine was intentionally "unstarted," and the other kept and full power. The torque was so great that the test aircraft lost part of the vertical tail. The controls were programmed to reduce the power on the other engine during any "unstarts." Although I had discussed the phenomena many times and we had practiced it in the simulator, I was quite terrified when we got an "unstart' at Mach 2.9, and the second engine power was "sympathetically" reduced. It got very quiet! I had all of the controls. With a lot of helpful guidance from the instructor pilot, I retarded the throttles, successfully repositioned everything, and advanced the throttles. Magically, we continued to fly and accelerate to Mach 3+.

During our one hour and twenty-eight minute flight from Beale Air Force Base (north of Sacramento, CA), we refueled, accelerated to Mach 3+, toured the northwestern quadrant of the United States (CA, OR, WA, MT, ID, WY, CO, and UT), and made three landings. I flew all phases of the flight except the later stages of the refueling. The SR-71 handles like a normal aircraft. My landings were "perfect" – but no video! When it flies at Mach 3, it gets very hot. Fuel is used to cool the leading edges. Otherwise the metal would melt. Even with the regenerative cooling, the aircraft still grows about twelve inches in length at Mach 3. It was a great joy to fly the U-2 and SR-71.

During my time as the SAC/DO, it was a tremendous honor to work for General Larry Welch and then General Jack Chain. They both showed utmost confidence and provided total support. During the build-up and execution of the El Dorado Canyon operations in Libya on April 14, 1986, I kept General Welch informed. He supported all of our activities. I was most impressed that he did not come to the Command Center during the execution late at night. I stopped by his home after it was complete to provide an update. As I mentioned earlier – since I first served as his escort during a visit to SAC, I regarded him as my mentor in the Air Force.

Jack Chain is also a dynamic leader. He is different from Larry Welch and brought his enthusiasm and focus to SAC. He was a very strong supporter and moved me to the Pacific Air Forces as the Vice Commander-in-Chief which began a series of moves that would broaden my experience and ultimately lead to my becoming the Commander-in-Chief of the U.S. Transportation Command.

We celebrated Linda's 50th birthday at Offutt. She liked pig charms. I ask my Executive Officer's wife, Shelly Fitzhugh, to help plan a party. I told Linda that we had been invited "next door" for dinner with Buck and Annette Shuler. She was a little "put out" that there would not be a party or that I would not take her out to dinner. Normally, we used the back doors to visit our neighbors. She first realized that something was up when I suggested we use the front door. When we arrived, the guests were wearing black armbands and "pig snouts." A

Linda and her Piglet!

short time later, the police arrived with their siren blaring, looking for Linda Johnson. "Some lady had arrived at the gate demanding to see Linda!" "Miss Piggy" and her little piglet were a great hit!

We did not recognize "Miss Piggy" and did not know who she was until later. I told the police that the pig did not stay. "Miss Piggy" kept the pig until it became too large to keep in its crib.

Jack Chain and the Command Surgeon General were concerned about several senior officers who smoked. One day in early November during a senior officer meeting, Jack said, "Several of us smoke. Everyone else with one notable exception drinks hard liquor. I proposed that on January 1st the smokers give up smoking and the rest of us give up drinking hard liquor." When it was my turn to speak, I said that I would be pleased to give up hard liquor. Jack responded, "You don't drink now! You must give up sex." I did not enjoy drinking hard liquor, and everyone thought that I did not drink at all. That evening I asked Linda for a drink of "hard liquor." Little did I know that I was about to be transferred to the Pacific Air Forces -- before the end of the year. Of course at our farewell party, Jack told the story that I arranged to get transferred prior to my "sentence."

Pacific Air Forces

To broaden my background in December 1986, I was assigned as the Vice Commander of the Pacific Air Forces. General Jack Gregory and his wife, Jane, were tremendous teachers and mentors. In our short seven months in Hawaii, I was involved in activities throughout the Pacific and gained better understanding of our tactical forces.

It was exciting and educational to learn so much about our tactical air forces and the Pacific. I was able to visit many Air Force units and countries in the Pacific. I was fortunate to fly the tactical aircraft and also participate in several tactical exercises with other countries. I was able to represent General Gregory at many activities and events.

Having helped develop the Air Force strategy through the Program Objective Memorandum (POM), I was most pleased to host a General from the Australian Air Force who had just completed a review of their strategy. To indicate the difficulties, he said, "You cannot image how difficult it is to build a national military strategy with no identifiable enemy!" I suspect it has also become more difficult for the US to openly identify large "enemies" for strategy and budget development.

During his visit to Hawaii, I escorted the Chinese Air Force Chief for his visit to our command. Our discussions were very interesting. During the Korean War, he was shot down by an American. On the day he was shot down, former US Air Force Chief of Staff, General Charles Gabriel, shot down a Chinese fighter aircraft. When he and General Gabriel met earlier, they wondered if they had indeed met in the air on that fateful day.

As part of the visit, I escorted him on his visit to the USS Arizona. He was quietly most respectful. I know his mind was wondering how the sinking of the Arizona and the attack on Pearl Harbor changed his and our lives.

I was most fortunate to have very capable lady as my assistant, Vera H. S. Estes. Her father was Chinese and lived in Hawaii. As was a Chinese custom, he married a "picture bride." His family sent a picture of a lady, he agreed to marry her, she came to Hawaii, and they married. They had 12 children. Vera's father was a Chinese merchant in Honolulu and was deceased. Vera retired during my tenure, I hosted the ceremony, and all of her family attended. Since the mother did not fully understand English, we asked an interpreter to translate our comments into Mandarin for her. It was a most exciting ceremony. After the ceremony, members of her family would invite us to events almost every weekend until we left.

I was most spoiled by my assistant, Vera Estes. She would make reservations for anything we wanted to do in Hawaii and for my travel. She would ensure that my airline travel was upgraded. When I checked in on one flight on a KAL 747 to Korea, I was told that I had been upgraded to first class in the upper deck. There were only two of us on the upper deck. On a multiple stop visit in the US, Vera gave me a list of people I should contact at various stops. On the first stop, her contact upgraded me to first class. At the second stop, the contact indicated there were no upgrades. Soon after I sat in the proper seat, the flight attendant told me that "they" had "double booked" my seat and I would have to move to first class. When we arrived at the last stop, the flight attendant asked me to meet someone at the door. The contact looked surprise when she saw me but escorted me to the VIP lounge and put me in business class on the flight out. When I asked Vera how she had arranged all of this, she indicated that she called the airlines at each stop and asked for upgrades. When the airline at the last stop was reluctant, she told them that I was a "BIG" man. Obviously, the contact was surprised that I was not a large person!

While we were in Hawaii, our daughter, Beth, married Doug McCombs in California. Of course, Linda was very active in planning the wedding. Unfortunately on one occasion, I asked Linda, "Whose wedding is this?" I got what I deserved! We were able to attend their wonderful wedding.

In August 1987, I was selected for promotion to Lieutenant General and required Senate confirmation. The process took a long time. Finally, we were assured that I would be confirmed on a Friday and General Gregory scheduled a promotion ceremony. For some unknown reason at the time, the confirmation did not occur. General Gregory suggested we go ahead with the ceremony and my departure. We arrived at the Central Command in MacDill AFB in Tampa, Florida on Saturday. My new boss, General George Crist had me at work on Sunday in civilian clothes. Linda was sure "they" would make us pay our own way back to Hawaii.

Promotion to Lt. General in Hawaii

The confirmation delay had nothing to do with me. A Senator placed a hold on the only open Air Force confirmation to demand some information. He never knew nor cared that it was me. On Thursday, I was confirmed and could wear the new rank publicly. Holding up confirmations to get something else done is quite common in our political system.

CENTCOM AND JOINT STAFF

U. S. CENTRAL COMMAND (August 1987 – November 1988)

My assignment as the Deputy Commander-in-Chief of the Central Command (DCINC CENT) started off with a bang and grew from there. I visited many of the Middle Eastern countries in support of our activities.

There was great urgency for me to arrive at CENTCOM and prepare to lead the Bright Star Joint Exercise in Egypt. I departed for Bright Star five days after I was confirmed as a Lieutenant General! I was to be the senior US military leader until the end when General George Crist would arrive. Unfortunately, General Crist was not able to attend, and I was the senior US leader throughout this most successful exercise. I knew very little about the exercise and the various military organizations involved. I was enabled and blessed by my assigned advisor and mentor, Marine Colonel Butch Neal who would later become the Assistant Commandant of the Marine Corps. I did many things for the first time. As the guest of honor at the banquet, I was to be offered the "eye of the lamb!" Before dinner, I declined the honor. In retrospect, I should have accepted. Earlier in survival school, I had "eaten" the eye of a rabbit. The secret is to swallow without chewing.

In 1988, I was the senior US military person at the 25th Anniversary of the Yemen Revolution in Sanah, Yemen. This was my first official visit to an Arab country. I had been warned about the coffee served at welcomes, and avoided drinking it as long as I could. When I finally tasted, it was very delicious mocha, and I wanted some more. Unfortunately, it was too late for "seconds." As we departed, I had several small cups.

There were several associated events. Perhaps the most memorable one was a series of musical dances showing men from various parts of Yemen dancing with their curved Jumbiya fighting knives. The program began with the heavy weight dancers from the Maritime Provinces. They were jovial and fun loving. The dancers from the most Northern provinces along the Saudi borders were tough and scary. The dancers were an indication of the tremendous differences in the various part of Yemen. Yemen was the home to the Biblical Queen of Sheba.

The main event was a very large parade along a six lane street. The setting was much like the Cairo Parade when President Sadat was assassinated while attending the eighth anniversary of the Yom Kippur war with Israel as Field Marshal of the armed forces on October 6, 1981. On the front row were the President of Yemen, Yasser Arafat, and President Mengistu Haile Mariam of Ethiopia. I was in the second row off to one side. As the parade proceeded, an Army truck stalled in front of the reviewing stand. It was most reminiscent of the setting for the assassination of Sadat. There was a very silent awe as the body guards surrounded the vehicle. The soldiers in the back of the truck sat very still until a tow vehicle pulled the truck away. Everyone watching was very tense and most relieved when the parade continued uneventfully!

There was a State lunch after the parade. According to protocol, I sat with other dignitaries. The others all spoke Arabic. They were very nice but would not answer me in English. After lunch, I had a wonderful conversation with one of the Ethiopian guests at our table in perfect English.

Pakistan Visit

Linda and I represented the Central Command in meetings in Pakistan, which included a visit with President Zia. Our trip was delayed due to an aircraft problem, which resulted in a direct 18 hour flight with two air refuelings from Tampa to Islamabad, Pakistan. We arrived at 6:00 AM with the first meeting at 8:00 AM. We were most graciously hosted by Brigadier General Wasson, the US Defense attaché. A short time after our visit, he would be killed along with President Zia and US Ambassador to Pakistan Arnold L. Raphel in the C-130 crash on August 17, 1988. The plane exploded minutes after taking off in eastern Pakistan.

On the way home, we stopped in Oman, Saudi Arabia and Bahrain. In all of these places, we visited with the US troops and the leaders of the host nations. In Oman, I visited the USS Iowa battleship and witnessed the firing of the 16 inch guns. In Riyadh, Saudi Arabia, we were told that I would be honored as we departed the aircraft and Linda would be pulled aside. As I joined the Saudi host for the traditional tea and coffee in the large hall, I saw Linda across the room with Bev Farrington, the wife of the US Military Liaison Officer to Saudi Arabia, Major General Jack Farrington. As we departed the hall the ladies joined us. The Saudi host shook Linda's hand. I kissed Bev on the cheek.

During our visit in Riyadh, we were escorted by a Saudi Lt. Colonel who had studied in the US. While we were in Riyadh, he would not make eye contact with Linda – as custom dictated. As we flew to Dhahran, the three of us sat together and had a wonderful conversation. On the ground, he reverted to the Saudi customs.

Our stop in Bahrain was wonderful as we visited the troops, received briefings, and got to better know our local leaders. The culture in Bahrain was much more like our style of living than in Saudi. The Crown Prince of Bahrain was a classmate from the Army Command and Staff College at Fort Leavenworth, KS.

Operation EARNEST WILL

CENTCOM played a large role in Operation EARNEST WILL, escorting the reflagged Kuwait tankers through the Persian Gulf and responding to aggressive action by the Iranians (1987-1989). Iran wanted to impede the movement of Iraqi oil through Kuwait and the Persian Gulf.

The Iran - Iraq War began in 1980 with Iran initially having the upper hand. Iraq gained the initiative in 1988. During the conflict, the United States was closer to Saddam Hussein and Iraq than Iran. CENTCOM worked closely with the Gulf Cooperation Council (GCC) (Bahrain, Kuwait, Oman, Qatar, Saudi Arabia, and the United Arab Emirates). CENTCOM encouraged the GCC to talk with each other and agree to cooperate.

Both Iran and Iraq used the Persian Gulf in their war activities. During the period of 1981 to 1988, Iran attacked 221 ships and Iraq attacked 322 ships in the Persian Gulf – mostly each other's.

Iraq used the Persian Gulf for commerce and over flight enroute to strike Iranian targets. Iraq primarily used the French F-1 and Exocet missiles. Iraq also used Soviet Badgers for the targets near Hormuz.

Iran used the Persian Gulf for over flight en route to Iraqi targets. Frigates and speedboats were used to harass shipping. The more prominent speed boat was the 21-foot Swedish Boghammer. Iran also used mining activities to stop commerce aimed primarily at Iraq and Kuwait. Both Iran and Iraq seemed to avoid hurting Saudi and the remainder of the GCC countries.

On May 17, 1987, the Iran - Iraq War became violent to CENTCOM when the USS Stark (FFG-31) was struck by Iraqi Exocet missile South of Farsi Island, resulting in the deaths of 37 sailors. The Iraqis convinced the US that it was an accident. Shortly thereafter at the request of the Kuwait government, the United States re-flagged, "transferred ownership to US entities," and renamed 11 Kuwaiti oil tankers to reduce some of the tension.

On July 22, 1987, Operation EARNEST WILL began. The CENTCOM's Middle East Force began escorting the reflagged tankers through the Arabian Gulf, the Straits of Hormuz, and the Persian Gulf to Kuwait and return. EARNEST WILL continued through August 16, 1990 (Iraq invaded Kuwait on August 2, 1990). CENTCOM conducted 480 missions escorting a total of 649 merchant ships through the Persian Gulf.

The US Central Command had the responsibility for EARNEST WILL and the activities within the Persian Gulf. The long term commander of the Middle East Force was Admiral Hal Bernsen. This position was primarily for US military presence in the Persian Gulf and provided logistics support and diplomatic functions.

The Pacific Command commanded the ships in the Arabian Gulf that were so necessary to support the escort activities. When Navy ships entered the Persian Gulf, they had been under the command of the Central Command's Middle East Force. The Pacific Command and the US Navy were not totally supportive of the Central Command approach. A Central Command Joint Task Force was established in the Arabian Sea under the Command of Admiral Brooks who was also under Pacific Command. The Pacific Command exercised great influence over the Joint Task Force. The Joint Task Force also made it much easier to communicate with Bernsen than Brooks.

Admiral Tony Less replaced both Brooks and Bernsen and was embarked on the Command ship at Bahrain. From the Central Command perspective, everything smoothed out with Admiral Less. I suspect Admiral Less received a lot of unofficial guidance from the Pacific Command and the Navy, but he reported to and was loyal to General Crist and CENTCOM. Tony Less was a great commander.

During EARNEST WILL there were several incidents. On July 24, 1987, reflagged tanker BRIDGETON struck a mine off Iranian controlled FARSI Island and had to be repaired in Dubai. Greatly troubled by Iran's intentional mine laying in the path of the first U.S. convoy, General Crist increased mine countermeasures to clear mines near Fujairah and in the Gulf of Oman. The US had very poor mine sweeping capabilities. In September, Belgian, British, Dutch, Italian, and French mine counter measure forces joined U.S. forces. The Iranians monitored the tanker radio transmission giving their position reports to their home office. They gained a good understanding of our convoy procedures, and it became evident that they were trying to ambush us.

On September 21, 1987, the Iranian ship Iran Ajr was caught red-handed laying mines in the Persian Gulf. U.S. forces including an Army OH-6A helicopter launched from the USS Jarret (FFG-33) attacked and captured the Iran Ajr, killing five and capturing 26 Iranian sailors. Iran Ajr was towed to a deep area away from shipping and sunk. (Later, when I was acting Secretary of the Navy, I learned that my Executive Officer, Captain Martin Jenkins, had been the officer who led the boarding of the Iran Ajr.)

Navy ships were not well equipped to handle threats from small boats. They were equipped with missiles and 5 inch guns. Later, Gatling guns were installed on the ships to handle air attacks; however, it was still difficult to depress the guns sufficiently to counter small boats. Two oil drilling platforms (Hercules and Winbrown 7) were leased from Brown and Root, placed in the Persian Gulf, and equipped with helicopters and boats to help patrol and control the sea lanes. They were outfitted with sophisticated target-acquisition devices and a variety of Army and Navy weapon systems including a wheeled variant of the Army Vulcan 20 mm Gatling gun manned by an Army crew. At one point, we even had dolphins acting as barge watchdogs. Navy Seals were also stationed on the barges. Army helicopters were operated from the mobile sea base Hercules. There was some concern that the Army helicopters were not "marinized" (prepared to operate in salty environments) to protect them from the effects of the salt in the air. The Army helicopters worked well. This was not a popular move within the Navy. The critics thought for certain that we had lost our minds. One senior Admiral later commented that he never wanted to hear the term "guerilla war at sea" again! (Guerilla war is normally conducted on land by the Army and Marines.) BUT IT WORKED!

In early fall, intelligence received information about an Iranian Plan called the "Hajj Plan." The plan called for a group to 50 small boats to proceed south from the Farsi area to attack a group of Khafji Saudi oil platforms. With the "Hajj Plan" fresh in everyone's mind on October 2, 1987, we received a report that 50 boats were detected moving from the Farsi area towards Saudi. The Commander in Chief of the Central Command (CINC CENT) and most of the senior Saudi military leaders were in Washington in a periodic review of our activities. The attack was taken very seriously. The Saudi leaders agreed to allow us to bring in some forces into Saudi – P-3 reconnaissance aircraft, KC-10 air refuelers, etc. In Tampa and the Persian Gulf, we were watching the progress of the boats very carefully. Thirty minutes before the anticipated time of attack, the tracks were lost and nothing happened! We later determined that a radar interpreter on a ship saw a return which was down linked from the AWACS. With Hajj Plan in the back of his mind, he reported that the "50-ship radar return" was the beginning of the plan. He gave the track the correct heading and speed for small boats attacking the oil platforms. Once the track was indicated, the computer automatically moved the "return" forward. I never heard how the track updates finally stopped. The whole affair was a MIRAGE. Some accused us of fabrication. It was not.

The Hercules was placed near Farsi Island and near the site of the *Bridgeton* mine incident.. On October 8, 1987, three Iranian gunboats fired on U. S. helicopters near the mobile sea base Hercules. U.S. returned fire and sunk the three gunboats. The same day, another U.S. helicopter was fired upon from the Iranian Rostam offshore oil platform. On October 16, 1987, Sea Isle City, another U.S. reflagged Kuwaiti tanker, in the vicinity of Kuwait's Sea Island Terminal was hit by an Iranian HY-2 cruise missile. Several people were injured, including the captain, who was permanently blinded.

National Command Authorities decided the U.S. should respond to Iran's attacks with some form of military force in self-defense. On October 19, Operation NIMBLE ARCHER attacked the Rostam oil platform. To minimize civilian casualties, we gave a 20 minute pre warning to allow evacuation of the estimated 30 people on the platforms – most heeded the warning. The three oil platforms were destroyed. After destroying Rostam, the Iranian attacks on merchant shipping in that area stopped -- validating the target selection.

On April 14, 1987, the USS Samuel B. Roberts (FFG-58) detected three mines lying approximately 55 miles off the Qatar Peninsula. She reversed engines and backed away only to hit a fourth mine. The 253 pound mine blew a 21 foot hole in the ship and injured ten sailors. Despite extensive fire and flooding, the Roberts crew was able to control the damage and keep the ship afloat. The crew literally tied the ship together with cables. The Roberts was towed to Dubai and eventually placed on the Mighty Servant II, a submersible ship normally used to transport oil platforms, and carried to Bath, Maine for final repair. Cost for Mighty Servant trip - $1.35 million. Cost of repairs - $60 million. Cost of a replacement - $400 Million. RADM George Gee, Director of Surface Combat Systems, said, "Her crew was able to save the ship – and most knowledgeable people would say that we probably should have lost her!"

U.S. and allied mine counter-measure ships conducted an extensive search and discovered eight more mines – the French found them, the Belgians localized the find, and the Dutch and British destroyed them. On April 18, 1988, CENTCOM carried out operation PRAYING MANTIS against SASSAN and SIRRI oil platforms. These targets were selected because they had been used for military purposes including support for Iranian speedboat attacks on neutral shipping and support of mining operations. Five minutes prior to the attacks, radio calls were made to those on the Iranian platforms to abandon the platforms prior to imminent shelling. There was eerie silence. As soon as the attack began, the Iranians occupying the platforms quickly abandoned their resolve to stand and fight. Three U.S. surface action groups and A-6 aircraft from the USS

Enterprise with orders to Sink the Sabalan and destroy the oil platforms in the lower Persian Gulf (SASSAN and SIRRI)

A wide ranging naval battle continued. A total of four Iranian vessels in the Murarak oil field were sunk or neutralized. American losses consisted of one AH-1T Sea Cobra. This was the biggest battle at sea since WW II. The attack occurred at almost the same time as the Iraqis were retaking the Al Faw peninsula and featured at least two instances in which technically superior communications allowed near real time decisions to be made in Washington which directy affected the outcome.

These very successful actions were being documented. Medal recommendations were being prepared. The pride of everyone involved soared to new heights!

As is so often the results, on July 3, 1988, pride turned to confusion and finally disappointment. The USS Vincennes mistakenly identified an aircraft as a hostile Iranian F-14 and shot it down. Most unfortunately, the aircraft was an Iranian commercial airliner with 290 people on board – all were killed.

As background, the USS Vincennes was an Aegis guided missile cruiser equipped with sophisticated surveillance and missile systems. During the work up period prior to entering the Gulf, the Vincennes crew practiced: Air intercepts with missiles, defense against small boats, and actions to respond to non-military "kamikaze attack." She entered the Persian Gulf under the command of Captain Will Rogers on May 16, 1988.

This was the first time the Vincennes, the most sophisticated Navy Aegis ship entered the Persian Gulf during the Earnest Will Operations. Earlier before the Earnest Will operations, some other Aegis ships had been in the Persian Gulf. The Vincennes Captain and crew were eager for action to show their capabilities. The entire US Middle East Force was alerted to a possible Iranian attack – including a suicide air attack – during the July 4th weekend. Iranian activity had been increasing for some time. Iran was under pressure to show some response to Iraqi victories on land.

During the prior week, Iranian F-14 fighters began flying from the Bandar Abbas airfield. F-14 can drop bombs and launch missiles but cannot normally launch Harpoon missiles. HOWEVER, it was widely rumored that the Iranians had modified the F-14 to launch Harpoons with a more than 13 miles range. Ships were being warned about Harpoons. Given widespread use of suicide in Iranian-backed irregulars in Lebanon, US crews also must have suspected that the Iranians might try a kamikaze attack on a ship. During the subsequent interviews, every crewmember believed the Iranians would use kamikaze tactics.

Prior and during the Iran Air 655 shoot down, Captain Rogers was preoccupied by an on-going small boat engagement and a fouled 5-inch gun in Mount 51. He believed the most immediate threat was to deal with the dense, aggressive high-speed small craft attempting to press home an attack. Early on July 3, the Vincennes launched a helicopter to investigate a report of small Iranian gunboats firing on merchant traffic. One of the boats fired on the helicopter. The cruiser moved to a position to drive the boats away. They did not leave even after the cruiser began to fire. After requesting permission, the Vincennes engaged the boats -- which were closing at high speed. The Phalanx close-in-weapon systems could not engage surface targets. The Vincennes also had USMC Stinger missiles on deck surrounded by sandbags. The forward 5-inch gun in Mount 51 failed after seven minutes. Only one 5-inch gun was available to engage up to four boats. The Vincennes had to maneuver violently (30-degree turns at 30 knots) to keep the remaining gun on the boats – especially one with a recoilless rifle. The engagement lasted 17 minutes; Vincennes fired 72 rounds.

An Iranian P-3 aircraft, which is used for surveillance and targeting, was detected inbound from the North and challenged. The "velocity leader" displayed on the radar showed the Iranian P-3 on the edge of the scope and headed towards the Vincennes. P-3 responded, "We are going about our business and will not approach the Vincennes or other ships." The P-3 mission in the US and Iranian forces was to target ships. It had "Passive Target Detection" (PTD) capabilities. It was not unusual for the US ships to talk to the Iranian P-3s, Iranian Air 655 was detected four minutes after the surface action began while the cruiser was still threatened. Vincennes Combat Information Center (CIC) identified contact as "unknown – assumed enemy." Radar echo was identified with a Mode III Identification Friend or Foe (IFF) response. But the operator also had a Mode II response at Bandar Abbas airport. The operator most probably left the radar "cursor" on Bandar Abbas area. Mode III is normally used by civilian aircraft. Military aircraft often use both Modes II and III. Aircraft was identified tentatively as a F-14 – "fitting the expectations." Normal visual identification using a TV camera was not possible because it was hazy with a ceiling of about 200 feet. The IFF system was not integrated into the situation display. The IFF information is displayed on the operators' consoles as a separate IFF character readout. It was at some stations and not others. Aegis equipment was designed to engage targets in dense, high-speed environments.

Rogers and his antiaircraft warfare (AAW) officer saw a vector, representing Iran Air 655, pointed at them and closing. Vincennes challenged the unknown air target seven times on both the Military Air Distress (MAD) and International Air Distress (IAD) frequencies. Normally commercial aircraft would monitor these "distress" frequencies and responded to warnings. ICAO confirmed that the pilot of the Airbus had been briefed on the distress frequencies prior to departing Bandar Abbas. The only plausible explanations were the pilot accidentally did not have distress radio working or turned off or the pilot used the normal distress radio to "get ahead in tuning in next check point frequency."

Warnings were copied in the Dubai tower and the Iranians at Bandar Abbas copied part of the warnings. USS Sides challenged the unknown air target five times and evaluated target as non-threatening -- it never replied, nor did it maneuver evasively. (This information was not relayed to the Vincennes.) The Tactical Information Coordinator (TIC) sat at a character read out console and became concerned that the air threat was being overlooked with emphasis on the ground action. He was relying on manual "read-outs" of altitude. The TIC called out the air target's altitude -- which he read as decreasing 1,000 feet per mile. Aircraft seemed to be flying directly at the Vincennes on a classic attack pattern.

Rogers could wait only so long. His Standard missile could not intercept targets inside a substantial minimum range. His only operating 5 inch gun was actively engaging the surface targets. Only one of Vincennes' two Phalanx Gatling guns was operational. As mentioned earlier, there were very short range Stinger missiles. His AAW (Anti-Aircraft Warfare) Officer asked to fire as soon as the unknown came within 20 miles. We all tend to accept the data that fits into a preconceived picture! Rogers authorized firing about seven minutes after the first detection. The target was ten miles away. Vincennes fired two missiles. The airliner was hit at a range of seven miles, 17 seconds after missiles left their rails.

As is so often the case in combat, when everything looks so great, one must be careful to avoid a catastrophe like this.

Under intense international political and economic pressure, Iran and Iraq agreed to a United Nations sponsored cease-fire on August 20, 1988. This brought to an end a long and extremely bloody war. Unfortunately, the Iran - Iraq differences were never been fully resolved and they both retained considerable military capabilities. As horrible as the event was, it cast a pall over everything with a profound effect on the entire world. This event offered honorable rationale to make a most difficult acceptance that the war had gone on too long – WITHOUT admitting total defeat.

A short time later, I was asked to go to the Pentagon to interview with Admiral Crowe to become the Director of the Joint Staff. With a night to prepare, my interview went very well, and we would again return to the Pentagon.

As we were leaving CENTCOM, George and Barbara Crist were most complimentary about our time together. In his farewell words, George indicated that he had heard great things about me and was most pleased to receive me as his Deputy Commander-in-Chief. He went on to say that I was very quiet, and he wasn't sure about me until several weeks later during a staff meeting. "The senior officer sitting next to him was fabricating some 'facts,' and HT figuratively took out his scalpel and cut the officer from ear to ear and he did not know he had been touched until he turned his head and it fell off! Then, I knew the treasure I had!" Linda and I learned much from George and Barbara Crist.

Director of the Joint Staff

As the walls of communism came tumbling down in 1989, I led the Joint Staff as our Nation responded to the fast paced activities. I was able to bring the military and civilian staffs much closer together at the highest levels in the Department of Defense.

After a short time as Director, the Chairman of the Joint Chiefs of Staff, Admiral Bill Crowe, asked me to stay after a meeting. He spent some time complimenting me on how well I was doing. I responded, "I don't visit too often to seek guidance!" He responded, "I have noticed, and I like it!" We had a most effective partnership during a historic time of world history. This (1989) was the year the "walls came tumbling down around the world!" The Soviet Union was dissolved and so many other countries gained their freedom.

The Joint Chiefs of Staff (JCS) meet regularly in a conference room referred to as the "Tank." As the Director of the Joint Staff, I chaired the three-star "Ops Deps" (Operational Deputies) meeting and acted as the executive secretary to the JCS meetings. There were five members of each: Army, Navy, Air Force, Marine, and Director/Chairman. To be most effective, the Director of the Joint Staff had to be neutral of Service interests. Early in my tenure at an Ops Deps meeting, there were even splits (Army - Air Force vs. Navy – Marine Corps) on two votes. Everyone assume that I would vote with the Air Force. Fortunately in both cases, the Navy/Marine Corps position was the correct solution, and I broke the tie in their favor. There was never any thought that I would let my background lead me in the incorrect direction. I could not have found a more dramatic way to show that I "was truly Joint" in my thinking and actions. After this, there was never a question about my listening and leading the group to truly Joint positions. We were able to gain consensus and votes were seldom needed.

Initially, President Bush nominated Senator John Tower to be the Secretary of Defense. During the preparation process, I hosted Senator Tower in the Tank for a briefing on the Single Integrated Operation Plan (SIOP), which outlines our nuclear war plans. There were four of us: Senator Tower, an assistant, the briefer and me. The building opposition to his selection and the details of the SIOP brought great pressure and perspiration to Senator Tower's face. He asked no questions; and at the end said, "This is a very complicated area, and I do not know enough to ask any questions. As I learn more, I will want to discuss the SIOP more." A few short weeks later, the new nominee to be the Secretary, Dick Cheney, came for a similar briefing. This time there were only three (Cheney, briefer and me). Mr. Cheney asked many questions. At one point, he said, "Did the previous slide say" the following? It was an intuitive statement. The briefer firmly disagreed, and I was about to agree when we went back and looked at the issue. Mr. Cheney was absolutely correct! These two briefings showed a very sharp contrast between Senators Tower and Cheney. During all of my meetings with Secretary Cheney, he always asked the difficult questions and very quickly gained the proper understanding.

Soon after David Addington became Secretary Cheney's Assistant, I had a long visit with David. He told me that he had met several senior Air Force officers and had been most unimpressed. For some reason, our discussions went extremely well. The next day, he had a direct phone link established between the two of us. Our friendship and great respect would continue and have a dramatic influence on my future activities. (David sponsored me to be a member of the 1993 Base Realignment and Closure Commission, and this experience led to my becoming an Assistant Secretary of the Navy.)

During my senior military career, I was fortunate and unfortunate to hear rumors of assignments being considered. It was most exciting to learn of the decision to promote me to four stars with an assignment to Stuttgart, Germany as the Deputy Commander-in-Chief (DCINC) of the European Command. We were very excited, and I was able to get copies of the floor plan for the DCINC home on Richard Strauss Street in Stuttgart. It was the most magnificent home that I had ever visited. Later, I heard that I would be interviewed by the Secretary of the Air Force for one of two positions – DCINC of the European Command or the Commander-in-Chief of the U.S. Transportation Command and the Military Airlift Command, which was much better. I used a 5x8 card to prepare for the interview. One side of the card provided facts about Europe and the other about Transportation Command. When my mentor and friend, the Air Force Chief of Staff Larry Welch called to officially tell me, I never "let on" that I had already heard. During the conversation, he kept referring to two positions but never identified them until the end. I was "of course surprised!" The Secretary only talked of one position, and we were most fortunate to become Commander and First Lady of the U. S. Transportation Command and Military Airlift Command! Neither Secretary Rice nor I had any idea about what would lie ahead.

My promotion ceremony was a little awkward. I worked for Admiral Crowe but the Air Force was promoting me. I asked Admiral Crowe to host the ceremony. It was held at the intersection of three halls on E Ring of the Pentagon. All three halls were filled. As Admiral Crowe, Linda, and I walked down the hall, he said, "Why don't we ask the Chief of Staff of the Air Force Larry Welch to 'pin you?' Of course, I was most pleased. Admiral Crowe said wonderful things, and General Welch and Linda pinned me. I had always said the Linda outranked me. When I was promoted to three stars, someone said Linda is "maxed out with four stars." The night before the promotion ceremony, a friend gave me a plaque with five large stars and an inscription saying, "Linda Johnson, the CINC's CINC!" As a new four star, my first action was to promote Linda to five stars. She and everyone thought it was most appropriate to recognize her. I then turned to Peg Ellis and acknowledged that the first star that she had pinned on was always hers. Tears flowed.

Everyone wondered why my promotion had drawn such a large crowd. After my remarks, the entire Joint Staff and I surprised Admiral Crowe with our recognition of his outstanding leadership – just prior to his retirement. On behalf of the Joint Staff, I presented him with a punch bowl and eight young officers representing the eight directorates presented cups. Admiral Crowe was "blown away" by the surprise and our utmost respect. After his gracious comments, he ensured that the attention was returned to me and my promotion.

One of the early Air Officers Commanding at the Academy, Colonel James B. Townsend, was present and filled with emotional pride in "his" cadet becoming the first four-star general from the Air Force Academy. After the ceremony, I invited him and Linda in to my office and asked them to change the rank that "really mattered" -- the rank on my shirt. Teary eyed, he shared our immense pride.

TRANSCOM

COMMANDER-IN-CHIEF OF THE U. S. TRANSPORTATION COMMAND

I served as Commander-in-Chief of the U.S. Transportation Command and Commander-in-Chief of the Military Airlift Command during a most demanding period of our history in operations JUST CAUSE in Panama, DESERT SHIELD/STORM in the Middle East, and a myriad of daily transportation challenges.

Welcome to TRANSCOM

Linda and I were welcomed by Duane and Rosalie Cassidy as friends and with great respect. Uncharacteristically, we were invited to share his farewell event the evening before our assumption of command. The mutual respect and assurance of a smooth transition was very helpful. The day after the Change of Command, our planned visit to St Louis was changed dramatically by Hurricane Hugo. I properly chose to visit the areas hardest hit by Hugo in Charleston, SC. I was amazed by the destruction. Large buildings would be cut in half -- half was gone and the other half was untouched. Two trees fell in front of a home and someone recognized it as the "Home of the Month!"

As with all changes, we received many most thoughtful notes. The one from the Commander of the Central Command, General Norm Schwarzkopf, was extremely touching and certainly foretold our very close relations in the future.

> HT, Heartiest congratulations on your promotion and assumption of command of our nation's military transportation forces. Few know better than you the enormity of the transportation challenges facing USCENTCOM. We, on the other hand, are equally aware that no one is more capable than you to tackle the pressing global requirements of your newly won mission. Recalling the leading roles you played in our past – as DCINC here and, more recently, on the Joint Staff – we at

USCENTCOM share in the excitement of your crucial assignment. In both previous positions, your unfailing support has been deeply appreciated.

Brenda and I wish you and Linda the best of everything. We know USTRANSCOM is gaining a great team and could not be in better hands. Look forward to working with you and welcome yet another opportunity to continue our mutually supportive relationships.

Warm Regards, Norm

Little did either of us know the full importance of his words in what would follow within a year.

Always stay humble

Soon after assuming command of TRANSCOM, Linda and I attended the retirement of Admiral Crowe at the Naval Academy. During the reception, a former Air Training Officer (officer upper classman) from the Academy, Charlie Cole, brought his new bride, Corliss, to meet "one" of his cadets who was the first Academy graduate to be promoted to four-star general. After he finished heaping great praise on me, I respectfully asked, "Would you have thought this would happen when we were cadets?" After a courteous pause, he answered, "No!" Of course, I agreed with him. We never know where our paths will lead, and we always need to be very humble!

Invasion of Panama 1989

During Operation Just Cause, the invasion of Panama, all the Air Force forces that took part in the invasion except the tankers and F-117s were assigned to MAC. As CINCTRANS and CINCMAC, we coordinated and directed the deployment and re-supply of all forces. Prior to directing the invasion, General Colin Powell called me, outlined the plan, and asked if we had the forces to support the timing of the plans. Despite unusual freezing rain at the Fort Bragg departure base, all operations were carried out on time and without any Air Force casualties.

The MAC Christmas Party was scheduled on the night of the deployment, December 19, 1989. In a show of total support of the "battle staff," I went to the party, as the first planes were to launch. All was going well until we received a message just before the main course that the aircraft were refreezing as fast as they were de-iced at Pope AFB, NC, and we could not make the departure timing. As you can imagine, I returned to the battle staff and was quickly reassured of Herculean efforts to get the aircraft airborne as soon as they de-iced, the aircraft held overhead until all were de-iced, and they coordinated the proper timing. The airdrop occurred only 30 seconds late!

Operation Just Cause began on December 20, 1989, at 0100 local time. The operation involved nearly 57,000 U.S. troops and over 300 aircraft -- including the AC-130 Spectre gunship, OA-37B Dragonfly observation and attack aircraft, and the F-117A Nighthawk stealth aircraft, and AH-64 Apache attack helicopter. The Panamanian Defense Force included 46,000 troops.

There are some vivid and difficult memories of Just Cause activities. One of the key military objectives was the securing of Noriega's Punta Paitilla Airport and aircraft by the SEALs. Unfortunately, four SEALs were lost. The SEAL team was being fired upon from the top of a hangar. For no apparent reason, the Panamanian sniper surrendered. When asked why he surrendered, he said, "When the helicopter arrived with the big gun, I knew it was over!" Of course the "big gun" was a harmless refueling probe on the helicopter. This was perhaps the most difficult early target, and the "refueling probe" had a decisive impact.

The entire operation was a great success. We provided every desired support. There were several examples of the AC-130 providing stark demonstrations of our abilities. To show its capabilities and gain the respect, the AC-130 was asked to "take out" a palm tree in the middle of a traffic circle. The tree was removed with no other damage. Later, to encourage surrender of a Fort in northern Panama, the US Army approached the Fort at night and asked the commander to surrender. There was some hesitation. To encourage the proper decision, the US commander invited the Panamanians to look south as the sky became bright with flares and an AC-130 destroyed several targets. The

Panamanian commander surrendered and there was little additional fighting.

The Nation and Panama were duly impressed by the tremendous job our people did in ensuring the success of the operation.

Quality Journey

As I prepared to assume command of the U. S. Transportation Command and MAC, our friends from our Evreux days, Bob and Shirley Marquette most graciously asked to drive Linda and me from Washington to Scott AFB. It was an amazing time to relax with Bob and develop eight programs I thought we needed to improve our performance, morale, and perception of ourselves and by others. These were accepted by all as "enlightened" leadership. As I was departing Washington area, I was given an article on "TQM" (Total Quality Management) and told I might enjoy reading it at some time. Initially, I was much too busy commanding the two commands to read about TQM! When I finally read the article and listened to others, I realized that all of "my programs" were embedded in the TQM principles.

Prior to the beginning of Desert Shield on August 7, 1990, we had begun a Quality Journey in the Military Airlift Command (MAC). The first step was wide participation in an off-site led by a TQM consultant, Dr. Sheila Sheinberg, to establish OUR Vision and gain "buy in". Before leading the session, I insisted she learn about our command. Just prior to our session, she visited with me and told me more about our command than I thought anyone other than I knew. Consequently, the visioning and "buy in" went very well as it was indeed OUR Quality Journey. Our Visions became: "Proud MAC – Suppport America can Always Count On!"

The Monday after the Desert Shield airlift began, all of the MAC senior officers except me were scheduled for Quality training. All weekend, "they" wondered when I was going to cancel the training because we were much too busy to worry about Quality. The proper focus was established when I announced that not only the Quality training would continue but I would also attend – and everyone attended! There were a steady stream of notes to me, and I am afraid I got very little from the training. HOWEVER, a powerful message was sent to all -- "Quality was even more important during the biggest airlift in the history of the world."

This Quality focus was picked up at all levels, and we did our part by outlining opportunities and letting the leaders at all levels find, execute and refine the processes! All of a sudden everyone was a leader and fantastic things just happened!

Don Loranger was a deputy in MAC Plans and orchestrated our Quality activities. After he was promoted, we moved him to the Inspector General (IG) position. As we sought very positive ways to focus on Quality, we changed the IG title to "Quality Support and Readiness" and changed IG Visits to Quality Visits. Normally, the IG briefed the results; the units would try to fix or find excuses just prior to the next IG Visit. Rather than have the IG Team out brief the visit, we had the commander brief the challenges and solutions – and gain "ownership" for the results.

I attended the first few out briefs. We required the unit being visited to highlight the findings and outline the solution. At the first out brief at Charleston AFB with John Handy (who would later become the Commander of the Transportation Command), the Wing Commander found the good things without raising many issues. During the third out brief with Woody Hogle at Altus AFB on a Thursday, the unit raised many issues and proposed solutions. There was one difficult computer challenge without a solution. I stated that it sounded like a communications challenge and asked who was the Communications Officer? Major Moore stood, acknowledged that he was the Communication Officer, and indicated that he had not heard of the problem. I responded that he should try to fix it in three days, and if he could not, I would find the solution. On the following Sunday, I received a call from the Base Operation saying that Major Moore was on the line for me. Of course, they had figured out the problems and fixed them. That was a relief for me – because I did not know how to fix it!

On subsequent out briefs, the unit and headquarters had figured out the solutions and fixed the challenges. It was indeed amazing how everyone began working together!

As in every organization, it was much too easy to say "no" than "yes" to a new "Quality" proposal. We instituted a suggestion program called Quality Eagle. Only the CINC (me) could turn down an idea. Intervening headquarters were only authorized to approve ideas. It was a "shot heard around the mobility world." Virtually every Wing and Numbered Airlift Commander asked, "He is not really serious, is he?" Everyone became very serious about Quality and Transformation. It was a resounding success. We received many good ideas from our young people, and they felt and were empowered!

In a separate pronouncement, the CINC indicated, "When someone presented a problem she or he also had to be prepared to present a solution – or at least the start of one!" Again, the Team achieved amazing results.

Later when criticized by the Air Force Chief of Staff McPeak for giving Quality credit for all successes, I proudly replied "Guilty!"

An author in writing a chapter on our Quality Journey asked where I was first learned about Quality. I responded, "From my mother and father, they just did not know the current titles!" Looking back, most of us have used these principles all of your lives.

As I was about to retire, a young NCO was asked, "What will happen to the MAC Quality Journey when General Johnson leaves?" He quickly responded, "What do you mean? It belongs to me; just let someone try to take it away!" The MAC Quality Journey did indeed belong to each member.

We were most fortunate to have Dr. Sheila Sheinberg facilitate our Quality Journey. As she led us to ever higher levels, she convinced each of us that our successes were OURS!

<u>C-5 participation in a Salinas, CA Air Show</u>

I received a call from Congressman Leon E. Panetta of California who later became President Clinton's Chief of Staff and President Obama's Secretary of Defense. He demanded that I allow a C-5 land at Salinas, CA for an air show. I knew the details. After he read his demands, I calmly explained that the load bearing capacity on both runways was well below that required for C-5s. Both runways were too short for C-5s and the longer one had the lower load bearing capacity. After explaining the details, I said, "If you want us to send a C-5 in, we will," implying that he would be responsible for any damage. He very quickly said, "No way! You should not send a C-5 to Salinas!" It is amazing how facts and placing a person in an accountable role brings clarity to their demands.

DESERT SHIELD

As with "Just Cause" earlier, General Colin Powell called to discuss our mission and asked if we could handle the demands. I assure him that we could, and we were off and running. He never had to ask for anything. I was most blessed to have Vice Admiral Paul Butcher as my TRANSCOM deputy. He brought wide ranging experience and was a decisive, wise decision maker.

One of General Powell's staff officers complained that we told countries around the world before the State Department. Each time a mission is scheduled, we had to gain "over-flight" clearances. The quick, heavy traffic certainly told others of our activities. A short time later, I began sending Colin an update from TRANSCOM each evening. He was most appreciative. In mid-November 1990, we began moving forces from Europe. In one of my "Personal For's" to Colin, we outlined the difficulties we would have in moving forces from Europe. We made the point that Europe had great experience in receiving troops and equipment but no experience in deploying their forces to other areas. This was sent widely and upset some. In the end, it was very helpful to have "others show us they could be very flexible and supportive!"

As Christmas and the New Year approached, the Army Commander in Europe thought it would be great if no person was deployed on Christmas or New Year's Day. I responded informally that I agreed, and we would have to stop flying three days before and after the holidays to ensure our crews were well cared for. We heard no more about the holidays and pushed hard to meet the goals of General Schwarzkopf.

Early in Desert Shield, I made three decisions that proved to be very important and wise. First: when told by the MAC staff that the CENTCOM Time Phased Force Deployment Lists (TPFDL) were not accurate and could not be used, I knew they were correct. To ensure the tool was corrected, I directed that nothing would move that was not in the TPDL. Within a day, the TPFDL became much more accurate and usable! Second: As each Service and commander demanded that their movements were the highest priority, I directed that the CENTCOM CINC General Schwarzkopf would determine the priorities. He did and everyone had to follow his priorities. Third: to ensure all reports were proper and timely, I directed the Historian to collect the Operations Center reports. He had a vested interest and the reports were very accurate and timely! These three decisions made our task much more efficient. (The Historian, Jim Matthews, later wrote a well-documented book, "So Many, So Much, So Far, So Fast.")

The TRANSCOM staff matured very quickly to meet the demands of Just Cause and Desert Shield. Our Operations Center had to be greatly expanded. All of the Services gave us many dedicated reserve members to meet our every need. I never knew if I were talking to an active or reserve member, and it made no difference. Everyone was equally talented and totally committed. As we drew down after the conflict, I invited all of the reserve members for a reception in the garden behind our home. Several times, I wanted to say, "I did not realize you were in the reserves," but it did not matter; and we were equally proud of every member of our team. For a few months, our Operations Center was more experienced on the weekends when many reservists were on duty than during the week when primarily new active members were working. What a phenomenal team of professionals!

As we were initiating our responses to the demands of the Desert Shield build up, I had to make a most difficult decision. I had picked a very sharp senior officer to lead MAC Operations. As the difficult decisions began to pile up, he had difficulty in pushing out ahead of all of the formal "permissions." One afternoon in late August 1990, I decided and cleared with the Air Force that we needed a more decisive MAC DO and asked him to move on to a different job in the Air Force. Major General Vern Kondra became the leader of MAC Operations. Everyone knew this decision had to be made. By eight o'clock the next morning, everyone knew about the decision, and there was an "extra quickness" in everyone's actions.

C-5 Crash and visit to Europe

On August 29, 1990, a C-5 crashed just after takeoff from Ramstein AFB in Germany. The final accident report indicated that one of the engine reverse mechanisms had malfunctioned causing the thrust to be reversed on that engine. It was fully loaded with cargo and personnel in the upper rear deck. A few survived. A few days later, I was visiting Europe and was able to visit the crash site. I was amazed that a passenger would survive when many sitting nearby had died. I had a most touching visit with a surviving crew member at the Memorial Service. I know throughout his remaining life he asked, "Why not me?"

On this same mission, we visited Torrejon AFB in Madrid, Spain. It was an exciting but also disappointing visit. Many passengers were spending the night on cots in the hangar. I was most impressed when I visited the Exchange in the hanger and asked what were the top selling items? Number two was wiring flowers to love ones at home. Number one by far was the American Flag. As our troops were going into war, they were proud of their families and their country. This speaks wonders for our society.

Torrejon was one of the two largest refueling points in Europe. As the flow increased, the ramp parking space became a premium. The Spanish units very quickly volunteered to move to give us more space, but the US fighter unit refused to make room for the MAC aircraft. The local base wanted to restrict the MAC and transient crews to ensure they did not disrupt their activities and refused to allow them to use the officers club. The MAC crews could use the Class Six store, which sold alcohol and sundries at a good profit. The local unit wanted MAC assistance in planning their move to theater but could not talk to me while I was visiting because it was a holiday! After a short phone discussion, all of these concerns were quickly fixed by my classmate, General Bob Oaks, the new Commander of US Air Force in Europe.

I continued to insist that we support the needs of General Schwarzkopf and all who supported him. Most of the airlift was supported by Industrial Funding (the customers paid). This was the first time such funding was used in a wartime movement. At one point, the MAC Comptroller told me that I was in violation of the "Anti Deficiency Act" (spending money that we did not have). I responded, "Great, let's continue supporting the war effort!"

As CINCMAC on August 17, 1990, I activated Stage I of the Civil Reserve Air Fleet (CRAF) for the first time. For many years, the civil air carriers had agreed to support MAC and the Nation in time of need. There were three levels of effort. I knew I had the authority to "call" the Stage I CRAF. When Colin Powell and I decided it was time to require their service, I merely signed and transmitted a memo and all the air carriers provided their services to meet our needs.

Later, I found out how it was transmitted: On August 6, the following transmission from the Military Airlift Command to all CRAF members flashed over ARINC (Aeronautical Radio, Inc.), a communications system serving commercial air carriers:

> CRAF STAGE 1 ACTIVATION NOTIFICATION. THIS IS NOT AN EXERCISE. THE COMMANDER IN CHIEF OF MILITARY AIRLIFT COMMAND HAS DETERMINED THE UNITED STATES HAS SUBSTANTIALLY EXPANDED PEACETIME MILITARY AIRLIFT REQUIREMENTS. HE HAS THEREFORE ACTIVATED STAGE 1, EFFECTIVE 0001Z, 18 AUG 90. THE GOVERNMENT MAY EXERCISE ITS OPTION TO INCREASE THE SERVICES TO BE PERFORMED UNDER YOUR AIRLIFT SERVICES CONTRACT TO THE FULL CAPACITY OF THE AIRCRAFT VOLUNTEERED TO CRAF STAGE I, AND THEREFORE ANTICIPATE A SELECTIVE UTILIZATION OF STAGE I. SPECIFIC MISSION SCHEDULES WILL BE SENT AT LEAST 24 HOURS PRIOR TO MISSION ONLOAD TIME ... CRITICAL: VERIFY RECEIPT OF THIS MESSAGE. THEN IMMEDIATELY PASS TO YOUR CHIEF OPERATING OFFICER AND CIVIL RESERVE AIR FLEET MOBILIZATION REPRESENTATIVE. RESPOND VIA AIRINC CIRCUIT ...

We became very close to the entire air carrier industry, and together, we served our Nation with utmost distinction. Every company and agency eagerly responded to every need I could ask for on behalf of our Nation! It was indeed a proud time for our country and all of us who were so involved.

Gas masks for CRAF crews for Desert Shield

As the potential chemical threats increased, we decided to provide gas mask protection to all military and commercial crews. Initially to ensure proper availability, we provided the masks after the commercial crews landed in the Persian Gulf areas. We realized the potential hazards of needing the protection on landing and crews not being familiar with the equipment. We very quickly began providing the equipment and an orientation at the intermediate refueling base. This allowed the crews to practice and become very comfortably with the equipment enroute to the Persian Gulf. There were several potential threats and the crews were well prepared. Fortunately, there were no actual exposures.

DESERT EXPRESS

As the troops and equipment were deployed to the Persian Gulf, the need for crucial supplies and spare parts became critical. As the commander of all transportation assets, I was held responsible (blamed) by all for any delays -- even if the part was not even in the transportation system. In this and past conflicts, "they" knew the system would not be responsive so each level "rat holed" extra supplies which made the deployment even more demanding. We (sometimes spelled with one letter) decided to establish a "FedEx" type delivery system. We picked the "on load" base, gave general guidelines, and empowered the base to determine how best to accomplish the task. A Senior NCO and his team planned the process. Together, we established the following guarantee: "If the service or other organization got the package to Charleston Air Force Base by 10:30 in the morning, it would depart at 12:30, and arrive in Saudi Arabia 17 1/2 hours later -- every day." There was only one delay at Charleston. When an aircraft had a problem after takeoff and had to return, the Team transferred the load to the spare aircraft, which was airborne 13 minutes after the original aircraft landed. This was an amazing feat; no one directed their actions; they were empowered. BUT they did not stop there because they had a guaranteed arrival time. They called ahead to the European refueling base and gained their tremendous support for getting the aircraft back on schedule. As one would well know, it arrived "on time" as just another "routine delivery." There were only two short delays: on the day the war began and another day due to adverse weather. This is a phenomenal tribute to empowered people.

One day at around 11:00 am, a vehicle came racing through the front gate at Charleston Air Force Base and would not stop even with the police chasing him! He was from Shaw AFB and had to get his "important cargo" on the departing aircraft. Of course after his success, he was treated as a hero!

All of this was easy for me because I did not have to do the work -- I only had to empower others. Wanting to recognize their accomplishments, I, "un-thoughtfully," arranged to visit the Charleston operation with a bag full of decorations during the critical 10:30 AM – 12:30 PM period. They were pleased and most proud to see me; however, they had an aircraft to load and decorations were less important. Needless to say, all those we supported and I shared their immense pride. All complaints went away, all parts of the supply system became more efficient, we established a European Desert Express, and such a system is now institutionalized in all planning for future operations. This was quite a feat for group of just ordinary men and women who truly cared and was empowered to make it happen!

Sealift Union Support

Sealift was divided into to several categories: the Afloat Prepositioning Force, the 12 Fast Sealift Ships, commercial ships, and the 96 ship Ready Reserve Force. All were manned by civilian crews. US flagged ships supported 73.4% of our sealift cargo. We were also well supported by foreign flagged vessels.

As we began activating the Ready Reserve Force ships, the Maritime Unions assured us that every ship would be manned when needed. With this strong support, we were assured of having the ship crewed when we needed them. Later, I found that the Unions had indeed met their commitment. Only one ship moved from its mooring position to the shipyard with less than a full crew. This was indeed a tremendous accomplishment by the Maritime Unions Leadership.

As the hostile threats increased, several foreign crews refused to enter the Persian Gulf and were quickly replaced. No American crew ever refused to go into harm's way.

Aeromedical CRAF

In September of 1990, it was obvious that we may have to medically evacuate many casualties in early 1991. I knew of plans to convert Boeing 767s to medical evacuation aircraft and asked the MAC staff how long this would take. The planned development was two years! I told the staff, "You have two months!" Industry and the Air Force had the aeromedical evacuation 767s ready in January. One of the airlines with the most 767s committed to this mission sent a representative to tell me, "We cannot spare the 767s for this mission. It is the only aircraft that is making money." I responded, "No problem!" and added, "Ask your CEO if he can stand the headline 'My airline refuses to fly the wounded soldiers home?'" The next day, the airline responded, "How many do you need and where?" The Airline and Aviation industry did everything we asked. If there were any shortfall, it was because I was not smart enough to know what we needed.

Visits to the Persian Gulf

During the Desert Shield activities, I visited those we were supporting and our troops in the Persian Gulf three times. Each time, I would join a regularly scheduled airlift mission from Dover, Delaware. We would land in Frankfurt, Germany or Madrid, Spain; change crews; and continue to the Gulf. I always planned to arrive in the Persian Gulf area around six in the morning so I could have a full day to visit the installations and the troops. I would stay two to three days and return along the reverse track. I would fly three of the four legs on a C-5 aircraft, which had a bunkroom for the crew and me. I would make all take offs and landings, visit with the crew, and arrange my sleeping patterns to be wide awake and ready for a full day's work when we landed. On these flights, I asked each crewmember to give me the name and address of a spouse, family member or a friend that I could write about their service to the Nation.

The first mission to the Persian Gulf was fairly uneventful. As luck would have it, we passed General Mike Dugan, Air Force Chief of Staff, who was returning from his ill-fated visit which led to him being replaced. He had carried a group of reporters who reported on some of his comments on the flight. I visited our mobility bases in the United Arab Emirates and Saudi Arabia and with General Norman Schwarzkopf and his staff.

General Tony McPeak became the Air Force Chief of Staff. Although we differed in leadership style, I was a strong supporter and worked hard to help him shape the Air Force. I always tried to adopt General McPeak's ideas as my own ideas. As I retired, General McPeak told a friend that I had supported him more than any other Four Star. The friend asked, "Are you going to tell him?" He replied, "No!"

The second visit began on New Year's Eve and established a new route. As a young pilot flying in Europe, we could not get clearance to fly over Austria – requiring us to fly from Germany through France into the Mediterranean Sea. As soon as we began Desert Shield, we asked for and received clearance to fly over Austria. Later when we were carrying some equipment from the East European countries, I asked for clearance to fly directly from Frankfurt to Greece. Unknown to me, we were to fly the first such flight on New Year's Eve, 1990. We departed West Germany and flew over former East Germany, Czechoslovakia, Hungary, Romania, Bulgaria, and Greece. As was my routine, I went to sleep. During the flight, some of the countries could not communicate with each other but all knew we were coming and welcomed our historic flight.

In Saudi, everyone was getting ready for the inevitable war. My visit with Norman Schwarzkopf was particularly interesting. He had two big issues that day. The Middle East members of the Coalition Force decided that they would only attack the Iraqi forces inside Kuwait. All of the Syrian and other forces that were on the border with Iraq had to be moved down to the Kuwaiti border and the two US Army Corps and United Kingdom and French forces moved up to attack through Iraq. This was a tremendous challenge in which our mobility forces played a very large role.

His second issue probably took more of his time, was much less important to the war effort, but was most important as a guest in Saudi Arabia. Every thirty minutes, CNN had been carrying a story showing women singing, dancing, and entertaining US troop in Saudi. (This is not allowed in Saudi.) Each time he saw it, the King would call Norman and read him the riot act. After he got to the bottom of it, Norman enjoyed telling the King, "The women are part of 'your' Saudi Aramco Oil Company, the TV crew works for your television, and my troops enjoyed the show!" His visit with me was relaxing after his hectic day!

My tours continued into January 3rd, my birthday. One should never want to be visiting on your birthday. Beginning at 6:00 AM, each place that I stopped had a birthday cake and wanted to celebrate my birthday. It was a great day—but too many birthday cakes!

One of the warmest joys was to see how much the "packages" from Americans meant to our troops. Many in the Nation sent gifts addressed to "Any Service Member." The volume was so great that the US Postal Service and USTRANSCOM set up a special operation from McGuire Air Force Base, New Jersey to handle the volume. In December, the airlift demands were so high that Colin Powell and I discussed slowing or canceling this mail in favor of "more important military cargo." As I watched the troops receive the gifts and write thank you notes, I realized how wrong it would have been to stop or slow this outpouring of love from the American people!

The third visit (May 24 –27, 1991) was after the fighting had ended. I arrived at Incirlik Air Base in Adana, Turkey at the normal six o'clock. After breakfast and some briefings at Incirlik with General Shalikashvili (future Chairman of the Joint Chiefs of Staff), I visited some of our troops at a port from antiquity in Iskenderun, Turkey near the Syrian border. We used this port for some of our cargo ships. It was exciting to see how a port with so much history was playing such a large role in Desert Shield. We then flew to the oldest walled city in the West at Diyarbakir, Turkey. After some briefings, I flew a C-130 aircraft over the drop zones in Iraq where we had re-supplied the Kurds and landed at Sirsenk, Iraq, Saddam Hussein's summer palace runway. In a helicopter, we flew over the area that the allied forces were occupying to support the Kurds in Northern

Iraq. We visited the allied forces headquarters and Kurd camps in Zakhu, Iraq. We returned to Incirlik for a dinner in the late (10:00 PM) evening.

The next day, we departed Incirlik at six o'clock for Athens, Greece. In Athens, we visited the Hellenikon airport and the seaport at Piraeus. Then, it was on to Pisa, Italy where we flew by helicopter to the Tombolo Dock in Livorno, Italy. After visiting Camp Darby, we rode back to the airport. There were four cars in our group. When we stopped at a railroad crossing, everyone in the other three cars got out with raised machine guns – they were our bodyguards! In Frankfurt, I took a briefing on an aircraft accident, had dinner, and flew home. The next morning at seven o'clock, I was back in the office. This was quite a trip!

Missiles to Israel

There was great concern at 0300 Zulu on January 18, 1991 when Iraq fired SCUD missiles into Israel. President Bush assured the Israelis that the US would help Israel defend against the SCUDs. At 0130Z on January 19, the US decided to send Patriot missiles to Israel within 24 hours and have them operational within 48 hours. At 0245Z on January 19, I directed MAC to deploy the missiles. We gave a short message to our commander in Rhein Main, Germany. "Find every C-5 you can. If it is loaded, unload it. If it is broke, fix it. A large number of Patriot missiles will arrive shortly, and they must be operational in Tel Aviv in less than 24 hours!" Everyone understood. Without any requests, the German air controllers gave top priority to these aircraft. The results were phenomenal: 30 missiles (8 more than required) were in place in Israel in 15 ½ hours -- 2 ½ hours early. The missiles were operational in 21 hours and 45 minutes after execution – well within the desired 48 hours! All of the required Patriot missiles were in place at 1855Z on January 20- -- 6 ½ hours early. The news commentators were impressed and indicated that the military had obviously been planning such a dramatic move for a long time! (As an interesting footnote: within 20 minutes after being congratulated for this tremendous effort, I was castigated for not being able to also carry more of the sustainment cargo at the same time. The time in the hero spotlight is fleeting at best – and more often ensure opportunities to do more demanding heroics!)

During the DESERT Operations, the Nation and the world came together to accomplish the most concentrated, largest movement in our history by air, land, and sea. We moved the equivalent of Richmond, Virginia half way around the world in four months!

CORONA and the forced retirement of a senior officer

It was exciting to attend my first Corona meeting of all the active four stars generals in the Air Force. It was a most impressive group of leaders. We all were proud of our leadership abilities. An interesting side story: All of the four stars entered an elevator, the doors close, we continued to talk. A short time later the door opened again, we were still on the third floor. A Lt Col reached in pushed the button for the first floor, and we continued to talk as we went down. All of a sudden, I realized we were just like everyone else!

During the senior officer discussion in November 1989, I asked if there were any positions that one of the senior MAC officers could assume to better compete for promotion. There was no support. When I returned, I told the senior officer of the response.

In a later senior officer discussion, I asked the same question and the Chief of Staff, General Mike Dugan, told me to tell the officer in question that he should retire the following spring. Again, I relayed the discussion. As always, I also talked to my predecessor about the decision. When the time came, I reminded the senior officer about the Air Force decision.

The senior officer was most upset and has never forgiven me for the Air Force's decision. I have always felt badly for having to relay the bad news; however, these tasks are the responsibility of commanders.

SUPPORT MISSIONS

Every day of the year, our forces are involved in support missions around the world. Two very interesting missions were the Emergency Resupply of the Ice Station Weddell and Operation Provide Hope.

Ice Station Weddell

The United States and Russia established a research station on drifting ice in the Weddell Sea north of Antarctica. The Ice Station was expected to drift along the same route as Shackleton Party drifted in 1915 after the Endurance ship was trapped in the ice around Antarctica. The Station was well supplied with provision, helicopters, and fuel. In March of 1992, it was determined that the fuel for the helicopters was contaminated and must be replaced. We received a request for an emergency airdrop of fuel to the Weddell Ice Station. On March 26, the Charleston 437th Airlift Wing was given the mission. The fuel was placed in 55 gallon drums. Four drums were placed on each drop pallet. The crews filled the area between the drums with fresh vegetables, "Twinkies", and other items that would support and excite everyone on the Weddell Ice Station.

This should have been a routine request except for the location. The Weddell Ice Station was moving and would have to be "found." There was great concern that the rear cargo doors could not be closed after the drop. To help prevent freezing, the grease on the aircraft's rear cargo door jack screws was removed. The drop zone was more than 1,000 miles from the nearest acceptable air field. In-flight air refueling was required on the outbound leg. The refueling aircraft had to return, refuel, and be ready to meet the airlift aircraft if the loads could not be dropped or doors could not be closed.

On April 1, 1992, the mission was executed with total precision. Twenty-nine bundles were dropped. The members of the Weddell Ice Station were so excited, they videoed the drop. As I watched the video, the narrator was very cool until he realized that he was standing on the planned impact point and the bundles were falling on top of him. There was a pause as he ran to a new location! His last scene showed the excitement as they discovered the AMC crews had filled the voids between the four barrels on the pallets with fresh food and Twinkies. The mission was 100 % successful: delivering 5,800 gallons of JP-4 fuel – 115 drums and 100 pounds of food totaling 48,000 pounds – over 7,000 miles to a floating ice station in the middle of the Weddell Sea without loss or damage, salvaging the joint US Russian expedition! Within 24 hours the Weddell Ice Station was back in operating order and the Station was most grateful for the strong support from "Team Charleston." This was a dramatic display of activities around the world every day.

Operation Provide Hope

In early 1992, the State and Defense Department directed TRANSCOM and EUCOM to visit eleven former Soviet Republics and deliver food and medical supplies. During the February 10 - 26, 1992 time period, TRANSCOM/AMC flew 65 missions, delivering 2,265 tons of food and medical supplies to 24 airfields. Wanting to ensure that we were most efficient in our efforts, I directed the crews to work under combat conditions and not remain over nights at the forward locations. Only one event required an overnight stay. When landing in Moscow, a C-141 blew a tire and broke the hydraulic line to the brakes. The next day, another C-141 aircraft brought a new tire, a jack that had been checked to fit a C-141, and a brake line. As far as I knew, the aircraft flew out fairly quickly. Many years later, the Operation Project Hope Commander General John Sams and I were discussing this mission at a public event, and John asked, "And would you like to hear the rest of the story?" Reluctantly, I responded, "Yes!" When the repair team had arrived, they found that the jack was for a C-5. It fit under a C-141 when all tires were inflated. The "brake line" was the wrong one. John Sams directed the repair crew to figure out a way to change the tire – he never heard how they did this. His vice commander took the proper brake line on a Delta Airlines flight into Moscow – without any diplomatic permissions. Due to the sensitivities, he was met in Moscow, delivered the brake line, and was escorted downstairs and back on the Delta airliner. The C-141 returned uneventfully.

Having had earlier flights into Armenia, we were most concerned about safety and directed the crews not to refuel there. On an earlier flight, a crew noticed the Armenian ground crew refueling an aircraft. The fuel pipe had many leaks, fuel was spewing from several locations, and the refueling specialist was standing by the aircraft smoking! Everyone understood our concerns. On one flight into Armenia, the "local" said, "We don't need food and medical supplies; we need guns and ammunition."

There were many anecdotal stories. All flights were very well received everywhere except Moscow --- where there was some embarrassment. Large crowd assembled to see this phenomenal event. During the "Cold War," most of the people at these locations thought the only American aircraft they would ever see may well be carrying a nuclear weapon. As the aircraft taxied in, the crew would open the top hatch and wave an American flag. The crowd would break into spontaneous applause!

On one flight from Frankfurt, Germany to Bakal, Russia, the crew was faced with a problem that could have scuttled the mission. The Russian navigator refused to guide the crew to Bakal saying it was improper to land there because it was a military airfield and the proper airfield was Balandio 20 miles from Bakal. Since the aircraft commander had been told to land at Bakal, he called back for instructions. Normally, the command would have directed the crew to land at Bakal or cancel the mission. Fortunately, we were well in to our Quality Journey. Our answer was, "We empower you to make the decision when you arrive in the area!" When the crew arrived in the area, they found that the large crowd was gathered to meet them at Balandio. The Russian Navigator was correct and our "empowered" crew was able to make the proper decisions! Empowered people can indeed do wondrous things!

Crews were well treated at all stops; however, the leaders in Kiev, Ukraine insisted on hosting the crew for lunch. Of course, there were to be many toasts. Remembering my direction, the crew asked to toast with juice. The host said, "We will toast with water!" The crew immediately realized the "water" was really Vodka. They changed drinks immediately and were able to fly out very sober with memories for a lifetime. I know there were many other stories.

Operation Provide Hope was a tremendous success in so many ways.

Bob Hope

For many years Bob Hope led USO visits with the armed forces. On a Saturday morning, Linda received a phone call with the introduction, "This is Bob Hope. I need to talk to 'the General' about a USO tour!" She was most impressed. Of course, we always met all of his requests to bring entertainment and joy to the troops around the world. I visited with Bob Hope at several events. He always enjoyed being with the troops.

White House Visits

We were invited to visit the White House twice. The first visit was to help pay President Bush's respect to Admiral Crowe, the retiring Chairman of the Joint Chiefs of Staff. I had been Admiral Crowe's Director of the Joint Staff and was the Commander-in-Chief (CINC) of the U. S. Transportation Command. Our driver had us arrive 15 minutes early. We were the third car in line. At ten minutes early, the couple (Commandant of the Marine Corps and Mrs. Al Gray) in the car ahead of us got out and went into the White House. We followed. The young lady who greeted us indicated that Mrs. Bush would be waiting for us in the family quarters on the second floor. When the two couples arrived, Mrs. Barbara Bush very graciously welcomed us. President Bush was following behind – straightening his tie.

The Gray's, Linda and I were alone with George and Barbara Bush for ten minutes as they discussed the evening activities. George wanted to show us the Lincoln Bedroom. Barbara said, "But someone is staying there!" George replied, "He knows the rules. He has to keep his room in

HT and Bob Hope

'inspection order'!" It was decided that Barbara would lead us on a tour of the family quarters. George followed the group and kept adding comments.

There were 50 guests in the large oval dining room. Millie, the First Dog, slept behind my chair. Linda's dinner partner was a little evasive about himself. Later, we realized that he was the guest speaker and gave a very patriotic talk. He was from Philadelphia, and President Bush had met him when he gave a similar talk. Of course, the Marine musical group entertained us.

Linda, George, Barbara, HT

After dinner, Barbara took the ladies into the family room to show them a rug that she had 'hooked' over a nine-year period. She also wanted them to see where, Millie, the First Dog, had inaugurated it. It was a beautiful "family" evening. As we were leaving, Barbara implored us to stay longer.

The second visit was to recognize the military's performance in the Persian Gulf. President and Mrs. Bush welcomed us more formally with pictures with each couple. After cocktails, we gathered in the Rose Garden and were entertained by a group from the Kennedy Center. Linda and I sat with President and Mrs. Bush at the head table, snacking on popcorn. We then moved to the other end of the Rose Garden by the Oval Office for dinner.

After dinner the President took us on an informal tour of the Oval Office, the putting green, horseshoe, and tennis areas. As we walked the grounds, we stopped by the ponds on the Washington Monument side of the White House. George and Barbara showed us some "ducklings" that were born earlier in the day. When the first ones were born, the crows attacked and killed them. The Secret Service then built a cage, which allowed the ducks to enter the pond but be protected from birds and animals. It was a beautiful evening as we strolled around the grounds with Millie and a couple of other dogs. When it was time to go, Barbara again insisted that we stay longer. Of course, we knew it was time to leave.

Visit with the Queen

One day, I brought home an invitation; and as normal, laid it on the counter. When Linda found it, she asked, "Where did this come from?" I responded that it had come to the office; however, we could not attend. She exclaimed, "What do you mean that *you* cannot attend!" -- implying that she was going. When I reminded her that she had 300 ladies coming to a party in the backyard, she told me that others would host them. All was ready for us to fly to Washington when a landing aircraft blew a tire on landing and closed the runway. Knowing the importance of our trip the base moved the aircraft to one side and let us depart. We arrived on time for the small garden party for 1,400 guests. As she made her tour of the guests, Queen Elizabeth stopped to talk to us. Her aide explained my role in taking every one to the Persian Gulf. The Queen exclaimed, "What a magnificent logistical feat!" We talked for a couple of minutes. When she was about to move on, she spoke to Linda. It was a most memorable day for Linda – and me!

Antarctica

One of the many responsibilities of the U.S. Transportation Command was to provide air and sea support of the National Science Foundation activities in Antarctica. C-5 and C-141 aircraft flew from Christchurch, New Zealand to McMurdo in Antarctica. The majority of the aircraft would land on an ice runway in McMurdo Sound. Cargo and tanker ships would bring supplies to McMurdo during the very short period of time in late December and January when the U. S. Coast Guard icebreakers open the sea passage.

As part of a series of visits in October 1991, I flew a C-5 aircraft from Christchurch to McMurdo. It was challenging to land a 650,000-pound aircraft on 7 feet of ice! I knew it would work; however, I was a little nervous. While the aircraft was on the ice, a surveyor's transit was used to determine if the aircraft was settling. If it settled more than four inches, it had to be moved.

Ski equipped C-130s used a snow runway in a much longer season. Earlier wheeled aircraft landed on a "blue ice" runway on the glacier. The ice never melted; however, during the summer months (December – January), it would partially melt and form humps or moguls, which made landing hazardous. On my visit, we brought some "laser guided" grader blades to smooth the "blue ice" runway and return it to use. (When I returned in December 1996, the "blue ice" runway was closed and insulated with snow. We were able to see it, and visit a C-121 Super Constellation that crashed in the 1950s.)

We were on the ground for four hours. The NSF Director of Polar Operations, Peter Wilkniss, was in McMurdo. Peter met the aircraft, and we toured the area in a helicopter and on the ice. It was an amazing tour. At one point the helicopter pilot kept asking if they could take me to the "Tongue." Finally, Mr. Wilkniss agreed. We landed beside a snow bank. All we could see was a "port-a-potty" that had blown over. I followed the pilot out, over the bank, and into a gully that led to a cave. At one point, we had to get on all fours to get through the tunnel. Finally, we arrived in a brilliant ice cavern – with giant crystals of ice coming up from the floor and down from the ceiling. Enough light came through the ice to make everything sparkle. Not knowing where we were going, I was not mentally prepared to fully appreciate all of the beauty. When describing the "Tongue" to people, they said, "That is Superman's Krypton cave!" Apparently, the "Tongue" got its name from the tongue of ice where it was found.

Later, we visited the research and support facilities and discussed the "ozone hole" with scientists. During this season, we supported the NSF in cleaning up all of the waste that accumulated over the years. It was a delightful visit. Little did I know that I would be so fortunate to return to Antarctica for five days in December 1996.

Mount Penatubo

On June 15, 1991, the Mount Penatubo volcanic eruption in the Philippines virtually covered Clark AFB with lava and ash and shut down operations. To evacuate people and equipment, everything had to be moved to Cubi Point Naval Field. Most of the people were moved by air to Andersen Field in Guam and on to other locations on the west coast – primarily AMC bases at Norton AFB, CA, Travis AFB, CA, and Fairchild AFB, WA.

We soon realized our first challenge was to find enough cages to transport the pets. Some airlift teams thought it would be neat to have a Noah's Arc aircraft filled with pets. To my knowledge, this was only done once. When the Arc arrived at Andersen, the smell was horrible and "they" finally agreed that this was not a good idea. The pets would often arrive on the west coast before the owners. Military families enthusiastically volunteered to care for the pets. One returning family was so excited that they ignored their children as they searched for their pets. When asked about the children, they replied, "They can care for themselves; we have to find our pets!"

The activities surrounding the eruption, once again reminded me that you have to be careful about directing things. MAC had several badly needed C-5 aircraft engines at Clark. I directed (and kept requesting updates) that these engines be transported to Cubi Point. When I was told of our success, I asked how they were transported. The response devastated me, "We did not have a truck, so we towed them on the small wheeled carts!" I suspect the engines were greatly damaged as these cart were towed around debris, holes, etc., en route to Cubi. Once again, I relearned the lesson, "BE CAREFUL WHAT YOU ASK FOR; you might not like the results!"

During a later Mount Penatubo eruption, a World Airways DC-10 was on the ground at Cubi Point, Philippines to support the military activities and evacuate people. We in the Military Airlift Command directed the DC-10 mission. As the DC-10 was ready to depart, the Navy airfield controller refused to let the DC-10 depart. In addition to the DC-10, there was a AMC C-141 on the ground. As the "ash" drifted over Cubi Point, each aircraft was covered. The C-141 crew kept the wing and tail swept of ash. The DC-10 received such an accumulation of ash on its tail that it sat on its tail – damaging the tail section and the engines. After the ash was removed, everyone was evacuated.

Linda speaking at Dining Out

During her time as the First Lady of the Transportation Command and Military Airlift Command, Linda was asked to speak at several events. On one trip, she was the speaker for a wives Dining-Out. At the head table, a senior NCO ran the agenda – everyone else was a lady. My Aide and I were invited and sat at a back table.

The gavel was given to Linda, and she sent the Aide and me to the "gorge" bowl to drink the horrible mixture of wine and other alcohol beverages. She was kind enough to make us repeat and refine our performance. The group went wild. Linda was their Heroine!

As she approached the lecture with her notes, she realized she had forgotten her glasses. Of course, she gave a magnificent speech.

IG Visit

On February 26, 1992, Senator Sam Nunn received and sent an anonymous complaint about me to the Air Force. The complaint accused me of inexperience, poor leadership, harassment of others, and firing or forcing out long time members of the command.

On Monday, March 9, 1992, the SAF/IG, Lt Gen Gene Fischer, called to say the Air Force had received an anonymous letter through Senator Nunn's Atlanta office about me -- making many non-specific allegations about fraud, waste, abuse, driving the troops too hard, etc. and generally questioning my ability to command. Such anonymous letters are normally discarded on receipt. The Secretary and the Chief sent the IG out to "snoop around" for three days.

On Wednesday, General Fischer arrived and in-briefed me. I told him to feel free to talk to anyone he wanted. He talked to many of the senior staff, staff members in operations, junior women, and others. He also announced and held an open IG session where anyone could come forward.

The IG found just the opposite feedback from the anonymous letter. "They" all liked two senior officers who were asked to leave, but they knew it was time for them to go. "They" remembered some incident (which I had long since forgotten) where the two of them were non supportive. They thought of me as an "outsider" but learned very quickly that I was taking the Command to new heights.

Interestingly, four people attended the open session. One Colonel was concerned about why he was SERBed (involuntary separation), and another about why he was passed over – he claimed all of his problems began when he "blew the whistle" on some medical activities. One NCO wanted the Air Force to stop typing airmen performance reports and Commendation Medal recommendations – he obviously had to type them. Another NCO had genuine concerns about how he was treated after being evacuated from the Philippines after Mount Pinatubo eruption. Apparently, he asked for advanced pay while others asked for assistance from the Air Force Aid Society. The Aid debts were forgiven, and of course, he had to repay his advance pay!

The IG gained a much better understanding of the tremendous workload the Command had to bear routinely and gave a "clean bill" on me. I suspect the Secretary and the Chief knew the results in advance. The visit was an embarrassment to me and the Command. On the other hand, it was reassuring of my strong support within the Command.

Retirement

As I was approaching retirement, World Airways submitted a claim for the damage to its aircraft at Cubi Point, The Philippines during an eruption of Mt. Pinatubo. When I heard about this, I ask my MAC claims people about how it was being addressed. They indicated that MAC and the Navy were arguing about who was responsible since the Navy refused permission to depart prior to the arrival of the ash cloud. I ask if the Department of Defense was liable to settle the claim. When assured that it was a legitimate claim, I directed our claims staff to take the lead on settling the claim for the Department of Defense – since we directed the aircraft to go to Cubi Point.

Subsequently, an anonymous caller filed an allegation with the Department of Defense Inspector General (IG) that I had directed the settlement of the claim and the amount. The IG conducted a formal investigation of the allegation. I readily admitted that I had directed that we take the lead in the settling the legitimate claim – but certainly had not been involved in determining the proper amount of the claim. I was shocked when the final question the investigators asked was, "Have you been approached about going to work for World Airways?" I responded that only USAA had asked me to join them, and I had fully disclosed my USAA agreements to the Air Force.

Senate confirmation was required to retire as a General. No nomination can go forward while there is an open investigation. A friend advised me that the Secretary of the Air Force planned to submit my replacement's nomination without mine. It is always awkward and there is no urgency to confirm someone for retirement after the replacement is approved. With the help of a lot of friends, the IG very quickly removed me from the complaint saying, "There was never any question that HT had done anything wrong." The White House agreed to expedite the request through the White House process. Senator Dixon, my senator of residence, put a hold on any consideration of my successor's nomination until my nomination arrived. My nomination arrived late on a Monday. Senator Thurmond, my Senator of birth, arranged an unprecedented approval two days later on Wednesday.

This once again reinforced an interesting lesson: "As your influence decreases, many will try to find unfounded fault and make life more difficult!"

As I approached retirement, I had many fond memories but two stories made me feel best as an American.

As we were taking troops to and returning from the Desert operations, many commercial and military aircraft would stop at Westover, Massachusetts or Bangor, Maine for refueling. In the deployment phase, I stopped at Westover and was most impressed that the communities provided many snacks and personal items for the departing troops. I learned that when the troops returned, the communities welcomed each with Red Carpet treatment as if they lived in the Westover area. I requested to visit and thank the communities for their generosity and respect. We agreed that Linda and I would arrive at a fixed time on a Saturday afternoon to show our respect. When we arrived, the normal base officials met and welcomed us – as normal! We were not prepared for what was to follow!

As we entered the Hangar, there were thousands of people to welcome us as if we were returning heroes. Linda and I walked down a Red Carpet with thousands behind ropes on each side. Each of us hugged and kissed our way across the hanger. As I turned the corner, I was greeted by veterans from my Vietnam War who had lost limbs. When we finally got to the stage, I was "blown away" by the welcome. Before, I was introduced by a "cheer leader" who got the crowd even more engaged. I am not sure what I said, but the crowd erupted after each sentence. After visiting with the leaders, we departed along the same Red Carpet and crowds. This time, the path to the aircraft was lined with big state troopers, Vietnam Veterans, and community leaders. I made sure that I greeted each one. When we finally got on the aircraft, we were emotionally wiped out; however, I knew that I must get in the pilot's seat, wave, and depart. This was a phenomenal display of what makes our Nation so great.

Bob Arnot was a medical reporter and described a medical evacuation in a TV report. During Desert Storm, a C-130 crew was directed to pick up some injured along the Saudi – Iraqi border. There was no runway.

The crew was to land on a section of a highway. The weather was so bad that the crew should have aborted the mission – but the injured needed them. After landing, the patients were brought aboard on stretchers. The doctors and nurses cared for them. As the aircraft was about to take off, Bob Arnot said and the "most interesting part is that the injured were not American or coalition – they were Iraqi!" "This is what makes our country so Great!"

It was indeed a tremendous privilege and distinct honor to have been a small part of such heroic and important activities.

During all of our activities in TRANSOM and MAC/AMC, I was most blessed to have a very strong team supporting me and helping me meet the many demands. Colonel Phil Lacombe was my very strong public affairs chief. He and Randy Larsen were extremely helpful with our communication within the commands and outside. His wide ranging experience was an immense asset to me and our commands.

My aides, Jim Droddy and Jim Greunke, and Executive officer, Kim Smallheer were very active in keeping me on track. The overall Boss was my Secretary Vance Huller! She moved us from the TRANSCOM and MAC/AMC offices and kept all of us well coordinated and "on track!" At home, Scott Emert took care of all details and was able to support any social function. He could even prepare a lunch for guests that we arranged on the morning of the lunch.

Everything was set for my retirement. As with most senior officer retirements, everyone was most gracious. Since I was the head of two commands, we had two retirement dinners and many smaller groups. Having witnessed many ceremonies, I suspected there would many "plaques" and other memorabilia. I told both staffs that I did not want any plaques and indicated it would be neat to have my medals mounted inside of a cocktail table. We still display the beautiful teak table with three glass panels inscribed with the shields of the two commands and my Service to our Nation. All of the medals, insignias, and many military commands where I served are well displayed. I was their hero until I relinquished command. We had a small reception for our family and close friends. Then it was off to Texas!

Postlogue

On August 25 1992, I was relieved by my friend, General Ron Fogleman. A year later, Ron called and said, "It has been one year today since I replaced you. You have not called. I knew you would not call, but I want you to know that I would be pleased if you called. And I know you will not!" He paid me a tremendous compliment of not trying to influence an organization after I left. I thanked him for his call, his outstanding leadership, and continued my approach of always looking forward and not hanging onto the past!

CIVILIAN LIFE

Federal Aviation Administration (FAA)

Prior to my retiring from the Air Force in 1992, the acting Secretary of Transportation, Jim Busey, told me that President Bush wanted me to be the FAA Administrator. I asked to think about it. During the Persian Gulf activities, I had become very close to the Secretary of Transportation, Sam Skinner. During the conflict, we worked very closely together to gain aviation insurance, appropriate waivers, and strong support for all of our Air, Land, and Sea transportation needs.

After much thought and consultation, I declined the offer and continued my plans to join USAA.

A couple of months later, Jim Busey called again. He indicated that the new Secretary of Transportation, Andrew Card, wanted to have the President personally call and ask me to be the FAA Administrator. Jim told Secretary Card that a call for the President would not be proper because as a dedicated American, I could not decline a request from the President. Jim then asked if I was still firm in my plans to go to USAA. When I responded positively on my desire to go to USAA, he said that the President would not call. A friend, General Tom Richards, USAF (Ret), was selected to serve as the FAA Administrator until the end of the Bush Administration.

President Clinton was looking for a new FAA Administrator in 1996. I was considered. I had several meeting with Secretary of Transportation, Rodney Slater, and the White House Personnel Office. When asked by Secretary Slater about FAA's largest challenges, I responded, "most people think the greatest challenges involve modernization of the air traffic system; I say it is people and procedures." Modern equipment will be of little value unless the procedures and mindsets are also changed.

On February 10, 1996, I was invited for a series of visits by the Liz Montoya of the White House Personnel Office. I met with Elaine Kamarck, Vice President's Senior Policy Advisor. Elaine had led the Vice President's National Performance Review (Reinventing Government) and the Aviation Security Review. She is an extremely talented and persuasive leader. Elaine would play a strong role in selecting the FAA Administrator and in "reinventing" the FAA. Fred Smith, CEO of Federal Express had called her after his visit with AMC and indicated I was the person to reinvent the FAA. He told her of the tremendous things AMC had done in Quality Assessments. Bob Stone, the Director of the National Performance Review and a long-time friend and supporter, had told her many tremendous stories about AMC and our Quality and transportation feats. She chided him for not telling her about me earlier since I had been under consideration for a long time.

Our visit went extremely well. Elaine and I were in agreement on the FAA challenges and proper approaches to leading the FAA. There was a strong push to name an FAA Administrator in December, but she and Slater convinced the President not to name an Administrator until after the Gore Aviation Commission's work was completed. They wanted to bring in the new team, charge them with their responsibilities, and begin work in a concerted manner. We were able to be comfortable with each other and make our points. I believed she would be a strong supporter. She, as everyone, asked why I would want to lead the FAA. Earlier in the day, she had talked to the Vice President about me. When she finished in amazement, he said, "And he wants this job?" – recognizing past performance and pride, but also implying the challenges.

Later in the day, I visited with Rodney Slater, Secretary of Transportation. He was also extremely impressive. He had prepared well for our discussions and asked insightful questions. He focused on my "attributes." We talked about the importance of pulling FAA together and building a true partnership among all of the players. We had an extensive discussion on personnel. I told him I did not bring a group with me but rather built the staff from within. We discussed my thoughts on the type of people to be the Deputy, General Counsel, and Chief of Staff. I indicated that I was not as interested in selecting the people as I was in ensuring talents and commitments -- and I had no one in mind. He appeared to agree with my thoughts.

He appeared to be genuinely impressed by my background, leadership, focus, and commitment. He asked why I would want to be the FAA Administrator and seemed pleased with my responses. I pledged my and the FAA loyalty to him. We may disagree in private, and he would have to "hold me back" on occasion, but I would be totally supportive in public and practice. He responded, "In military terms, you are saying you will be a 'good soldier'" I responded, "But not in the 'blindly (and stupidly) following orders' that 'soldiers' are sometimes properly accused of." He indicated that he would interview several others and try to reach a good decision quickly.

During the process, I talked to many airline CEOs, former FAA administrators, and others. One former administrator said, "The FAA Administrator has the second most stressful job in the Administration" – second only to the President. That was a very sobering thought.

The White House vetting process was begun and pretty well completed. During the process, the airline industry began expressing concern about having a former military person leading the FAA. For some reason, my friend, Carol Hallett of the Air Transport Association (ATA), led the concerns. An influential congressman wrote a letter expressing concern about having a former military person lead the FAA. He indicated that he did not know the candidate and their concerns had nothing to do with the candidate. Title 49 USC 106: states the FAA "Administrator must be a citizen of the United States; be a civilian; and have experience in a field directly related to aviation." Congress is required to grant a waiver for a former military person to lead the FAA. I never realized that a former military person was not a "civilian." Several retired military officers did become the FAA Administrator with Congressional waivers.

In light of all of this, Secretary Slater indicated, "it would require a lot of heavy lifting to get you approved." He then indicated that his greatest challenge, as Secretary of Transportation, was to integrate all modes of transportation. He went on to say that in the history of our country only one person had ever been successful in achieving this "intermodal" approach to transpiration. I responded, "But, we had a war" – referring to our Desert Shield successes in integrating all modes. He then offered me a Presidential Appointment to be his Under Secretary of Transportation for Inter-modalism. After a couple of days, I respectfully declined. Secretary Slater's former Assistant Administrator of Highway Administration, Jane Garvey, was nominated and confirmed as the FAA Administrator for a five-year term. If I had been selected, I would have been the FAA Administrator on September 11, 2001!

USAA

As we were going from the Pacific Air Forces to the Central Command in 1987, The Chairman and CEO of USAA, General McDermott, asked me to join the USAA Board of Directors. General McDermott had been the Dean at the Air Force Academy, and we had utmost respect for him and USAA. I was honored to join the other most distinguished directors. Each of us became very active in leading USAA. I became the Chair of the Audit Committee and was highly respected – hopefully for my contribution rather than my senior military rank.

Throughout our duties at the Central and Transportation Commands, I was able to participate in all board meetings except one during the height of the DESERT SHIELD deployment. The next meeting was at Opryland in Nashville. After this meeting, the Opryland leaders asked if they could publish in their internal news a letter that Linda had written. Of course, I quickly agreed. "They" said, "Perhaps you should read the letter first." Linda had written a very nice letter thanking the Opryland Team for their warm hospitality. She briefly outlined our hectic activities during the build-up for DESERT STORM and indicated that this was the first time we had been able to relax a little in a long time. Opryland published her letter under the headline, "You never know who you are serving." I trust this story indicated how we were just ordinary people asked to Serve our Nation during times of crisis.

As I approached retirement in 1992, General McDermott asked if I would join the USAA Leadership Team. We did not talk any specifics; however, I readily agreed. I retired on September 1, participated in a USAA Board Meeting in Europe, and became an Executive Vice President in October. During the initial three months, I participated in an extensive orientation program to include visiting the Homestead AFB, Florida area to survey the damage for Hurricane Andrew. It was interesting to tour the devastation and see our "USAA" name on the outside of several homes. We visited one and could feel the devastation and not understand how the family survived. Blades of a ceiling fan had "cut through the walls like they were paper!" Fortunately, the family gathered in a bathroom and were unharmed! It gave new meaning to the force of nature and how serious families have to be in planning to survive.

During this short period, a USAA securities expert tutored me, and I successfully passed all three examinations required to become a Registered Securities Broker. It was exciting to learn about the securities market and regulations. Taking the extensive examinations was even more exciting. At the end of the computer based exams, you are asked, "Do you want to change any answers?" When I responded, "No," the computer indicated, "Stand by for your score!" Within seconds, I knew I had done very well on the exam. It is amazing that a person could learn about the securities world in two and one half months and still enjoy the holidays!

In early 1993, I was scheduled to become the Chief Administrative Officer and another leader was scheduled to be the Chief of Staff. Without any discussion with me, McD reversed this. I became the Chief of Staff much to the disappointment of the other leader. He was the first to tell me of the change. Although he was openly very supportive, human nature would indicate that he was not helpful in my future USAA activities.

As the Chief of Staff, one of my big tasks involved working on the purchase of the Spurs Basketball Team by USAA and a group of San Antonio companies. I was also deeply involved in ensuring a smooth transition from Robert McDermott to Bob Herres. McDermott had long advertised that he would step down and Bob would become the Chairman and CEO of USAA. I am not sure that Bob was confident that it would happen until it was announced by McDermott at a leadership meeting. Later, McDermott had a difficult time 'letting go' and would always "regret" his decision. Bob Herres promoted me to Vice Chair of the Board and President and CEO of the USAA Capital Company, asked me to work the San Antonio issues, and indicated that he would retire at age 65 and I would move up.

At USAA as with previous positions, I listened to the leaders of the various companies and entities under me and with their help, outlined where we should go. Initially, not all of the leaders agreed, but after a short time, "we" had a blue print on where we could and should go. This initial course changed a little over time but has been amazingly accurate and embraced. Together, we produced great results:

As Vice Chairman of the USAA Board of Directors, and President and CEO of the USAA Capital Corporation (CAPCO), I was full partner on Bob Herres' leadership team in taking our company to new heights.

USAA was an insurance and financial service group with $37 Billion in owned or managed assets. Wholly owned subsidiaries provide a complete line of insurance, investment, banking, and other services to 2.7 million customers worldwide. The mission of USAA was to facilitate the financial security of its members and their families through provision of a full range of highly competitive financial products and services.

Capital Corporation (CAPCO) was a wholly owned subsidiary of USAA and acted as the holding company for all the USAA non-insurance subsidiaries. Its role was to support the USAA CEO, USAA Board, and USAA Membership by overseeing the company's investment and debt portfolios and providing a full range of competitive non-insurance financial products and services through its subsidiaries. The Presidents of each of these subsidiaries reported directly to me, and I chaired the various company boards, which included outside and inside directors.

USAA Federal Savings Bank was a $5 Billion bank and offers a full range of consumer banking products. We were selected as 'The Best Bank in America" by Money Magazine in June 1995. We embraced technology to better serve our customers through Direct Banking on personal computers and via touch tone phones, voice response which handled 62% of our phone calls, "FAX to Image" which allows for paperless routing and action, and the proposed e-mail to image pictures which would soon be available. Through my strong encouragement, we established a trust department for corporate and personal trusts. The bank and investment company very successfully implemented a full service Asset Management Account (AMA) program.

USAA Investment Management Company (IMCO) managed the $13 Billion USAA insurance portfolios, $16.3 Billion in 32 mutual funds, and 1,000 trades a day in its brokerage services. I aggressively reorganized and pushed the investment company to focus more sharply on the USAA portfolios and improve the performance of these and the mutual funds. The brokerage operations almost doubled in trades per day. I was tenacious in encouraging the use of technologies to more completely integrate our mutual funds and brokerage activities. IMCO implemented a Direct Investing process on personal computers and touch tone phones which would allow an increased flow of information and the ability to buy and sell securities and funds. This increased the already impressive service of 50% of the calls via voice response systems.

USAA Real Estate (REALCO) managed a diversified $1 Billion portfolio. The President of REALCO and I were able to quickly address long festering real estate challenges and gain enormous results. We brought in a consultant who helped us right size and organize the company with savings which brought our G & A expenses in line with the industry. My focus on the sale of units and management of a retirement community provided better living for the residents and greatly reduced our headaches and losses. We were able to refocus our portfolio and emphasis on lease management to return the first ever dividend to the parent company.

USAA Buying Services (BSI) operated a claims replacement service for USAA insurance operations, along with a travel agency, and offered a broad range of products and services for the USAA membership. I was very active in refocusing BSI on our primary responsibilities of supporting the insurance company. We refined and enhanced our alliances with car rental companies, SPRINT long distance service, cruise and travel groups, and Signature Road and Travel. We forged new relationships with ADT home security and Federal Express. In the process, BSI gained in employee pride and stature within USAA and with our members.

In addition to CAPCO CEO responsibilities, I initiated efforts to consolidate cash handling throughout USAA; instituted policies to appropriately upstream dividends from diversified subsidiaries to the USAA parent, improving regulatory liquidity; facilitated the financial and debt ratings process with the three primary rating agencies; initiated customer access effort spanning all USAA activities, formalized surplus and liquidity planning for the association; and maintained and enhanced banking relationships with over 30 highly rated institutions.

1993 Base Realignment and Closure Commission (BRAC)

My wide-ranging Air Force experience was a strong factor in my selection to the 1993 Base Realignment and Closure Commission (BRAC). I believe that David Addington in Secretary Cheney's Office pushed my candidacy. David and I had utmost mutual respect for each other. I was selected by President Bush and confirmed by President Clinton after his election. I provided senior military experience to the commission. Having been associated with many bases and all the Services, I worked hard to help the staff prepare. All commission discussions were held in public. Being well prepared and wanting to ensure that all facts were available to the public and the process was truly objective and very importantly, perceived to be unbiased. I became the informal "prosecutor" during the hearings. Most of the witnesses were on our staff and became very uncomfortable with my questions but also became much better prepared. In several cases, the sense of the Commission and the outcomes were totally changed as a result of my insistence on getting the facts on the table. I was never perceived as working an issue in a particular way -- in fact, I made motions opposite to my personal desires when the "facts" did not support my thoughts.

The BRAC General Counsel, Sheila Cheston, and I became good friends. She subsequently became the General Counsel of the Air Force. Many years later she told me an interesting story. "I was always fascinated when you would begin asking a series of naïve questions that changed the whole discussion. Then, you looked surprised by the outcome that your questions inspired the Commission to make."

The BRAC actions touched many lives. It was always interesting to visit the various bases identified for potential closure. We received very warm welcomes. Some communities were quite persuasive; others made emotional defenses without substance. One of the more difficult decisions for me was to close the Aviation Depot at Pensacola and replace the workload with the Training Center from Memphis. To the Pensacola community, the economic impact was small. However, the "physically challenged" men and women who worked at the depot, it was catastrophic. The depot had the largest percent and number of physically challenged workers in the Department of Defense. They were strong performers and most proud of their contributions. I visited with them and, later, gave an emotional "speech" when I voted to close the depot.

Perhaps the most controversial decision was to keep McGuire AFB, NJ open and close Plattsburgh AFB, NY. The Air Force proposed to close McGuire and make Plattsburgh a "mobility base." Plattsburgh was a great base, but it was difficult to get large quantities of fuel in the winter months, and there were no forces or supplies in the area. McGuire was in a congested area but also in the middle of supply and resource activities. As a "mobility base," McGuire was much superior. This was by far the most difficult decision for me – the vote was 6 to 1. I suspect the lone voter to keep Plattsburgh open was supporting DoD recommendation. After the decision to keep McGuire open, Commissioner McPherson (who had been Lyndon Johnson's counselor) made the motion to close Plattsburgh. Sometime later, Senator Monahan's staff asked McPherson why he made the motion to close Plattsburgh when the Senator had asked for his support in keeping it open. The wisdom of the decision was so great and the motion was considered "procedural" that McPherson was comfortable in making the obvious motion – and did not place the decision in the context of his earlier discussions.

As we discussed closing Alameda Naval Air Station, California, I sensed that the majority wanted to keep it open. I did not feel strongly either way, but we were required to fully discuss each decision. As I began asking some "naïve" questions, all the answers drove the Commission to vote 6 to 1 to close Alameda. I and everyone else were quite surprised by the answers and results.

Our processes were totally objective, the decisions were perceived as proper (except by some of those directly affected), and the Nation fully accepted our results and process as a better way to make hard decisions. This was possible because our leader, Jim Courter, ensured openness, fairness, and national views.

Alamo Bowl

With opening of the Alamo Dome in 1993, the San Antonio sports leaders decided to host an Alamo Bowl football game each year. The first two years, we hosted PAC Ten teams (California and Washington) and mid-west teams (Iowa and Baylor). The bowls were organized on an ad hoc basis, the organizers and attendees had a "good" time, but there was no fervor. At the last minute, there were many challenges, and among other requests, the big businesses would be asked to buy tickets to give to groups to make "the Dome look more full." After the first two years, the "bowl' was in debt around a half a million dollars. Beginning with the 1995 game, the leaders were able to get the "number four" picks from the Big Ten and the new Big Twelve Conferences. The Chairmen were picked at the last moment for assumption in March. In the spring of 1995, there were indications that I would be drafted. I sent "word back" that our CEO should be approached to gain his support before approaching me. He enthusiastically gave his support. I had supported most activities in San Antonio but was not a sports leader.

My first actions were to bring structure to the organization with clearly assigned tasks and accountability, to establish an "advisory Group" of all leaders in the city (all accepted except one who insisted on being a part of the working group!), to select a "Chairman Elect" with general duties but a big stake in the outcome, and to make the "executive Director" the "President and CEO." We met throughout the year and planned ahead for events and finances. We were able to generate enthusiasm, support, and funds. We also participated in NCAA events including a visit to Pasadena and the Rose Bowl stadium. To be most successful, we were told to select teams that traveled well!

With the help of good team selection, Michigan and Texas A&M were teams that traveled well with many supporters. We sold out the Dome several weeks prior to the game. All events were sold out; the teams arrived early and had most memorable visits! The game was well played and widely watched across the Nation; the schools were paid 129% of the guaranteed $1 million; and the Alamo Bowl was well established and placed on a financially sound basis with some $400,000 in excess cash. As in all activities, good fortune of team selection is very helpful, but the principles of leadership, empowerment, accountability, stake in the outcome, infectious enthusiasm, joy, etc. are just as important here as in business --NO, more important!

During the build-up to the game, we participated in many activities. At one event, Linda met the Texas A&M field goal kicker. During the game, he became a hero and participated in the trophy presentations. When he saw Linda, he hugged and kissed her as he would honor his mother.

Community Activities

Linda and I have always been very active in a wide variety of community activities. In San Antonio, I chaired the contribution committee at USAA. Consequently, we were in great demand to serve on the various boards. We were active in the University groups, Children Hospital Board, Cancer Therapy and Research Foundations, library foundation, economic development foundations, and the Chamber of Commerce. I was also a director on the Spurs Basketball Board. Linda enjoyed the McNay Art Museum Board and became the Treasurer. She was also a director of the Air Force Village. She was also able to become deeply involved in her love for libraries on the San Antonio Library Foundation. We enjoyed all of our activities. It was most heart-warming to be able to make a very positive difference at the Santa Rosa Children's Hospital, the Cancer Treatment and Research Center and the March of Dimes.

From our family's early association with the March of Dimes and Warm Springs, Georgia, I became active in the local March of Dimes. I was asked to be the chair the San Antonio Chapter. During my tenure the National President, Jennifer Howse, came to San Antonio. During a reception, she talked to Linda about me. Linda told her I could do anything but sing and that I could not even keep time while clapping. The next morning, Jennifer and I were at the annual March. Before beginning, the program included a Gospel Singing Group. I worked hard to "clap in time." Jennifer turned to me and said, "Linda is right!" Linda was absolutely correct; I have no musical talents.

I did not realize that Jennifer was interviewing me to become a national director. I was most fortunate to be selected to serve on the National March of Dimes Board with such distinguished people as Mary Ann Mobley, former Miss America; CEO of J C Penney; and Anna Eleanor Roosevelt, granddaughter of President Roosevelt.

Departure from USAA

Bob Herres became very comfortable as the USAA Chairman and CEO. At his direction, I became very active in the community and throughout the company. Others were not always supportive. I suspect that Bob Herres was also uncomfortable with my popularity. It was time for me to move on. He and USAA were extremely kind in ensuring that I would retire with full benefits, and we would retain full health coverage for Linda. The transition went very well. I must admit that I enjoyed our activities in USAA and with all of the people.

During my service to our great nation, USAA, and our community, I was blessed and am most grateful for the tremendous support from my superiors, compatriots, and most importantly, those I was fortunate to lead and serve.

As in all transitions, new challenges immediately kept me extremely active. I stayed in San Antonio for about a year and worked the transition of Kelly AFB.

LOCAL REDEVELOPMENT AUTHORITY (LRA)

Because of my experience as part of the 1993 BRAC, I became a behind-the-scenes advisor as San Antonio defended its bases during the 1995 BRAC. For a variety of reasons, the largest San Antonio installation, Kelly AFB, was directed to be realigned over the next five years. The day after the closure was announced; Mayor Bill Thornton appointed groups to seek the best way forward. In the initial considerations, I was selected to chair the important Privatization Committee. There was a strong push to select me to chair the seven-member Local Reuse Authority (LRA) Board of Directors. During the San Antonio Council deliberation and votes on prospective board members, only two of us received unanimous votes. When the Mayor called a news conference to introduce the LRA, he said, "I will introduce the Chairman. Then, we will literally and figuratively step aside and let the LRA do their job." I was introduced and introduced the other members. The LRA was charged with implementing the privatization of the defense work at Kelly and bringing in commercial work, which would use these extremely valuable facilities and provide employment for the current Kelly work force and bring additional jobs to our city. Our task was to bring the competing interests together to gain the greatest economic value for our City in terms of employment and economic opportunities. As we did our work, I would ask the Mayor if we could brief the Council. He would respond, "You can brief us but do not ask for guidance." With strong total support, we were able to work things in a very business-like way without becoming involved in City politics and bureaucracy. Consequently, we were perhaps the most successful LRA in the country.

Early on, we decided that we should select a private company to help with transition rather than using the municipality government agencies. We were successful in gaining strong bids from several companies. In the end, we down-selected to two companies: Johnson Controls and EG&G. We had a public "brief off" in the San Antonio Council Chambers. We did not discuss the result until a public discussion among the LRA members. Frank Herrera asked to make the motion. I did not know Frank's planned motion. I recognized the various members for their comments. I recognized Frank last. After his comments, I asked if he had a motion. I fully expected a split vote. Frank recommended EG&G. There was no other motion and the vote was unanimous.

Rudy DiLuzio headed the EG&G Team. Everyone on the base and in the community was most supportive. Because of the strong support of the Mayor, we did not have the normal "municipality" suggestions. We were able to have unity of effort. We also received strong support from Henry Cisneros and President Clinton.

Our initial focus and much hard work and commitment from the community produced tremendous results. In a very short time, the community was so successful; they "wondered why they had not sought the closure!"

As always, I was involved in outside activities. With my previous support of activities in Antarctica, I was asked to join a panel to work Antarctic issues.

Antarctica

In 1996, the National Science Foundation established an "External Panel" led by Norm Augustine, CEO of Lockheed Martin, to review the U.S. programs in Antarctica. The eleven member team included:

Dr. Norm Augustine, CEO of Lockheed-Martin
Astronaut Rusty Schweickart
Mr. Ed Link, U.S. Army Corps of Engineers Cold Regions Research
Admiral Rudy Peschel, US Coast Guard retired
General HT Johnson, USAF retired
Dr. Rita Cowell, Microbiologist at the University of Maryland and later NSF Director
Dr. Ed Stone, Director of Jet Propulsion Lab
Dr. Susan Solomon, Atmospheric Scientist at NOAA (proved the cause of the Ozone Hole and featured in the Smithsonian American History Museum)
Dr. John Anderson, Head of the Rice University Geology Department
Dr. Charles Hess, Environmental Horticulture at University of California at Davis
Dr. Richard Alley, Glacier Dynamics at Pennsylvania State University (Richard was unable to join us on the visit to Antarctica)

We were also accompanied on our visit by:

Dr. Jack Gibbons, Presidential Science Advisor
Dr. Neal Lane, Director of the NSF – who later, succeeded Jack Gibbons as the Presidential Science Advisor
Neil Sullivan, NSF Director of Polar Exploration

We had a great trip to Antarctica and the South Pole from December 26, 1996 to January 4, 1997. We spent a day/night at the South Pole, four days/nights in McMurdo, Antarctica, a day each way in Christchurch, New Zealand, and a night to and from Los Angeles.

This impressive group worked very hard. After a very long flight from Los Angeles through Auckland, NZ and the loss of a day, we arrived in Christchurch, New Zealand on December 28, 1996. After a visit to the NSF Center in Christchurch to receive briefing and clothing, we departed on December 29 for a very long 8½ hour flight on a C-130 aircraft equipped with skis. We landed on a snow runway. (The McMurdo Sound runway was melting and the "blue ice" runway had to be covered with snow to insulate it from the summer heat.)

The McMurdo Station provides support for most of the U.S. and International activities in Antarctica. This thriving community would be the center of our activities in Antarctica.

After one half-day in McMurdo, we flew to the South Pole Station on a C-130 Ski aircraft. After a three-hour flight over the Antarctic terrain, we landed at an elevation of 11,000 feet of ice – eager to explore the many activities at the top of the world (or bottom, depending on your perspective). In any case, we were all on "top of the world" with excitement. As we were meeting after dinner, Ed Link, our youngest man, "passed out." Susan Solomon first noticed him. There was great scurry of activity. We were most concerned. The next morning, we found that he had become overheated as we were still dressed in our cold weather gear. After we found out he was in good shape, we were a little envious – he got to sleep in the dispensary with an adjoining bathroom. .

After a "town hall" meeting with everyone at the South Pole, we were shown our summer quarters on the ice. To show their needs, we were quartered in the ""summer camp" on the ice in "Janesway" buildings-- insulated canvas and wood structure originally developed for use in the Korean War. My cubical was 200 yards from the bathroom. I must admit I did not need to go to the bathroom all 'night' and found I did not need my daily shower. Despite the continuous daylight, we were able to sleep well with the very active schedule and eye coverings.

The Antarctic ice sheet accounts for 90 percent of the Earth's ice volume and 70 percent of its fresh water. The South Pole Station was built on two miles of frozen fresh water. Until 1994, fresh water was chopped and melted by the heat of the generators. Someone (I assume Rodriguez) developed the Rodriguez Well. A hole is drilled to approximately 230 feet into the ice, hot fresh water is pumped down, and an ellipsoid "bulb" is formed with the melted water being pumped up in another pipe. Using the heat from the generators, a continuous cycle is completed to provide ample fresh water. As the cavity goes lower, at some point (estimated to be 10 years) another hole would need to be drilled to begin a new well.

One of the most interesting scientific activities is the AMANDA (Antarctic Muon and Neutrino Detector Array). Enormous numbers of high-energy Neutrinos, sub atomic particles, hit and pass through the earth without interacting. They do collide from time to time with water molecules and become muons. The detectors were built in the Mediterranean, Lake Baikal in Russia, and at the South Pole. The South Pole detectors are placed in two-kilometer deep holes in the AMANDA array. These can detect neutrinos that impact the earth anywhere north of the equator. The purity and depth of the ice makes AMANDA the best neutrino detector in the world.

It was exciting to walk around the world at the South Pole. It does not take very long to walk around the flag designating the South Pole.

The South Pole was quite impressive. During our 24 hours at the South Pole, we visited all the support and science activities. There are some truly unique scientific activities. The environment is very harsh on the support structure. The reason the National Science Foundation asked the "External Panel" to review their Antarctic programs was to have us recommend building a new South Pole Station – with government funds in addition to their current funding. The Nation <u>did need to begin building</u> a new South Pole station to replace the facilities under the dome and some outlying buildings. During high winds the ice would blow over the Hemisphere structure and build up on the windward side causing that side to sink. With my "programming" background, I was instrumental in recommending a less costly, phased approach, and that the NSF programs be reduced to pay for a large portion of the costs. The new facility would be built on stilts allowing the ice to blow under with no build-up. (I called it a "Motel on Stilts." The new facilities were approved and have been built.

I brought a T-Shirt home that says, "Ski South Pole; 2 miles of base; 2 inches of powder." This tells the story! The altitude is over 11,000 feet with a "pressure altitude" of a couple of thousand feet higher.

The Panel was divided into three sub groups. Our group included Dr. Susan Solomon who proved the cause of the "ozone hole," and Dr. John

Anderson who headed the Rice University Geology Department and had led 18 visits to Antarctica. Susan was so highly respected that the Antarctic Solomon Glacier and a Saddle were named for her. One evening, the three of us "commandeered" a helicopter and departed McMurdo at 10:30 PM for the Dry Valleys. The Dry Valleys were formed when lifting action raised the area and "shut off" flows of ice. We picked up another geologist and two female graduate assistants in a distant valley with three little tents. Before arriving back at McMurdo at 3:00 AM, we had toured the valleys; landed on glaciers and mountaintops; heard some deep discussions by the geologists about things that happened 6 million years ago; and enjoyed a majestic evening.

In addition to looking at all of the logistics functions, we visited a Penguin rookery. We saw the full cycle from the eggs, to the little Penguins sheltered between their parents' feet, to the mature Penguins (six weeks). They came to within six feet of us. If we had stayed longer, they would have come even closer.

We flew over Lake Vanda. John Anderson on our team had joined the Lake Vanda Swim Club a few years before when the New Zealanders had a camp there. The Kiwis would cut a hole in the ice. The swimmers had to go in naked. John and his female graduate student both joined the Lake Vanda Swim Club. The Kiwis said it was not embarrassing for men and women to swim together. When the swimmers came out, they could not tell the difference between the men and women. Fortunately, the swimming hole was closed. I am not sure they would have let a "sinker" go in – even if I were foolish enough to want to swim. Many years later, a Navy Captain told me that she had flown the C-130 Ski aircraft in Antarctica. I asked if she had joined the "Lake Vanda" Club. Embarrassingly, she assured me that she had!

On the entire trip, I flew a total of 64 hours (five on helicopters). We thought it was amazing that C-130 # 03 had been abandoned at an Antarctic field site for 17 years and recovered to fly again. A JATO (Jet Assist Take Off) bottle had come loose on takeoff and went through the wing in 1975. The U.S. expressed interest in recovering the aircraft but did nothing. Finally, the Italians asked if they could recover the C-130 – then the U.S. decided to get on with the recovery. In 1992, the U.S. recovery was complete – in the process "we" crashed another C-130. All of this was not nearly so funny when we were assigned # 03 for our return flight. After departure, we experienced a hydraulic leak and had to return for repairs. As you can well imagine, we were quite relieved when #03 land safely at Christchurch.

After leaving USAA, I sought opportunities where I could contribute.

Credit Union National Association (CUNA)

The Credit Union National Association has a business office in Madison, Wisconsin and a political office in Washington, DC. In 1997, I was asked to serve as the Chief Operating Officer in Madison. Dan Mica, the Chief Executive Officer, had his primary office in Washington. Initially, the main office was in Madison with a government affairs office in Washington. As the business activities decreased and government activities increased, the primary focus moved to Washington. The Credit Union Movement provides a tremendous service to the members of the credit unions around the country. It was rewarding to visit with some of the smaller and larger Credit Unions and feel the immense pride is serving their members.

Living in Wisconsin

We enjoyed living in Wisconsin and were most impressed by our many friends. From my background, I often "got into trouble" by being my gracious self: holding doors open for ladies, offering to help other, and just being nice. I was once accused of treating ladies different; I responded, "Guilty!" Wisconsinites are a hearty group and do not expect courtesies. After getting "over it,' they found that they really did like my courtesies.

It was a tremendous privilege to work with Dan Mica and the Credit Unions that serve so many around the Nation. I led a financial review of CUNA. Among other things, I recommended reducing the number of Executive Vice Presidents. After careful consideration, Dan Mica agreed, and I led the reduction.

Worst Day of our Lives

Our son, David, was diabetic since age six. After working as a lawyer, he decided to get an MBA. He lived in Hollywood Hills and was engaged to Corine Zygelman. In January 1998, our daughter, Beth, called and asked for my help in finding David. He had been missing for a couple of days and neither she nor Corine could find him. Somehow, they found out that he had used his USAA credit card but not where. I called my friend Mark Wright, President of the USAA Bank. In a very short time, he was able to tell me that David had used his credit card at a hotel in Santa Barbara and gave me their phone number. I called and asked to speak to David, but there was no answer. I told them that he was diabetic and asked them to check on him. After they were able to get into his room, they would not tell me his status but said, "We are so sorry!" Expecting the very worst, I called Beth. After our cry, we decided that we would not tell Linda until Beth could confirm David's death.

When she called back, I put Linda on speaker phone, and Beth and I relayed the worst news a mother can ever receive. This is the most difficult thing that I have ever had to do. We flew to California. Richard, Beth, Corine, and we began the very difficult tasks of closing and celebrating David's life. Our lives would never be the same!

Much later, Corine would marry Jonathan Hartman. They have two children. With a total lack of our knowledge, they named their daughter Julia – my mother's name, and their son Benjamin – Linda's father's name! Linda treated all of them as a full part of our family and showered the "grandkids' with gifts.

Return to Washington DC

EG&G

EG&G had an impressive history dating back to the Manhattan Project to build the first Atomic Bomb. An MIT professor Harold Edgerton partnered with two graduate students Kenneth Germeshausen and Herbert Grier to form Edgerton, Germeshausen, and Grier" and ultimately "EG&G."

After working for CUNA for a year, the CEO of EG&G asked me to lead their Washington office and serve as the CEO of EG&G Technical Services. We had a wide range of services primarily for the Department of Defense, NASA, and the Department of Energy. It was interesting and educational to learn of the many challenges and opportunities in the private sector. In early 1998, we moved back to the Washington, DC area to be a part of the EG&G Team.

Carlyle

The EG&G leadership decided to purchase the Perkin-Elmer Company and sell EG&G Technical Services.

It was a very interesting and stressful time and as many firms showed interest in buying EG&G Technical Services. I would host each group beginning with a dinner and meeting the next day until 3:00 pm. A new group would arrive at 6:00 pm for dinner.

When the Carlyle Group won the competition, the Carlyle leader called our home, and I modestly received the news as I was doing the weekly ironing. The Carlyle Group purchased EG&G Technical Services and the name EG&G, and made me the CEO. The "closing" was done in New York City. It was a busy day with discussions going back and forth until 3:30 pm; then everything came together to allow the funds to transfer before 4:00 pm! I was feeling on "top of the world" as I traveled to LaGuardia for my flight home. The flights were cancelled, I caught a train from Grand Central Station, Linda picked me up at Union Station in DC around midnight, and I was just a normal guy again! It was a tremendous privilege to work through the acquisition process and serve the Carlyle leadership.

EG&G had a wide range of activities support government activities from operating the Cape Canaveral launch site to De-Militarizing (destroying) Chemical weapons. It was an exciting time for me.

I retired from EG&G on my 65th birthday in 2001.

Church

During our entire married life, Linda and I had been members of Methodist churches. As we always did when moving to new locations, we visited many churches in the Washington, DC area and were most impressed by the National Presbyterian Church and its minister, Craig Barnes. After completing the orientation and joining the church, we were ask "where we wanted to serve" from a list of church activities. We both chose to be greeter, and Linda worked in the church library. I indicated that I wanted to serve the homeless. National Presbyterian has a wonderful relationship with the Inner City "Third Street Church of God." I agreed to help prepare and serve breakfast every other Friday. Many of those participating in the Morning Prayer service and breakfast were recovering alcoholic and drug users. A wonderful Danish lady friend, Inger Sheinbaum, asked to go with me most of the time. We would work closely with the morning minister, Rev Hervin Green, and a long time church worker, Sister Martha Mable Estell Jones. There were several others who would help us. We would arrive at 6:30, prepare breakfast, and serve around 7:30 or 8:00. And I would arrive at work at EG&G around 10:00.

It is a small world. The National Presbyterian coordinator of these activities was a Clemson classmate, Rufus Hill. It was fun to renew our relationship and talk about our time at Clemson.

Falcons Landing

Falcons Landing is a continuing care community primarily for retired military officers. The board of directors is the Air Force Retired Officers Community (AFROC). When Falcons Landing was opened, there was a need to fill it quickly and the eligibility was open to military officers and other government executives. After the initial fill, the eligibility was restricted to retired military officers.

Linda was part of a book club that included several residents of Falcons Landing. In early 2001, I asked for a tour, and we joined AFROC. A short time later, I was elected to the AFROC Board and became the Chairman. I was very impressed and enjoyed working with Falcons Landing. Unfortunately, when I joined the Department of the

Navy, I was required to give up the Chairmanship and withdrew from the board.

After I left the Navy, I was again asked to join the AFROC Board and was elected as Chair. Linda and I were associated with several continuing care communities (Air Force Village and the Towers in San Antonio), and Falcons Landing is the best of all. As with all such continuing care communities, there are always many suggestions and challenges from the residents. Falcons Landing continues to grow and provide great care for all of the residents. It was a great honor to lead the AFROC Board.

Little did I know that I would become a resident in early 2011.

DEPARTMENT OF THE NAVY

Selection to be the Assistant Secretary of the Navy (Installations & Environment) in 2001

Over the years, we have been fortunate to be called on to serve in some very interesting areas. When I served on the 1993 BRAC Commission, Jackie Arends worked in the White House Personnel Office under President Bush. When Clinton became President, she was one of our many talented members of the BRAC staff. When I learned that she was head of White House Personnel for the Department of Defense, I wrote her a congratulatory note in early 2001. She responded, "You do not get off that easy; send me your resume." A few days later, I interviewed with all three prospective service secretaries. As you would expect, I did not want to return to the Air Force. The other two asked for me. The Secretary of the Navy, Gordon England, asked me to be his Assistant for Installations, Environment, and Safety – unsaid was that I was also a BRAC expert.

The confirmation process is long and laborious. The entire life of a nominee must be carefully reviewed. Any unsubstantiated stories must be reviewed. Anyone can say anything without any facts. Having made some difficult decisions, there are always some who want to cause difficulty. When I was being considered to the FAA Administrator in 1997, the White House Personnel Office asked if I had left USAA under "sexual harassment charges." I responded, "No!" A couple of weeks later they asked the same question. I asked if they wanted me to prove the accusation false. They said, "No 'they' say those sorts of things about everyone!" She went on to relate that on a recent panel she had worked each prospective panel member had some such totally unsubstantiated accusations. The "accusation" must have still been in the rumor file. Of course, the FBI background check proved it totally false. Towards the end of the background check, the FBI agent asked me a question about some unsubstantiated derogatory comments while I was at the Credit Union National Association. I responded that it was not true and asked, "Did you not just talk to my boss at CUNA this morning?" She responded, "Yes, and he was most complimentary in every way." That was a short lived unsubstantiated story. Some must wonder why anyone would want to be a part of Government. Unfortunately over the years, there have been many examples of unacceptable conduct for various nominees.

While at EG&G, we did not have a PAC (Political Action Committee) where members of the organization make contributions, and then the PAC makes political contributions. Without a PAC, I often made personal contributions to help EG&G. One such contribution was a $1,000 contribution to Al Gore. All political contributions are part of the public record. The Gore contribution as well as one to Ted Kennedy showed up. The Gore reception was sponsored by an "Energy" group and EG&G was trying to gain some contracts in this area and needed to attend. The EG&G home office was in Massachusetts, and I represented EG&G at a breakfast for Senator Kennedy. In business, you really do not think much about such contributions – they are a "cost of doing business." Since Linda wrote most of our checks, only the unusual ones associated with EG&G were under my name. When they looked at both of our political giving, they were not concerned except for the Gore contribution. (I later found that only two people who contributed to Gore became Presidential Appointees, Senate confirmed (PAS) under President Bush.) Later, the White House asked who could confirm my allegiances. I responded, "Dick Cheney, Colin Powell, Senator Hutchison, Frank Carlucci, and others." When my nomination was considered by the Vice President, he allayed any concerns with his extremely strong support! During the last discussion with the White House prior to the nomination, the staff member said, "We are not sure we can always count on you to do what the President wants!" I responded, "You can always count on me to do what is best for our Nation, and I believe that is what the President wants!" There was no more discussion. When I sent the mandatory list of contributions to the Senate as part of the confirmation package, I annotated the company related contributions as "On Behalf of EG&G." The Senate leaders asked the White House to ask me if I had been reimbursed by EG&G – which is clearly illegal. When I visited with them, they were laughing about it.

At the time, there were only two confirmed PAS (Presidential Appointee, Senate confirmed) appointees (Rumsfeld and Wolfowitz). Jackie Arends took me to Paul Wolfowitz for the formal interview. Jackie introduced me and asked Paul to interview me. Paul quickly replied, "I will not!" Jackie was mortified. Paul went on to say, "I know HT very well, and we will be most honored to have him in any position in our department." Jackie was relieved, and we had a wonderful discussion.

The confirmation hearing was very straight forward. Prior to the hearing, Senator Warner said, "Just because we ask you a question doesn't mean you have to answer it!" He was saying not to try to "make any waves in the answers." At the Hearing, Senator Thurmond came in to introduce me and Mario Fiori who had worked in Aiken, SC. He had very nice words. Senator Warner also gave a glowing introduction. Linda was impressed when I introduced her as my wife and partner for my entire adult life.

The Senate confirmed me on August 3 and the President appointed me to be the Assistant Secretary of the Navy (Installations & Environment) on August 6, 2001. I was part of the Navy and Marine Corps Defense Team and worked for Secretary of the Navy Gordon England.

Under Secretary England's leadership, I served the Navy and Marine Corps in providing the Sailors, Marines, and civilians the proper facilities and quarters in which to live and work in a good environment. I worked with installation, facility, environmental, safety, and many other activities.

From my initial overview, there were plenty of challenges and opportunities to keep me very busy. It was great to get back into the full swing of things.

As I lamented to Secretary England that I would not be able to accompany Linda on our planned trip to Russia, he smiled. He and his wife had planned to go to China. Their daughter went with her. Our daughter-in-law, Colleen, went with Linda.

9-11

A little over a month after I became Assistant Secretary, 9-11 occurred. I was visiting the Marines in the Navy Annex south of the Pentagon when the first aircraft hit the Towers in New York. As we were returning to the Pentagon along the route the third aircraft would follow to crash into the Pentagon, we heard of the second attack in New York. After returning to my office, I was visiting with a couple of out-of-town guests when we heard a loud noise. We continued our conversation until someone came running in to tell us about the crash into the Pentagon, which hit one face away from our offices. We found our way out of the Pentagon.

I had been scheduled to attend a meeting on the fifth floor of the E (outer) Ring immediately above where the aircraft hit the Pentagon! The Under Secretary of the Navy attended. When the aircraft crashed, the room and the hall were filled with smoke. The group got out of the room and crawled to the wrong end of the hall. Fortunately, someone at the opposite end began yelling and everyone was able to crawl to a good exit. They were not hurt – other than carrying a most horrible experience for the rest of their lives! Again, I was blessed not to be at the "wrong place."

After realizing that we could not provide any assistance, the guests left. I tried unsuccessfully to call home – as the cell phones in the DC area were maxed out. Later, I received a cell call from our son Richard from California, and he was able to call his mother and tell her I was OK. Later, I learned that Linda had seen the crash on TV and was afraid I had been hurt or worse. Some workers were repairing the ceiling in our basement; noting Linda's concern, they helped her sit and got her some water. Almost immediately a close nurse friend, Inger Sheinbaum, called Linda and asked if she could help. Sensing Linda's concerns, she immediately came and remained with Linda until I arrived home.

Things were chaotic for a short time in the Pentagon before we all moved forward in more determined efforts. These attacks inspired major improvements in the security of all of our installations worldwide. This changed our world forever.

Serving as the Assistant Secretary

As the Assistant Secretary of the Navy for Installation and Environment (and Safety) (ASN(I&E)), we had many challenges that we quickly transformed into opportunities. My previous experience was valuable in finding solutions that helped the communities as well as the Navy and Marine Corps.

Partnerships with the Department of the Interior and communities resolved many environmental issues. We were able to clean and transfer several BRAC properties. We chose to sell three very valuable BRAC properties in California. Communities soon discovered that we could sell properties and the developers would bring more value to the communities than if we merely "gave" the property to the communities. In partnership with the General Services Administration (GSA), we developed a most effective bidding process.

Gordon England and I inherited a major problem of closing the Vieques Bombing Range in Puerto Rico. We were finally able to transfer it to the Department of the Interior. There were strong feelings for and against the transfer. On the night of the transfer, the demonstrators got out of hand and even embarrassed the Government of Puerto Rico. Puerto Rico was pleased to get the Island of Vieques back but disappointed to lose the jobs. Since Naval Station Roosevelt Road, PR existed primarily to support activity on Vieques, the Congress allowed us to also close Roosevelt Roads. The Government of Puerto Rico finally realized that they should be careful about what they asked for!

Public Private Partnerships (PPV)

The military services always had many challenges in providing good housing to military members. There had been several private partnerships over the years that were not very successful. Prior to my arrival, the Army, and Navy/Marine Corps had developed some tremendous Public Private Partnership for military family housing. The Service would provide the land and invest up to less than 50%. The "PPV" (the Army uses a different name) would be operated as a private venture with funding for continual upkeep and replacement in the future. If the private investors had financial difficulty, the public partner could become the receiver. The PPV leadership was focused on serving the military families. If there were not enough military families, the PPV had to be competitive in attracting private tenants. PPV managers would live within the PPV project and ensure all the needs were met and the turnover time between occupants was a minimum. It is amazing how much better and more efficient the PPV projects are over the traditional military projects. These PPV projects have radically changed how military family housing services are provided. It was a joy to see the results.

Safety

Safety is a continuing challenge and opportunity to not only save lives but also make organizations more safe and efficient. We were able to change our approach to Safety and gain strong support. By using technology, we found ways to improve safety, predict equipment failures, offer better training aids, and provide data to better maintain the fleet.

By showing helpful interest, we also found that we could return the injured civilians to work more quickly and retain their pride and self-respect. It was satisfying to work with the installations, environmental, and safety experts and all the leaders of our Navy and Marine Corps in caring for our member and national needs.

Selection to be the acting Secretary of the Navy

The rumors of Gordon England's departure were rampant in November 2002. There were strong rumors that the Under Secretary Susan Livingstone would not become acting Secretary. She had not played a large role in leading the Department. Everyone was reluctant to tell her of their concerns. In January, Secretary Rumsfeld and Wolfowitz had talked to her but been indecisive.

Normally, the Assistant Secretaries for Installations and Environment have breakfast with Ray DuBois, the Deputy Under Secretary of Defense (Installations and Environment), on Tuesday mornings. In mid January, Ray asked if he could visit with me after breakfast. Without looking me in the eye, he told me that Susan Livingstone would be the acting Secretary of the Navy. I told him that I was relieved and would strongly support Susan.

A couple weeks later, Ray DuBois told me that I would be the acting Secretary. A short time later (January 29, 2003), Secretary Rumsfeld asked me to visit with him. Since I was on his "calendar," everyone assumed that I was being interviewed. As I walked in, he greeting me and said that he just wanted to positively place a face with a name. We talked about things in general without any indication that I was being considered. I was very careful to tell Susan Livingstone about the visit. By this time, Susan understood that she probably would not move up. During the same time period, Secretary Rumsfeld asked Assistant Secretary of the Navy for Research and Development John Young to be the Director of Program Analysis and Evaluation (PA&E). John discussed a long list of accomplishments, but declined to lead PA&E.

In January, we were preparing Susan Livingstone to represent us during the Congressional hearings. Our Installations and Environment preparation session went very well. She indicated that she would want to carry many backup books with her to the hearing. She told me some anecdotal stories about her hearings as the Assistant Secretary of the Army. Reportedly, others expressed concerns to Secretary Rumsfeld about her representing us in Congress. A little later at about the same time, Susan and Ray DuBois told me to begin getting prepared to testify. At the first preparation meeting, John Young was very upset that I would be so presumptuous in having preparation meetings. I explained the directions from Susan and Ray. Later during the preparation session, John was called out for a phone call. He returned much more supportive.

As my potential selection became more obvious, I gave much thought to how I could best serve. Our National Presbyterian Church minister had departed, and a new interim pastor, Dr. Tom Erickson, was most impressive. After church services, I told Tom of my potential designation and asked if I could seek his advice. He enthusiastically agreed, and we had a most helpful discussion on February 7.

I told him that like him I would be asked to serve in an "acting" role and wanted to learn from his approach as the Interim Pastor. He outlined four principles he used as the interim leader.

1. His first task was to assist the congregation through the grief of losing a pastor.
2. He would carry forward the current ministry – not make substantive changes.
3. Tom would try to help church reconnect with national church.
4. Finally, he would help the congregation prepare to receive a new pastor.

He recommended being: absolutely positive, encouraging everyone, being very visible, and in his case, say – "a new and different leader is coming – prepare for a new minister." In my situation, prepare everyone for a new and different leader. (We did not realize that Gordon England would return.)

Tom Erickson's advice was very helpful. On August 22, 2003, the Marine Commandant honored me at an Evening Parade at the Marine Barracks. Tom and Carol Erickson were most proud to participate and beamed when I told this story.

During the interim period before I was officially designated, Robin Pirie and I talked about his action when he was "acting" before Gordon was confirmed. He was the Under Secretary and chose to stay in the Under's office. He cautioned that the "acting' should never be presumptuous and not make any decisions that could wait. On February 1 at a Carabao Wallow (a group that goes back to our early American days in the Philippines.), a senior OMB official, Robin Cleveland, asked me how I intended to operate. I explained my plans along the lines that Robin Pirie had done. She very bluntly told me, "We do not want a 'figure head!'" On this stark thought, I reevaluated my approach and decided to move into the Secretary's Office and "act" -- and be the only "Secretary" the Navy and Marine Corps would have for an extended period – but not place my name on the door.

Alberto Mora told me that paperwork had been sent to the President to designate me as the acting Secretary of the Navy. He assured me that he would know the instant that the President signed it.

After returning from an ASN (I&E) party on Saturday afternoon (February 8), I had a voice mail from Ray DuBois saying that the President had signed the order designating me on Friday. The NCIS protective service was already scheduled to pick me up on Monday.

On Monday morning, I moved into the Secretary of the Navy office. There were rumors up and down the halls that I was presumptuous. I invited Alberto Mora down to listen to the voice message. I visited with Susan Livingstone. We decided that we both would go to the normal "Secretary's" update with her chairing. We were both extremely complimentary about each other. A short time later, Alberto Mora got the

Presidential Designation letter that was signed on Friday, February 7, 2003.

Susan Livingstone was most supportive, and I was extremely courteous. She agreed to continue serving while I visited the Persian Gulf

Some News Releases

THE WHITE HOUSE

Office of the Press Secretary

FOR IMMEDIATE RELEASE
February 7, 2003

President George W. Bush today announced his intention to designate one individual and nominate two individuals to serve in his administration:

The President intends to designate Hansford T. Johnson of Virginia, to be Acting Secretary of the Navy. Mr. Johnson currently serves as the Assistant Secretary of the Navy for Installations and Environment. Mr. Johnson has been a leader in the military, public and business sectors for over 41 years. He previously served as the Commander in Chief of the U.S. Air Force Transportation and Military Airlift Command and served as Deputy Commander in Chief of the Central Command during operation Earnest Will, the U.S. re-flagging of Kuwaiti oil tankers and escort operation in the Persian Gulf. During Viet Nam, he was a forward air controller and flew 423 combat missions. After his combat tour, he served as an assistant professor of aeronautics at the Air Force Academy. He is a graduate of the U.S. Air Force Academy, earned his master's degree from Stanford University and his M.B.A. from the University of Colorado. He went on to further his military training at the U.S. Army Command and General Staff College and the National War College.

InsideDefense.com
Friday, February 07, 2003

Hansford Johnson To Replace Livingstone As Acting Navy Secretary

Feb. 7, 2003 -- The Pentagon is expected to announce today that Hansford Johnson, assistant secretary of the Navy for installations and environment, will be the new acting Navy secretary, replacing Susan Livingstone just weeks after she assumed that role.

Livingstone, the Navy Under Secretary, automatically became acting Navy secretary Jan. 24, when Gordon England resigned as Navy secretary to start work at the new Department of Homeland Security. A week earlier, during an appearance at the West 2003 conference in San Diego, CA, Livingstone told Inside the Navy she was not in the running to succeed England as Navy secretary. "I'm not a candidate," she said, noting "a number of names" have circulated.

The timing of Johnson's appointment suggests the Pentagon did not intend for Livingstone to become acting secretary, but instead failed to identify another candidate for the acting position before England's resignation. Sources indicated that Livingstone might stay on as under secretary for a few more weeks, before resigning from the Navy.

Johnson, a retired Air Force four-star general who flew 423 combat missions in Vietnam, is expected to manage the Navy for a short period, until England's successor is nominated by the White House and confirmed by Congress. Johnson served in the Strategic Air Command, the Pacific Air Force, Central Command, the Joint Staff, Transportation and Military Airlift commands. After leaving the Air Force, he entered the private sector but was appointed to the 1993 Base Realignment and Closure Commission.

Michael Wynne, the Pentagon's principal deputy under secretary for acquisition, technology and logistics, and Pentagon Comptroller Dov Zakheim have been mentioned as potential successors to England.

-- Jason Ma and Christopher J. Castelli
© Inside Washington Publishers

Livingstone Steps Down As Navy Secretary
Washington Post, February 9, 2003

Acting Secretary of the Navy Susan Morrisey Livingstone is stepping down from the Navy's top administrative post, Defense Secretary Donald H. Rumsfeld announced.

Hansford T. Johnson, assistant secretary of the Navy for installations and environment, is to replace Livingstone while tending to his normal responsibilities.

Livingstone, who had served as undersecretary of the Navy since July 2001, was appointed acting secretary when Gordon England left the position Jan. 24 for the Homeland Security Department. She asked not to be chosen as his successor.

© 2003 The Washington Post Company, Page A12, 9 February 2003

I retained my Assistant Secretary position and would have the acting Under Secretary and acting Secretary as "additional duties!" Needless to say, I had plenty of help. We expected that it would take five to six months to find and confirm a new Secretary – it took eight months. I told everyone that I would be a strong, decisive Secretary until the afternoon before the new Secretary arrived. To my boss, I added, "I assume that is why you picked me." He assured me that this was the case.

During the rumor stage, Linda was not too excited -- until the President "designated" me as acting. Later, she was quite pleased and enjoyed our activities. She had a knee replaced in October 2002 and the second one replaced in April 2003. She was extremely pleased with the first results and the second one was much less painful. The knee was replaced on a Monday. She came home early on Friday and was feeling so well on Saturday that she was resorting the drawers in her dresser!

It was indeed be a most interesting time. I obviously was in the right place at the right time. The Chief of Navy Operations and the Commandant of the Marine Corps and I were strong partners. Earlier in the Transportation Command, I had worked closely with the CNO, Admiral Vern Clark. We were extremely close friends and partners. The Commandant, General Mike Hagee, assumed his position just before I became acting Secretary and we developed a strong respect, friendship and partnership. Linda and I worked close and enjoyed being with Vern and Connie Clark; and Mike and Silke Hagee. This was a crucial time during Operation Iraqi Freedom.

USS Intrepid in New York Harbor

The first official trip that Linda and I took as the acting Secretary was to visit a ceremony on the aircraft carrier, USS Intrepid, in New York Harbor. The new Commandant of the Marine Corps, General Mike Hagee, and his wife, Silke accompanied Linda and me. When we arrived at LaGuardia Airport, the Hagees and we were ushered into different cars in a "caravan of cars and escorts" for the ride downtown in the midst of the afternoon traffic jam.

With sirens and loudspeakers the caravan parted the traffic to let us through. Linda was so embarrassed, she wanted to hide. Silke had similar feelings. It was a most exciting ride. We were given an extremely exotic suite at the Plaza Hotel to freshen up. The event on the USS Intrepid was also very impressive. Linda always remembered her first trip during this interesting time of our lives.

Visit to the Persian Gulf -- February 17 to 23, 2003

During my second week as acting Secretary, Assistant Secretary John Young and I visited the Persian Gulf as the Sailors and Marines prepared for Operations Iraqi Freedom. It was most exciting to visit the ships, Marine camps, and Navy, Marine, and Combined Land Forces Headquarters. Our son, Richard, was a Marine Liaison Officer at the Combined Land Forces Headquarters. As a most proud father, it was a joy and privilege to visit with him.

Richard & HT

Many years later Richard told me a story about my visit to his headquarters. He told his senior Marine that his father was going to visit. The Marine General responded, "So?" Richard told him that I was the acting Secretary of the Navy. He was very upset that Richard had not told him earlier!

While in Bahrain, the Minister of Defense said, "You went to the US Army Command and General Staff College at Leavenworth the year after the King." The records showed the King going in 1971 and me graduating in 1972. I assured him that we were classmates. Needless to say the next day, the King and I had a wonderful visit. He said that at Army Command and Staff College he learned more than any other year of his life! There were 113 officers from other countries, and he worked very hard.

HT and the King

Testimony

In various positions, I had testified before many committees in the Congress. As the acting Secretary, I was very fortunate to have the first hearing before the House Armed Services Committee (HASC) with the Chief of Naval Operations, and the Commandant of the Marine Corps. The three of us were a tremendous team before the HASC.

The Senate Armed Services Committee (SASC) hearing was with Air Force Secretary Roche, Army Secretary White and me. The Air Force Academy sex discrimination story had just broken. Jim Roche was really under the gun. Tom White and the Army had some disagreement with the Secretary of Defense. I had a very easy hearing. Interestingly, that same afternoon as the Assistant Secretary, I had a hearing with a subcommittee of the SASC. "They" did not quite know how to handle the protocol of my two hats: Secretary and Assistant Secretary. Needless to say, I was treated very well.

Meeting with Nancy Reagan

On May 17, 2003 prior to the Commissioning of the USS Ronald Reagan, I gave a medal to Mrs. Nancy Reagan at the Bel Air Hotel in Los Angeles. I met her at her car. She took my arm and never let go as we walked across a very steep bridge, greeted many Sailors and a few Marines. At the end of the line, we were prepared to present the Medal.

She said, "I belong in the middle!" We moved her to the middle and she most graciously received the medal. It was a great day for Mrs. Nancy Reagan, the Sailors and Marines, and me. Being a brave person, I admit that I was scared as I walked her across the bridge, etc. I must admit that when I got her back in her car, I was most relieved and proud.

During the Commissioning of the USS Ronald Reagan later in the year, I sat across the aisle from her. Mrs. Reagan was not as relaxed – saying, "My speech is nothing." When it was time for her speech, she said "Man the Ship and bring her to life." As 3,000 sailors began running up the gangplanks, her eyes were filled with excitement! It was a long difficult ordeal for her. After the commissioning she said, "I have to go home to see Ronnie!"

On September 9, 2003, we went to a foundry in Amile, Louisiana to participate in melting 50 tons of steel from the World Trade Center and pouring the "bow" of the USS New York LPD (Landing Platform Dock) Amphibious ship. This was very exciting. I helped pull the lever that pours the steel; however, the ship sponsor, Secretary England's Dotty England had the honor of being the sponsor and official "Pourer!"

Travels

As part of my duties, I had to be outside the Washington area for four days (11 people rotate) as part of the "continuity of Government" activities (in case of an attack, at least one senior leader had to be away from the Washington area). It was rewarding to travel and visit the Sailors and Marines around the world. Early on I chose to visit Europe with Ray DuBois. We visited Sigonella, Gaeta, and La Maddalena in Italy; Souda Bay, Crete in Greece; Rota, Spain; and London and Devonsport, UK. As we were visiting the Souda Bay Sailors Recreation Center, they said, "Sailors can 'sign on the internet." I gave them my AOL account and I was on the net in a flash. I was most impressed by our Naval team of Sailors and Marines and how well they were treated at each location. I had always known of the very strong role the Navy League (the professional organization that supports the Navy) plays around the world. As I saw them in action, the Navy League's reputation is extremely well earned and deserved.

Social Activities

There were many social activities where I represented the Navy and Marine Corps.

Two of the most exciting were the Gridiron Dinner and the White House Correspondents' Dinner. The Gridiron Club is best known for its annual dinner which features the United States Marine Band, along with satirical musical skits by the band members and remarks by the President of the United States and representatives of each political party. The skits and speeches by various politicians are self-deprecating and sharply comedic. I sat at the head table and enjoyed the many activities orchestrated by the Marine Band Director.

The White House Correspondents' Dinner was held at the Washington Hilton. As with the Gridiron Dinner, the Marine Band provided the music and orchestrated the many speakers. The featured speaker has usually been a comedian, with the dinner taking on the form of a roast of the President and his administration. After "harassing" the President, the speakers would always apologize and honor the President. The famous actress, Ann Margaret, was also a guest. I told her about our earlier meeting, and she said, "Of course, I remember meeting you!" We had our picture taken after a short conversation.

Ann Margaret and HT

As the acting Secretary of the Navy, there were many rewarding opportunities to represent the Navy and Marine Corps. Serving in this position was an exciting time and I was very honored to have been chosen to serve.

Colin McMillan selected to be Secretary of the Navy

The White House indicated the intent to nominate a friend of mine, Colin McMillan, to be the Secretary of the Navy. During the DESERT STORM, he was the Assistant Secretary of Defense for Logistics. We worked closely together and had great mutual respect for each other. As he prepared for confirmation, we had several very meaningful discussions. He told me that he had some earlier bouts with cancer, but he thought all was well. Before he was formally nominated, his health deteriorated and he took his life. I was told of his death during a Ceremony on a Japanese ship in Baltimore. We immediately excused ourselves. After getting in the vehicle, I told Linda and the others. We were all extremely shocked. I would have enjoyed working for him.

After Colin McMillan lost his life, Gordon England was selected to return from Deputy Secretary of Homeland Defenses to be Secretary of the Navy.

Gordon England returned as Secretary of the Navy

On Friday, September 26, 2003, the Senate confirmed Gordon England as the 73rd Secretary of the Navy. After confirmation, the President has to sign the "warrant" before an office holder can assume the position.

After the Senate confirmed him, Gordon called the SecNav office and indicated that he should be picked up by the NCIS team on Monday morning. I had cleared out of the office on Friday and welcomed him on Monday morning. Although I was still acting until the President signed his "warrant" on October 1, he assumed the position. During Monday morning, we attended two ceremonies. At the second one, I was told that I would sit where Assistant Secretaries sat. During the retirement ceremony, several documents and letters were read. I had signed the appropriate one as the acting Secretary. As they read the Secretary of the Navy letter of congratulations, everyone was surprised that Gordon had signed it as the Secretary. On the way back to the Pentagon, the General Counsel kept repeating that "it was not right!" He talked to Gordon and convinced him that he could not sign anything until his warrant was signed by the President.

Secretary England was only the second person in history to serve twice as the leader of the Navy Marine Corps Team. The Honorable John Mason served as the 16th Navy Secretary from 1844-1845 and 18th SECNAV from 1846-1849.

We all welcomed Gordon home to his Navy and Marine Corps family. It was been a distinct honor to serve as Acting Secretary during this important time in our nation's history, and I am grateful to President Bush for the opportunity to serve. I also greatly appreciated the outstanding work of our Sailors and Marines, and the support of Secretary Rumsfeld, Admiral Clark and General Hagee.

Chief of Naval Operations Adm. Vern Clark praised both of us. "Our institution is honored to welcome home Mr. England as Secretary of the Navy. His leadership, focus on mission accomplishment, and commitment to improving both our business practices and the quality of service for our Sailors and Marines, are valued and needed qualities as we build the future Navy.

"We owe a debt of gratitude to H. T. Johnson for his remarkable service as acting Secretary of the Navy. With his steady hand and commitment to Sailors and Marines, the Department of the Navy never missed a beat. We will undoubtedly continue to benefit from his continued service as Assistant Secretary of the Navy for Installations and the Environment."

Gen. Mike Hagee, Commandant of the U.S. Marine Corps, said of the two leaders, "The Marine Corps is honored and pleased to have Mr. England return as SECNAV. His efforts in leading the Navy-Marine Corps team into the 21st century are especially welcomed because of his impressive and established record of accomplishments, particularly with respect to improving our combat capability and readiness. We look forward to continuing our role as the world's preeminent fighting force under the direction of Mr. England."

"We also are grateful to Mr. Johnson and his untiring commitment to the Marines as acting Secretary. I look forward to his continued leadership as Assistant Secretary of the Navy for Installations and the Environment."

Navy League Support

Thanks Acting Secretary for Superb Service

Considering the unusual length of time Johnson served as Acting Secretary of the Navy, the Navy League would like to recognize Johnson's leadership during these trying times for our Navy and Marine Corps, and our nation.

Along with the outstanding uniformed leadership of Admiral Vern Clark and General Michael Hagee, Johnson immediately got to work ensuring that America's Sailors and Marines had the materials they need for war and that their families had what they needed on the home front.

Holding down three jobs at once, as Acting Secretary, Assistant Secretary of the Navy (Installations and Logistics), and unofficially, the gapped Under Secretary position, Johnson, a retired 4-star Air Force General got cracking as war in Iraq loomed.

As a career military officer with more than 400 combat missions during Vietnam and the person responsible for the largest and fastest logistic effort in history during the first Gulf War when he commanded the United States Transportation Command, Johnson recognized the importance of remaining close to the Sailors and Marines on the front lines and communicating with their families at home.

The first of the more than 65,000 miles traveled as Acting Secretary over the past 7 months took him to the desert camps in Kuwait and facilities in Bahrain and Qatar. There he met with thousands of Sailors and Marines in the desert and at sea. Johnson understands that the people who are the Navy and Marine Corps are its most precious asset.

Johnson treated each and every person he met with dignity and compassion. From deck plate Sailors to Marines wounded in combat, Secretary Johnson's special way with people endeared him to those who wear our nation's uniform and their loved ones.

I've watched this true leader in action," said McNeill. "I'm amazed at how well he manages all of his responsibilities – fighting the war in Iraq, the war on terrorism, transformation – and he still puts Sailors and Marines first, period."

The service of these men and women, appreciated by all Americans, had a very personal interest to Johnson and his wife Linda. Their own son, a Marine Corps Reserve officer, was one of the tens of thousands of brave military personnel assigned to Operation Iraqi Freedom.

Dealing effectively with tough issues like as the Navy's departure from Vieques, the basing of F/A-18 squadrons on the East Coast and the untimely death of the prospective Secretary of the Navy, Colin McMillan, were all handled with Johnson's trademark, grace, style and quiet, effective leadership.

The Navy has been blessed with great leadership and the results have set a high mark for the services. America is likewise blessed to have these selfless public servants working day and night to ensure our freedom.

To H. T. Johnson the Navy League says "well done" and to Gordon England, "welcome home" and to all those who serve, we say thank you.

October 4, 2003 Navy –Air Force Game

As I represented the Secretary of the Navy at the Navy - Air Force football game, I had many memories of the Navy - Air Force game two years before. At that game, Linda was unable to walk from the "tailgate" to FedEx Field. Since that time, she was blessed with wonderful medical care. A "stent" and medication had taken care of her stamina. It was much better. Two new knees helped her walk and feel much better. An Acupuncturist took care of her lower quadrant pains from "shingles" with three "needles" in her ears. She was much healthier. Both of us were showing the effects of our age and were not as active as we have been in the past. I was not sure how much longer I would be able or want to work. As shown below, I still keep very busy.

The game was exciting. We had planned several activities prior to Gordon England returning. He continued his plans to spend this week with his family in Hawaii. I represented the Secretary at the "coin toss," pre-game reception, visiting the wounded troops, cheering the team, etc. – I even got credit for giving the Midshipmen extra privileges. Linda was well dressed - complete with a small anchor around her neck - and Falcon under her collar! The game could have gone either way. Navy had more desire to win. Air Force was surprised. After the game, we hosted a party for our Air Force Academy classmates. Mike Reardon's son, Joe was a midshipman at the Naval Academy. He also brought another Midshipman "whom I had given extra privileges to." Our classmates did not give me a hard time for leading the Navy to victory.

Farewell from acting Secretary Position

As I was leaving the acting Secretary of the Navy position, my assistant and traveling partner, Navy CAPT Kevin Wensing, wrote the following about our adventures:

> Secretary Johnson has a gift, a gift with people. He has the uncanny ability to make everyone who works for him and with him feel at ease, yet inspires and motivates them like few people have the ability to do.
>
> Whether it is one of the Sailors in the chow hall in

Sigonella, Italy or the Commanding Officer of the 24th Marine Expeditionary Unit, Secretary Johnson makes you feel special, purely because he feels that you are, and truly values what we do day in and day out to keep the Navy and Marine Corps running.

How many four star General's or Secretaries take the time to write a Sailor's or Marine's parent's to tell them what a superb job he is doing? How many senior executives learn not just the spouse's name of the people they are meeting with, but also the names of his or her children? Acting Secretary Johnson does.

He believes in forming positive relationships in order to develop a strong, unified team. His commitment to people extends to the deepest roots of the Department of the Navy. Since his appointment as Acting Secretary, he has worked diligently in fostering the Navy and Marine Corps relationship, encouraging jointness at every level. He ensures both Sailors and Marines are represented at every level and always refers to them as one unified team. Having served as a four star General in the Air Force, he brings a piece of Air Force to the Navy/Marine Corps team, helping to encourage the necessity of jointness and Navy and Marine Corps integration ... His selfless work ethic has contributed to making our Department of Defense a more efficient and effective organization, with jointness as the key ingredient.

To Secretary Johnson, people are our most precious asset and the focus on what we do. He feels at home at every level with people, making each person feel important. He traveled extensively to visit Sailors and Marines, see where they lived, what they did and worked diligently to improve Quarters and facilities on base.

He made numerous trips to Bethesda Naval Hospital to visit the wounded Marines from the war in Iraq. He was overwhelmed by the strong, fighting will, and commitment he saw in the Marines and Sailors. He thought he was going there to cheer them up, but instead, they cheered him up.

Safety is a part of everything he does. We would remiss in taking care of our people if we don't practice and preach safety each and every day.

He turned the loss of Vieques Training range in Puerto Rico into a positive training environment.

He transforms challenges into opportunities!

It was indeed a tremendous honor and privilege to serve as the acting Secretary of the Navy and Marine Corps.

The Navy Staff gave me an "Oscar" as the "Best Acting Secretary of the Navy!"

Secretary of the Navy (Acting)

Return to Assistant Secretary

As Gordon England was preparing for confirmation, we talked a great deal. Once he asked what I wanted to do. I told him that I would like to be the Under Secretary and continue to lead our BRAC efforts. He indicated that he did not need or want an Under Secretary. He suggested that I become the Special Assistant to the Secretary of Defense for BRAC and lead all BRAC activities for Secretary Rumsfeld. Later, he told the Secretary of Defense that he did not want an active Under Secretary. When I understood his concerns, I was honored not to be asked. I would have a very difficult time in trying to not make a positive contribution to any group. He was not given a choice and selected Dino Aviles to become the Under Secretary. He also arranged for John Young to move to the Office of the Under Secretary of Defense for Acquisition, Technology, and Logistics.

During my early tenure as the Acting Secretary, the Military Assistant was Rear Admiral John Morgan. He was overly qualified for the position. The Secretary of Defense's office and everyone else strongly suggested that Admiral Morgan leave this position. I finally agreed and he left. Gordon brought him back as his Military Assistant. Fortunately, he also brought a brilliant young leader, Bob Earl. Bob attended the Naval Academy and went on to be a Rhodes Scholar and serve in the Marine Corps. After retiring from the Marine Corps, Bob Earl worked for General Dynamics and with Gordon. He had also worked with Gordon at Homeland Security. Bob Earl continued to be a wonderful advisor and partner to Gordon.

During the initial days after the return of Gordon England, I wanted to help reestablish him as our Secretary. I worked very hard not to offer too much advice and to distance myself from the Secretary's front office. He seemed to appreciate my effort, and we very quickly reestablished our old close partnership.

On May 15, 2004 at the Navy Marine Corps Relief Society Ball, Lt. Gen. Bob Magnus, USMC talked to Linda about me. He said, "Of all the Secretaries of the Navy that I have known, HT was the best decision maker. Early on, he told us if we do not want a decision, we should not ask. He listens and makes decisions. We miss him as the Secretary."

As the Assistant Secretary for Installations and Environment, I continued my duties and contributed to the BRAC activities. Although it was a great privilege to work for Gordon England, I soon realized that it was time to move on.

On July 16, 2004, I resigned my position as Assistant Secretary. I was honored with medals from Secretary Rumsfeld, the Army, and Air Force. I had already received the highest Navy Civilian Medal.

CIVILIAN LIFE SECOND ROUND

IDA

When I decided to leave the Department of the Navy, I wanted to become a Senior Fellow and work three days a week. My first choice was to work for a Federally Funded Research and Development Center (FFRDC). Over the years, I had worked closely with the Center for Naval Analyses, RAND, and the Institute for Defense Analyses (IDA). I also considered some "not for profit" analytical companies and serving on boards of some large companies. Large boards normally retire board members as they approach 70.

On August 16, 2004, I became a Senior Fellow at the Institute for Defense Analysis (IDA). This was my first choice. Initially, we agreed that I would work four days a week – this quickly became five days a week. The CEO, Admiral Dennis Blair, was most gracious, and we agreed that at some point I would become an Adjunct and could work as much as IDA needed and I desired to work. On June 11, 2007, I became an Adjunct.

The IDA Team is filled with extremely talented professional, with virtually all having advanced degrees and many having earned their PhDs. I was indeed most fortunate to work with a wide range of experts.

In a most interesting world, on November 12, 2004, I was asked to lead a Red Team (an outside group) to evaluate the Defense Base Realignment and Closure proposal. Although I did not become the "Special Assistant to the Secretary of Defense for Base Realignment and Closure (BRAC)," I was asked to review the final product. The Red Team was able to carefully review the recommendations and make some very helpful suggestions which were accepted by DoD. It was exciting to participate on my third BRAC: 1993 on the BRAC Commission, on the Local Reuse Authority for Kelly AFB which was closed by the 1995 BRAC, and 2004 as leader of the Red Team. As always, I was proud to serve to the best of my abilities.

As part of IDA, I was most fortunate to work on a wide variety of "organizational" studies with Dr. David Graham. We have done multiple studies for the Marine Corps, the Special Operations Command, the Transportation Command, and the Congress. We were able to work directly with leaders at the very highest level to include the Service Chiefs, Comptroller General of the Government Accountability Office (GAO), the Commanders of the Combatant Commanders, and senior leaders in the Department of Defense. Most importantly, the studies were well accepted and made an extremely positive impact.

Dr. Barry Crane brought his experience as the Deputy Drug Czar back to the military, as we looked at how all illicit activities supporting the insurgences around the world. Together with Dr. Rich White and Dr. Amy Alrich, we were able to translate their research into very helpful information for the military. Many realized that it is better to take away the support than try to kill their way to victory against insurgents.

DSSG

The Department of Defense invites a group of university professors to participate in the Defense Science Study Group (DSSG). As a Senior DSSG Mentor, it has been exciting to learn from and share with the many members of the DSSG. During the two year DSSG cycle, the members visit a wide range of defense and defense supporting activities around the country. As a Senior Mentor, I was able to travel with the DSSG and share in their experiences.

Honors

Several honors came very quickly. During the fall of 2005, I received a call from Retired General Eberhart, a member of the Air Force Academy Association of Graduates asking if I would be available on April 7, 2006. When I confirmed that I would be available, he said, "Congratulations, you have been selected as a Distinguished Graduate."

On November 6, 2005, I received a call from Speaker Hastert's office asking if I would be his only non-Congressional one year appointee to the Air Force Academy Board of Visitors (BOV). Of course, I agreed and asked what I needed to do. She responded, "Nothing, the Speaker will sign it today and it will be in the Congressional Record tomorrow!" Having worked with the White House Personnel Office, I was blown away with the simplicity of the appointment procedures. The next day, I received the official call about being select to be a DG. Needless to say, I was most pleased with both honors to serve our Academy.

A short time later, I was invited to be inducted into the South Carolina Aviation Hall of Fame. It was a wonderful ceremony. My brother and sister were able to join us. I was presented a plaque which included a hologram. From one view, one sees an older general and from another angle, a 17 year old freshman at Clemson College. It is most impressive.

The Distinguished Graduate presentations were beyond belief. Our entire family participated and was well hosted by the Academy. I was able to interact with a wide range of cadets and our family was able to visit all parts of the Academy. I was honored at Friday noon in the Cadet Dining Hall, evening dinner, and Saturday morning parade. It was a busy but most productive time.

I could not figure out how the younger grandchildren were so well behaved at the long evening dinner until I saw the iPOD cords. The six year old finally went to sleep in his brother's lap. During the choir singing, he awoke and sat up. The people who could see him were watching him more than the choir to see which way he would fall out of his chair. His mother took away the excitement when she put him in her lap. We were honored that so many of our Academy classmates Air Training Officers, families and friends were able to attend the events associated with Founders Day.

Johnson Family at the Distinguished Graduates Awards

U. S. Air Force Academy Distinguished Graduate Citation
General Hansford T. Johnson
Class of 1959

General Hansford T. "H.T." Johnson's lifetime of distinguished service to our Nation represents the highest ideal of the Air Force Academy. He was the first Academy graduate to rise to the rank of General. After serving in the Air Force, he was the Assistant and acting Secretary of the Navy. He was awarded a Silver Star, three Distinguished Flying Crosses, and 23 Air Medals for his exceptional courage during combat as a forward air controller in Vietnam and Laos. After his combat tour, he was an assistant professor of Aeronautics at the Academy. Cadets praised him as an enthusiastic, motivating, and encouraging advisor and mentor. He served in a wide variety of operations and staff positions that shaped the Air Force. As the Deputy Commander-in-Chief of the U.S. Central

Command, he was intimately involved in preparing for the inevitable war with Iraq. He culminated his military career as Commander-in-Chief of the U.S. Transportation and Military Airlift Commands. His command provided all the airlift and special operations forces for the extremely effective invasion of Panama. During Desert Shield, he commanded the largest, most concentrated movement of troops, equipment, and supplies in American military history. He served as President and CEO of the USAA Capital Corporation. President George H Bush appointed him to the 1993 Base Realignment and Closure Commission. As the acting Secretary of the Navy, he led the Navy and Marine Corps during the initial Operation Iraqi Freedom victory. General Johnson also served his beloved Academy as a member of the Academy's Board of Visitors. Throughout his service to our Nation, General Johnson believed that individuals can be inspired to achieve the impossible. He transformed challenges into opportunities and always gave credit to others for positive results. As each daunting task became an opportunity to make a positive difference, he consistently lived our highest core values of Integrity first, Service before Self, and Excellence in all we do.

DISTINGUISHED GRADUATE AWARD-2005

Introduction as a Distinguished Graduate by the
First Graduate of the Air Force Academy,
Lt. General Brad Hosmer

The Class of 1959 and all of us have been blessed with the friendship and fine example of the Honorable Hansford T. Johnson for over a half a century. H. T. already stood out around cadets 51 years ago as a special person. Even in a class that entered the Academy with more college semesters under its belt than any class since, H. T.'s maturity was obvious–as were his unusual ability and his affinity for hard work. From the time we first knew him,

H. T. expected more of himself than anyone else–and he delivered. And he never changed. H. T.'s gifts and talents in the classroom, in command, and as a valued friend were recognized first as a cadet and throughout our lives because there are obvious in what he does, not in what he says. And while his talents are outsized, they come packaged with great humility.

We can all admire General Johnson's professional life because we have seen his rare potential so well matched with big responsibility, serving the Air Force and then the Nation. His remarkable contributions have been briefly outlined tonight. But what stands out for his classmates is H. T.'s continued concern, his interest, his care for classmates and others, and his unchanging humility despite over 50 years of continued success with bigger and bigger responsibilities.

We have all known unusually able and successful people who find professional demands somehow push their lives out of balance. That is not H. T. Johnson. Unlike them, H. T. has a full personal and family life. The demands of his professional challenges have never pushed aside the satisfactions of a private life and a large circle of friends–and his classmates are proud to number themselves in that circle. H. T. Johnson is a balanced, complete person, and Linda Johnson is very much a part of that completeness. We cannot think of H. T. without thinking of Linda, her warmth, her dignity, and her great decency. The H. T. Johnson story-line is very much a team product.

H. T.'s leadership and character have marked the Air Force throughout his military career. He tried to retire. But as our class-scribe Pete Todd put it that just didn't work out–and H. T.'s remarkable record in the government and private sectors after leaving active duty simply "extends the streak." So, with Linda at his side and a large and admiring circle of friends looking on, he remains a citizen of the Nation very much in demand. We, his classmates, are his strongest supporters and proudest friends.

I am on order to keep this very short. Otherwise, like most of us who know and respect H. T., I could go on and on. Instead, I will close by thanking the AOG for this opportunity to declare that the Class of 1959 enthusiastically applauds the selection of H. T. Johnson as an outstanding graduate of the Air Force Academy for 2005.

Air Force Academy Board of Visitors

The BOV meets four times a year: twice in the Capitol and twice at the Academy. In the past, attendance had not been too good. The various challenges at the academies have increased the role of the BOVs. The current law indicates that a member who missed more than two consecutive meetings without a good reason will be removed. When I joined the Air Force Academy BOV, my friend former Governor Gilmore was the chair.

After a year, the Speaker appointed someone else for the next year. During my year on the BOV, we were able to gain Air Force and Academy support for establishing four committees to work with the Academy -- Character and Leadership, Academic and Course of Instruction, Infrastructure and Resources, and Admissions and Graduation.

The Board of Visitors was an excellent opportunity to make a positive difference at the Air Force Academy. It was a privilege to serve on the BOV.

Port Hueneme April 08

In April 2008, I was invited by my Quality Mentor from my Scott AFB days, Sheila Sheinberg, to address the Naval Warfare Center Port Hueneme Division (PHD) Sentinel Whole Systems Transformation Conference. The PHD was trying to transform its processes and increase it competiveness perform naval support.

The Conference was held at the Reagan Library in Simi Valley, California. It was exciting to address the group and participate in their activities. I discussed our activities to engender quality ownership throughout the years. My comments were well accepted as the keynote to their work. During the question and answer discussion, I was asked what my most rewarding job was over the years. To everyone's surprise and then understanding, I responded, "The one I had at the moment!" They realized that we always have to focus on and enjoy the activities we are involved in at the moment.

From my host, Karen Bower, I received a magnificent complement:

> You are an amazing man--truly one in 10 Million. Thanks for your kind words and wishes. Most importantly, thanks for who you are. In 37 years of government service, I have never met, nor seen, anyone like you. As senior as you are and with all the experiences and (I'm sure) all the political dancing you have been involved with, you haven't lost your soul, your heart and your humanity. It was a pleasure and a privilege to meet you and to learn from you. Thank you.
>
> Karen

It was truly a most rewarding experience for me and the PHD.

50th Anniversary

Linda and I were extremely proud of our strong marriage. Linda was always most supportive and encouraging during our Journey together.

To properly celebrate our 50th Anniversary, we invited the entire family to join us on an Alaskan Cruise. Everyone was able to join us. We all met in Anchorage, rode the train to Seward where we boarded the Royal Caribbean "Radiance of the Sea" for seven exciting days at sea. Along the cruise, we visited the Hubbard Glacier, Juneau, Skagway, Icy Strait Point, Ketchikan, the Inside Passage, and Vancouver.

The "Radiance of the Sea" had activities for all ages. The grandchildren joined us for formal dinners and sometimes for other meals. Emily (15) and Katie (11) roomed together and enjoyed ordering room service breakfasts. Zac (19), Jeff (17), and Kyle (10) roomed together. Kyle was able to keep up with the older boys except in courting the young ladies. Connor (13) roomed with his Uncle Richard though he spent most of his time with the other grandchildren and in the arcade. There was a rock climbing wall and many athletic and game events.

The four hour train ride gave us an opportunity to see the magnificent Alaskan countryside and visit with the family. Although Linda and I had visited Alaska, I did not fully appreciate the beautiful terrain with very few residents.

It was amazing to be on a very large cruise ship as it approached to within 300 yards of the 400 foot face of the Hubbard Glacier. The Glacier advances with creaks and groans as it moves forward as a very active caving glacier. We were told to yell to encourage the "calving" of the ice on the very high face. I am not sure our yells made any different; however, it was exciting to see huge chunks of ice fall into the bay creating a wonderful sound called "white thunder" by the locals.

Juneau is a relatively small town. I was surprised to learn that there is no highway access to the State Capitol of Juneau. Everyone, except Linda and me, went into the mountains and slid down the zip lines. Even the younger grandchildren enjoyed the excitement. Linda and I visited a salmon hatchery and learned a lot about salmon.

Skagway comes alive when the cruise ships (5) arrive to multiply the population by many fold. Beth and the three younger grandchildren took and train and tram ride, while the others went biking – mostly downhill. Linda and I visited the Klondike summit and the historic city's gold rush cemetery. It was a very active day but cool and rainy.

As we passed Icy Strait Point, we were able to go ashore in launches to watch tribal dances. Icy Strait Point is also "whale country." Our tour was fortunate to find and follow a pod of beluga whales for a couple of hours as they "spewed, dove, and "flumed."

Ketchikan is the southernmost large city in Alaska and filled with adventures. Richard, Zac, Jeff, Emily, and Connor kayaked in the streams. Beth, Doug, Katie, and Kyle flew around the area in a small plane. Linda and I took a bus tour to visit the Totem Poles, a Light House, and watch the eagles. It turned out to be a wonderful tour of these areas with many more baby sea lions, migrating salmon, eagles, birds, and land animals. The last day, we relaxed on board and tried to repack our suitcases as we sailed through the Inside Passage.

The sights and activities were wonderful; however the times with the family as a group and individually were most joyous part. Each of the grandchildren was very self-assured, found many exciting activities, was very much at ease in formal dining, and found warm moments with their Granny and Granddad. The cruise left us with memories we will all treasure forever.

My Linda, Partner for Life and Love of my Life

We do not always fully appreciate the impact that others have on our lives. My Linda had many medical challenges during her life but was always had more concern about caring for others. As a quiet, warm caring, giving, loving Lady, she touched the lives of so many of us in tender, helpful ways. She was a strong partner in our amazing journey together. She always kept me focused on the positive approaches – pulling me up in difficult times and pulling me back down when things were too good. I could not have found a better partner.

As her health deteriorated, she reserved a great apartment for us at Falcons Landing, entertained our family at Christmas, sold our home, and entered the hospital. During the last few days of her Wonderful Life, she knew her time had come and "asked permission to die!" Of course, I told her that it was not yet her time. After talking to her doctors, I called Beth and had her listen to the doctors' visit with Linda. At the end of the call, Beth said, "I will be there tomorrow!" A couple of days later, we were able to bring Linda home for two days, and she passed very peacefully on January 23, 2011. Family and friends got me through these most difficult days.

Linda loved to travel, read, watch sporting events, and volunteer with the Red Cross in support of our troops. She went through life with grace, determination, and a beautiful smile. Her love and devotion to her family and friends were unwavering.

The entire family and many friends participated in her Memorial Service in McLean and internment at the Air Force Academy. As always, I heard many most laudatory stories about how Linda had a positive impact on so many during her Life's Journey.

<u>Life at Falcons Landing</u>

Beth and a tremendous "moving coordinator," Linda Edwards, were masterful in helping me down-size and move to Falcons Landing. It was interesting as we carefully tried to share things with the family, I suggested the Ladies go through Linda's jewelry and select items to keep. The Grandsons were most upset that they were not included and they were allowed to select a pearl necklace each.

Beth and Linda Edwards arranged the new apartment at Falcons Landing. For several months, I had to call and ask where they placed things!

I was very well received at Falcons Landing. The first Mix and Match meeting that I attended, there were seventy-five widows and five widowers. The ratio is not that low, but many men did not attend.

Soon after losing my Linda, I received a letter from a Lady who lost her husband two weeks before I lost Linda. She told me how much I had meant to her husband and he had kept a letters from me many years before in a special folder that she found. I had known both of them at USAA. In a series of correspondence, she told she had promised her husband that she would visit the Vietnam Memorial for him. I offered to get a room for her and escort her for the visit. We had a wonderful weekend together, and Ann and I were married eight months later. Her letter (and my letters to her husband) certainly changed our lives and brought great joy and happiness to both of us.

Soon after Ann's visit, I visited San Antonio and met her son and his family. His wife Kristi told me that I was smitten! Later, Ann and I visited California to meet all of my family. On our last evening we were having dinner with my Grandson, Jeff. His mother sent him a "text" that told him to show his granddad how to read a text! Beth's text said, "You should propose!" Later that evening, I proposed and we were married in a lovely wedding with both of our families in Boerne, Texas on February 19, 2012.

Ann and HT

Ann and I became very involved in activities at Falcons Landing. It is a great continuing care community. We chaired the New Year's Gala, deliver Meal on Wheels, work at the Dulles USO, and many other activities. Having chaired the Board, I am honored to serve on the Residents' Council. I am still an Off-Site Adjunct at the Institute for Defense Analyses. I work more at Falcons Landing and work less as an Adjunct at IDA. It is still a privilege to serve others, and I will serve others as long as I can.

LIFE'S LESSONS

Health

Over the years, I have had amazingly good health.

As a youngster, my teeth were very fragile, and I broke both front teeth. One was due to a fall. Another one resulted from a chain over a limb of a backyard tree. We would attach an old tire and use it for a swing. Once when the tire was not attached, I got hit with the chain and had a front tooth broken. I believe that I also broke one a second time in football. They were replaced with a partial bridge and eventually with fixed bridges.

I played high school football as a tackle and end. At some point, I hurt my leg and was told to stay in bed. After a half day in bed, I got up and used crutches. After a few hours, I put away the crutches. As difficult as the crutches were to me, I have no understanding of how my brother, Dent, has been able to use crutches virtually his entire life!

As a freshman at the Academy, I ran track. During a two mile run, I noticed my foot began to hurt. Of course, I finished. When I took off the track shoe and stood up, I could not put any pressure on the foot. It was diagnosed as a "March Fracture." I was excused from all running for two weeks. It did not get better; then, the doctor put a cast on my foot for a week and everything got better.

During freshman Christmas at the Academy, we were not allowed to go home. During this time, one of my eyes began to "flutter" and hurt. After a couple of days, I went to our flight surgeon. After examining me, he said, "It is nothing. Forget about it and it will go away!" I stopped noticing, and it went away!

While I was at the Central Command and visiting the Middle Eastern countries, I started having "night sweats." I would wake up in the morning in a pool of sweat. I was given various medicines, but it never went away totally.

In the later years in the Air Force and at USAA, I had a continual "hacking cough." The San Antonio doctors did many tests to determine the cause. I had continuous bronchial congestion but nothing in the lungs. I tell others that they did a CAT Scan of my head and found it empty – they were looking at the sinuses and found them clear. Finally a throat doctor "scoped my wind pipe and lungs." He found no congestion but commented, "You have the longest 'uvula' I have ever seen. It is probably acting as 'wick' to pull mucus up and drop it into the windpipe while you sleep." He recommended removing the uvula. After a second opinion, I told them, "If there is 51% chance that removing the uvula will stop my bronchial problems and 60% probability of stopping my snoring, have at it." It was removed; my bronchial problems went away, and I stopped snoring.

In San Antonio, I exercised on a treadmill with an "ear pulse meter." I would normally get my pulse rate up to 160. In late June of 1995, the pulse rate went to 175; I pressed on and completed the run. The next day, it went to 185 and I slowed but completed the run. The next day it went to 195, and I got off the treadmill! I was having difficulty climbing steps and every other symptom of a heart attack -- which I knew. All of the children were coming for the Fourth of July, and I could not tell anyone. At a party on the evening of July 3, I saw General Paul Carlton, the Air Force Commander of Wilford Hall in San Antonio, told him of my problems, and asked if I could get a "stress test." On the 4th, we visited Fiesta Texas Amusement Park. The children wanted to ride the "sky coaster." Up to three people were pulled up 182 feet and released to swing back and forth. I knew that I would have a complete heart attack but could not "wimp out" and not ride with the children. It was an exciting ride, and I did not die. At one o'clock on July 5, my assistant and General Carlton had me on the stress test. Enroute, I called Linda and told her that I was going for a stress test but she did not think it was a big deal. During the walking portion of the test, I was still walking at the 15 minute point that normally required one to run. At the end, General Carlton and the experts said, "We cannot find anything wrong with you!" A couple of days later, I got a new "waist" pulse meter, and all was well. A bad pulse meter convinced me that I was having a heart problem – then, I "felt" every symptom that I knew of! It is amazing how our heads can "simulate" such pain!

During an annual physical in early 2007, my doctor found elevated cholesterol, blood sugar, and weight. These had been creeping up over the years and were not of great concern – except that I needed to lose some weight. He also noticed an irregular indication on the EKG and asked me to visit with a Cardiologist. A new EKG indicated near normal conditions, but to ensure there were no problems the doctor gave me five tests (EBCT, Cardiac Heart Stress, Nuclear Stress, CT Radiology Scan, and Cardiac Cauterization). I passed both stress tests; however, there was always a little concern. On March 8, 2007, the cauterization confirmed all concerns and indicated a 90% blockage of my Left Anterior Descending Artery. The surgeons used angioplasty to clear the blockage and emplaced a chemically treated stent. After an overnight stay in the hospital, I was released and healthy. Linda was working at the Walter Reed Red Cross Center and took me home and went back to work. When she came home from the Red Cross, I had scattered 30 bags of mulch!

At each step of the process the doctors could have dismissed the "slight indications" and a massive heart attack would have occurred at some point in the future. They and I suspected the blockage had been building for many years. I am most grateful for the doctors' and professional staffs' perseverance.

Opportunities

Many opportunities have come our way. I was able to make some choices; however, most opportunities were offered rather than being sought. Someone gave some very good advice. "Always be prepared and opportunities will come!"

Others gave some very good advice about being patient. When I was being considered for a teaching position at the Air Force Academy and was selected a year later than I would have liked, a much more senior and wiser friend told me that things normally happen just a little later that one would like. So many become discouraged and seek other paths or "just quit." Only once in my Air Force career did I seriously consider "getting out." Even before I could prepare my resume, a new assignment came, and we never considered leaving the Air Force again until the "proper retirement time arrived."

I only remember asking for an assignment once and being denied. I was considering a teaching position at Air University. My commander told me that I should not apply. Of course, his decision was correct. A short time later, I went to graduate school and subsequently became an instructor at the Air Force Academy.

There are other missed opportunities. In early 1997, I was the "front" runner to be the Federal Aviation Administrator. Although, "they" did not know me, Members of Congress decided that they did not want a former military officer as the FAA administrator. If I had been selected, I would have been the Administrator when 9-11 occurred! Or perhaps it would not have occurred!

I was once considered to join WorldCom in the early days. We were invited to join the WorldCom leaders at the Sugar Bowl, but nothing materialized. Of course, as things fell apart in 2003, I was again most fortunate not to be a part of WorldCom.

EPILOGUE

I have been fortunate to serve in some interesting staff and leadership positions. The principles I have attempted to always follow are much the same in all situations. I always tried to prepare for discussions or operations with a clear understanding of the objectives and a concept of a possible solution. Then, I listened carefully to the discussion without giving any indication of any predisposition other than the "objective" and a commitment to achieving it. When the group believed it was truly an open discussion, their fertile minds did wonders. It is easy to empower when "all of us" have developed and "own" the plan. Once the objectives and plan of action were well known, the "owners" ensure success. They will encourage and even "push" those who need help.

I tolerate mistakes or needed changes that are discovered and "fixed" early by those involved. I never willingly tolerate lack of integrity, commitments to "prove" known errors or misjudgments, or passing "blame" on to others. I am anxious to accept responsibility and find ways to improve shortfalls before they become harmful. I try to widely share credit and take personal responsibility for any shortcomings. I must admit that I reward successes with more opportunities.

This approach has held me in good stead in war, peace, and business situations. The people actually performing the work know more about their jobs that I ever will. My job as a leader is to set the objectives, facilitate initiatives, empower, ensure accountability, and witness the expected fantastic results.

Throughout my life I have been a simple, extremely trusting individual.

In the normal course of my professional lives, it is always exciting when someone says, "You are a Christian!" When I say, "Yes," I will often ask, "How did you know?" The response, "By the way you act and treat people," always brings me tremendous inner pride.

I have a very strong conscience. The Lord speaks to me through this strong conscience and dreams. When we lost our 33-year-old David, he lived in California near his sister, Beth. She was deeply involved in tracing the details surrounding his death and was very pregnant. Our granddaughter, Katie was born four days after losing her Uncle David and before the funeral. It was a very traumatic time in our lives. Over the years, David has visited me in three wonderful dreams. During Christmas in 2003, we were with all of our children and grandchildren in California. During our trips to California, Linda and I always tried to visit David's resting place. Beth and her four children joined us. The four grandchildren seemed to know of their Uncle David and understand why we should visit. As they were in solemn thought, five-year-old Katie asked, "Can we kneel and pray for Uncle David?" They knelt and gave individual prayers. We were most impressed about their thoughts for their departed uncle – but even more that religion is a big part in their lives. What a Wonderful Experience!

Many of us never know where our thoughts and character are developed. I would like to tell a story that was such a shocking remainder. When we returned to the Washington area, we joined the National Presbyterian Church. Representing the Church in "Serve the Homeless" at the 3rd Street Church of God in downtown Washington, I served breakfast on alternate Friday mornings. Normally, three of us would prepare and serve the breakfast. One morning, only Reverend Green who grew up in Jamaica, and I were in the kitchen alone. He asked how I came to know the Lord. I responded, "I never remembered not knowing the Lord." He was shocked. I suspect he and all of his members of the Prayer Breakfast group "had come to know the Lord" after some traumatic event. On reflection, I was extremely pleased by our early teachings. I trust that our children, grandchildren, and each of you can on reflection say the same thing

Prayers are a very private time for me – I can talk to the LORD, and I am also talking to myself. I never ask for things for myself. During one of his sermons, the National Presbyterian minister, Craig Barnes, talked about "my thoughts," and I was most impressed. He said and I practice, "I always ask the Lord to show me HIS path." Not "my" path but "HIS" path. Of course, unsaid is "HIS" path for me. All of a sudden my talks with the LORD took on even more understanding.

In an earlier life, I had many security clearances and was required to take a "random" polygraph. As part of procedures, I was asked two "bench mark" questions that I was to answer "NO" and the instruments would indicate that I was not telling the truth. The first question was, "Have you ever lied to your wife?" I responded, "No." He asked the same question again and said, "It shows that you are telling the truth!" Then, he asked, "Have you ever been asked to do something that you could not do with a good conscious?" The operator had difficulty believing the results and said, "I have never met anyone who could answer both correctly."

I take this as a compliment but also as a realist who looks at life in a trusting understanding way. My girlfriend, as I called my wife Linda after 51 1/2 year of marriage, reminded me that the Cadet Honor Code says, "We will not lie, cheat or steal nor tolerate among us anyone who does." BUT its teachings say that you can complement someone as being more beautiful than she is -- That is called TACT. Realism also says one does not have to blurt out the truth or draw distinct lines when things are often in the eye of the beholder. Early in our service to our Nation, many of my classmates had a difficult time with each issue being either "right" or "wrong." I recognized that most things are gray and many have quite different meanings to the speaker and the listener. I must admit that I have most blessed. First, when Linda asked a question that I could not or did not want to respond to and evade, she did not insist. I have suspected on some occasions that someone would want me to do something that I could not in good conscious do. By crafting the discussion properly, we can communicate without ever being confronted with such a question.

In a previous life, I built the financial Programs for the future of the Department of the Air Force. Normally, we were charged to find "good" reductions. Initially as the chair of a committee, I was the "fetcher" - to identify the reductions and propose. I quickly learned that no one would offer to give up their programs. We soon established an "engine room" that would develop a set of changes that would meet the requirements. Everyone knew "we" had some ways to meet the program limits. I would then ask for suggestions. When few were forthcoming, I could suggest some. When there was disagreement, I would allow the responsible office to suggest better solutions. The results were tremendous! Later, I was

Chair of the reviewing group, and I took the results to the very top levels. We were extremely successful in presenting balanced proposals that received strong endorsements. During the entire three-year in these two positions, we never took a vote and never failed to achieve consensus!

On assuming command of a very large organization with a poor reputation, I had many programs and focus areas. Everyone "dutifully" accepted "my" proposals! When we discovered TQM (Total Quality Management), I realized that everything I was trying to do was within the TQM principles. Gaining the support of our inspired Quality Facilitator, Sheila Sheinberg, we were on our way! In a very short time, the entire command was on a Quality Journey. "My" focus areas were overshadowed by "OUR" focus areas. Many were the same—but now ours!

Recognize others

Throughout my adult life, I have tried to properly recognize others with compliments and notes. Some examples of notes are:

During three visits to Persian Gulf during Desert Shield/Storm, I would fly with four crews of 8 to 10 members. I requested each crew member give me the name and address of someone that I could write about them. I flew with one young man twice. On the second flight when asked who I could write, he replied, "Last time you wrote my mother, please write my Grandmother!" I received some nice notes in return and still meet people who say, "I still have the note that you wrote me."

In 2008, a BGen introduced me to his wife as the "one who saved our marriage!" He had volunteered to fly some missions against the wishes of his wife. He was on the 1990 New Year's Eve flight over the Eastern European countries. When she received my note, she forgave her husband!

It is not just young people. Once as a three star, I wrote the wife of a one star and described the great work he was doing. After I retired, we visited the home of Chairman of the Joint Chiefs of Staff Hugh Shelton.

He pulled me aside to tell me that his wife had my note framed, and it was on his wall for many years.

I once visited the office of a Senior Civil Servant who was quite ill. His assistant asked me to come over to his desk, and she showed me a letter that I had written many years before and said, "When things are difficult, he would open his top drawer, read your letter, and Smile."

Of course, I am most grateful for the many compliments that I have received. We never fully recognize the positive effects we can and do have on the lives of others!

Acceptance

I learned early on not to lament over the past or things I could change. I am particularly impressed by the Serenity Prayer and try to live by its tenets.

Serenity Prayer

God grant me the serenity to accept
The things I cannot change,
Courage to change the things I can,
And wisdom to know the difference.

Praise

In all things, I try to pass praises on to others. While we were in San Antonio and I served as the Chair of the Kelly Air Force Base Reuse Authority, Mayor Thornton would always very publicly thank me for our doing many positive things. As is my custom, I would always pass full credit to others. After a while, the Mayor began saying, "HT, shut up and just say 'thank you!'"

I am also guilty of giving more praise to others than is perhaps deserved. Soon, they deserve more praise that they are receiving. I most like to give credit and praise to someone who was not 'too sure' of success in the beginning.

Treat Everyone with Respect as Full Partners

Often, military organizations try to differentiate between the "combat or warfighter" and other leaders. Every person in an organization is extremely important. During my time in the Navy, I would often confuse my hosts by walking into the kitchens (or galleys) and show my respect for everyone. The leaders are certainly ultimately in charge; however, the best leaders share leadership at all levels. Most of us do not prepare all of our meals or other activities and depend on others to properly care for many needs. **Show your respect and appreciation to everyone!** If you respect each person as a leader, you will be amazed by how things will improve

Reverend Barry Black

In 2003, the Chief of Navy Chaplains, Admiral Barry Black, became the Chaplain of the Senate replacing Lloyd Oglivie. As the acting Secretary of the Navy, I had the opportunity to work with Barry. As he was making his "out calls," we talked about personal beliefs. It was a marvelous discussion. Then, he asked if we could pray – he is as impressive on a personal basis as he is in the pulpit. I felt most blessed.

Life is like this: We learn so very much as we are growing up. Sometimes, we lose our way; however, these early teachings set our course through life. It is always reassuring to go back to our roots and understand and appreciate the teachings of our talented and loving parents.

CLOSING

A Lifetime of Serving

As we go through our lives, we find some challenges and many opportunities to serve others. As we focus on the opportunities, the challenges are transformed into opportunities or become insignificant.

I have committed my life to serving others and our Nation.

Appendix

Awards and Citations

APPENDIX

Distinguished Flying Cross 18 May 1967	225
Silver Star 2 July 1967	226
Short Round Incident 4 July 1967	232
Distinguished Flying Cross (First Oak Leaf Cluster) 12 August 1967	234
Vietnamese Cross of Gallantry with Silver Star 20 October 1967	237
Vietnamese Armed Forces Honor Medal 25 October 1967	241
Distinguished Flying Cross (Second Oak Leaf Cluster) 19 January 1968	242
Meritorious Service Medal 1 May 1968 – 16 July 1971	245
Legion of Merit 12 June 1972 – 31 July 1975	249
Legion of Merit (First Oak Leaf Cluster) June 1976 – February 1981	251
Distinguished Service Medal 26 February 1981 – 2 December 1982	254

Defense Meritorious Service Medal 260
    30 October 1985 – 18 December 1986

Defense Distinguished Service Medal 265
    August 1987 – November 1988

Defense Distinguished Service Medal 269
(First Oak Leaf Cluster)
    December 1988 – September 1989

Distinguished Service Medal 270
(First Oak Leaf Cluster)
    21 September 1989 – 31 August 1992

Defense Distinguished Service Medal 271
(Second Oak Leaf Cluster)
    September 1989 – August 1992

Certificate of Appreciation 272

Distinguished Public Service Award 273
    7 January 2003

Medal for Distinguished Public Service 274
    July 2004

THE DISTINGUISHED FLYING CROSS
to Captain Hansford T. Johnson, 18 May 1967

CITATION

Captain Hansford T. Johnson distinguished himself while participating in aerial flight as a Forward Air Controller in an unarmed O-1 Bird Dog Aircraft in Southeast Asia on 18 May 1967. On that date, Capt Johnson was directing a defoliation mission being flown by six C-123 aircraft with two F-4Cs flying cover. As the aircraft approached the end of their spray run, they began receiving intense ground fire from either .50 caliber or 12.7 mm machine gun positions. Capt Johnson immediately aborted the spray mission and moved into the area vacated by the C-123's in an effort to locate the enemy gun positions. As the anti-aircraft fire was re-directed toward his aircraft, he was able to locate three of the gun positions. Despite the low altitude, he rolled in through the curtain of fire, marked the target, and directed the fighters against the guns. Due to his accurate mark, the strike aircraft were able to score direct hits on the positions before the wingman was hit by ground fire and the flight had to depart. Capt Johnson quickly called for additional flights of fighters. Pending their arrival, he continued to search the area for additional gun positions and fleeing troops. He directed three subsequent strikes in the area, destroying the third known gun position and silencing all ground fire. Capt Johnson remained over the target area for over two hours making five marking passes. The intense and accurate ground fire to which he voluntarily exposed himself was attested to by the fact that all aircraft except the last flight received fire; one fighter was hit, and the six C-123's received a total of ten hits. In the past three months, not one spray mission has been flown in this area without receiving heavy ground fire, including small arms, 12.7 mm, and 37 mm. That Capt Johnson produced the first confirmed destruction of heavy weapons in this area was a direct result of his willingness to make slow, unarmed aircraft a target for the heavy anti-aircraft fire. His calm professionalism and devotion to duty with utter disregard for his own personal safety not only reflect credit and honor upon himself but are in the highest traditions of the United States Air Force.

THE SILVER STAR
to Captain Hansford T. Johnson, 2 July 1967

CITATION

Captain Hansford T. Johnson distinguished himself by gallantry in connection with military operations against an opposing armed force as a Forward Air Controller directing fighter aircraft near Con Thien, Republic of Vietnam on 2 July 1967. On that date, Captain Johnson was flying in support of friendly forces in imminent danger of being annihilated. Flying low through intense .50 caliber anti-aircraft fire to locate and mark the hostile positions, he directed successful airpower that routed the hostile forces. When his marking rocket supply was depleted at a critical point in the battle, fighter aircraft were no longer able to accurately locate the target. With complete disregard for his own personal safety, Captain Johnson used his unarmed O-1 aircraft to mark the unfriendly troops by making repeated passes at dangerously low altitude directly over their positions. By his gallantry and devotion to duty, Captain Johnson has reflected great credit upon himself and the United States Air Force.

NARRATIVE

6 July 1967

On 2 July 1967 around 0945, Trail 64 was flying a visual reconnaissance mission near Con Thien. He was asked to contact Ruggles 14B and to fly cover for Ruggles B, a USMC Company. When Trail 64 checked in with Ruggles 14B, the company was pinned down by fire from a trench and bunker complex. Trail 64 circled the trench complex at low altitude but was unable to see any enemy troops Air support was requested to bomb the trenches and bunkers. At around 1020 as Trail 64 increased his area of search, he saw what appeared to be trees crossing a road approximately 500 meters east of Ruggles B. The trees were determined to be uniformed troops with branches on their backs. Trail 64 immediately advised Ruggles 14 B of the sighting. Ruggles 14 B confirmed that there were no Marines in the area wearing camouflage. The troops were identified as NVA regulars. As Trail 64 continued to circle, he saw first 40 NVA troops cross the road and continue south along a hedgerow. Then 40 more crossed. Trail 64 notified all Marine agencies of the number of NVA and their direction of movement. Trail 64 requested armed helicopter and fighters with napalm and 250 LB GP bombs, and asked that all available air support be diverted to this position. He also advised of the overwhelming force opposing the USMC Company. While waiting for air support, Trail 64 circled low over the area finding all elements of Ruggles B and briefing Ruggles 14 B on the movement of the NVA troops.

The first air arrived on station around 1030 with 500 LB GP bombs. Trail 64 directed the fighters against NVA in the open at the point where the NVA had crossed the road. This was 400 to 500 meters from the friendlies. As the strike continued, the drops were moved closer to the friendlies until the friendlies said not to come any closer. By this time the NVA troops were within 100 meters of the friendlies on the east and south. When the strike began so did the ground fire directed at the fighters and Trail 64. Despite extremely intense ground fire, Trail 64 continued to circle the friendlies and advise Ruggles 14 B of the enemy and friendly ground situation. Ruggles B was getting hit very hard and began to withdraw.

At this time armed helicopters arrived. Trail 64 directed them against the NVA in the open within 100 to 300 meters east of the friendlies. The helicopters were again worked nearer the friendlies, where the majority of the NVA were located. Trail 64 kept constant communications with Ruggles 14 B and was able to bring the strikes as near the friendlies as possible. Throughout the helicopter strikes, the intense ground fire continued, and one of the helicopters gunners was hit.

After the helicopters expended their ordnance, another flight of fighters arrived with 500 LB GP bombs. By this time, the forces were in very close contact. Working with Ruggles 14 B, Trail 64 brought the strikes dangerously close to the friendlies. Each pass was cleared with Ruggles 14 B on FM radio before Trail 64 cleared the fighters on UHF radio. The ordnance was placed as close as humanly possible to the friendly lines. It is a great tribute to these fighter pilots to be able to get so close to the friendlies with great accuracy. Trail 64 realized the great risk involved, but he also saw the many NVA troops about to overrun the greatly outnumbered Marine Company, and he was willing to take the great risk to save the company from complete annihilation and provide time for reinforcements to arrive.

While waiting for the next flight of fighters, Trail 64 flew very low over the lines and was able to point out well camouflaged NVA troops moving within 10 meters of individual Marines who were unaware of the NVA presence. He also flew north of the Marine position and spotted a deep heavily wooded gulley filled with NVA troops. He saw at least 50 NVA and estimated there were many more. Now, the NVA were attacking Ruggles B on three sides. This new group of NVA was pointed out to Ruggles 14 B, and the Marines were able to change their defense to moot this third threat.

By the time a flight of fighters had arrived with napalm and 250 LB GP bombs, Trail 64 discussed hitting the gulley with Ruggles 14 B. Although it was only 75 to 100 meters away from some friendly troops, Trail 64 felt that if the napalm could be placed in the gulley, it would wipe out the NVA in the gulley and the gulley walls would shield the friendlies. Ruggles 14 B was unable to mark friendly positions since the enemy was only 120 meters away. Trail 64 briefed the fighters in great detail on the location of the friendlies and the enemy concentration. Trial 64 directed the fighters to place the napalm in the gulley or just north, but definitely not south. Trail 64 and the fighters decided to drop the first napalm just north of the gulley. With clearance from Ruggles 14 B and Trail 64, the first fighter did a magnificent job of hitting the northern rim of the gulley. Unfortunately, Ruggles 14 B advised that the fighter could not bring the napalm any further south into the gulley without injuring friendlies. Trail 64 and the fighters did an outstanding job of covering all NVA entrances to the gulley with napalm and 250 LB GP bombs. In this strike, one of the fighters took a hit attesting to the intense ground fire environment the fighters and the FAC were flying in.

After this strike, Trail 64 was out of marking devices and dangerously low on fuel. Trail 64 briefed an airborne Marine A. O. on the ground situation and suggested future targets.

The overall Battle Damage Assessment of 5 KBA (confirmed) and 40 KBA (probable) is low considering the number of NVA hit in the open, but the FAC did not have time to fly low over the area just struck looking for KBA. Trail 64 was much more concerned with keeping Ruggles 14 B informed about the enemy movements and spotting new NVA concentrations.

As Trail left the area, three relief groups of Marines were approaching Ruggles B's position. The battle continued to increase in size. Before the day was over, five Marine Companies were committed against what turned out to be a well disciplined and well equipped NVA Regiment. The overall friendly losses were high and two fighters were lost. The friendly and enemy casualty figures are not available, but they were extremely high, and this battle was a most important battle.

STATEMENT FROM MARINE Lt. O'Dell, USMC

On 2 July 1967, Bravo Company of the 1st Battalion 9th Marines engaged an NVA force later determined to be at least two battalions reinforced. With this engagement commenced a week long battle that was billed as an invasion attempt by the NVA. Certainly the number of troops, ferocity of the fighting, and the weapons employed supported this contention. In the first two days, ground forces were hit with massive artillery barrages, and support aircraft encounter flak and SAM missiles south of the border. In any event, it is clear the NVA made a major attempt to secure a decisive victory.

On the first day of this battle, Bravo Company bore the brunt of the enemy attack. They were greatly outnumbered and subsequently badly mauled by the NVA. During the early critical hours of the battle, Bravo Company was supported by Capt. Johnson, an ARVN system FAC from Quang Tri. As Marine Liaison Officer at Quang Tri Sector, I was asked by the survivors of Bravo to submit a statement commending the gallantry of this FAC during the intense battle.

When Capt. Johnson arrived, Bravo was already under fire. As the NVA moved into position for an all out assault, Capt. Johnson was able to detect their movement and warn the embattled Marines. This early warning enabled the Americans to improve their defensive positions at strategic points against the enemy attack.

As the attack began, Capt. Johnson made repeated low passes through intense anti-aircraft fire including multiple .50 caliber positions to distinguish between the opposing units and direct successful fighter strikes to within 30 meters of the friendly positions. When the contact became too close for additional fighter strikes, Capt. Johnson secured Huey gunships to continue his assault upon the enemy.

Capt. Johnson succeeded in thwarting the enemy attack and prevented the NVA from encircling the Marine position. This allowed reinforcements to reach the trapped Marines. In view of Bravo's extremely high early casualties, and the vastly superior size of the enemy force, the friendly survivors stated unequivocally that Capt. Johnson saved them from complete annihilation.

The outstanding support provide by Capt. Johnson was all the more significant in view of the fact that the Company's ground FAC was killed almost immediately, and this required Capt. Johnson to perform all coordination with the friendly units through a FAC radio operator.

By week's end, over 800 confirmed by body count and 300 probable NVA had been killed. The majority were killed by air. There can be no doubt that Capt. Johnson was directly responsible for the early survival of Bravo Company, the successful reinforcement of their position and the resulting shift in the tide of this important battle.

STATEMENT FROM ONE OF FIGHTER PILOTS
Major H. D. Bradshaw, USMC, Section Lead
Castor Oil Flight 060 on 2 July 1967

Forwarding Note: It is indeed a pleasure to receive and pass such glowing comments on the professional airmanship displayed by one of our Forward Air Controllers under the stress of an active combat situation. The ground troops required accurate ordnance delivery to support them in their engagement with hostile forces. The FAC had to be a cool professional airman to direct the air strikes for maximum effectiveness. Captain H. T. Johnson more than filled the bill. Please extend to him my congratulations for a job very well done.

LT. Col. Russell D. Brewington, USAF I DASC, Deputy Director

Pilot's words: On the morning of 2 July 1967, Trail 64 conducted an air strike by my flight, Castor Oil 060, in a rapid professional and commendable manner under emergency circumstances. We scrambled at 1022 from Chu Lai and 18 minutes later were on target north of the firebreak in the DMZ under the control of Trail 64. He quickly and thoroughly briefed us on the strike, explaining that a USMC Company was deeply engaged with a NVA Regiment, who were firing from a wooded gulley running East and West. Trail 64 pointed out prominent landmarks, set us up to run in parallel to the gulley, and emphasized that we were not to drop South of the gulley because of the danger to friendly forces, who could not mark their position because of their close proximity to the enemy. Talking on both UHF and FM, he constantly coordinated with the ground unit.

Under Trail 64's expert and continuous guidance, we were able to deliver our ordnance in such a manner as to provide some relief to the USMC Company and give tanks time to advance and remove the wounded. Bombs and napalm were dropped in the gulley and on the North side, effectively suppressing the enemy fire. Enemy fire was intense during the strike (both our aircraft were hit), but Trail 64 remained at low altitude in the target area, controlling each pass with precisions and aplomb. His bravery under fire and his professional conduct of the strike (and those that followed) under emergency conditions are to be commended. It was a pleasure to work under his control and I'm sure the Marine Company on the ground especially appreciates his efforts.

SHORT ROUND
July 4, 1967

STATEMENT
Captain Hansford T Johnson

At approximately 1100 on 4 July 1967, I received a request from Landshark B through Trail 61 for me to take off at 1200 and replace Trail 61 who was directing air strikes for Oldfield K USMC Company. Between 1215 and 1400, I directed six flights of fighters in support of Oldfield K. I was in radio communications with Oldfield 14 K on FM 35.2 during all strikes. Oldfield K was located south of a road running from YD134719 to YD110710. Oldfield K marked their position and I was told that all friendlies were south of this road. I was directing the strikes against a hedgerow. I put in the napalm and 2,000 lb and 500 lb GP bombs on this hedgerow. I put in two flights of 2,000 lb GP bombs 400 to 500 meters north of the hedgerow. All targets were cleared by Oldfield 14K. The bombs were going where Oldfield 14K wanted them. Since I had run out of smoke grenades and rockets, Oldfield K was marking the target with 60 mm white phosphorous round fired from a tank locate at their position.

Miss Muffet flight (two A-4s) checked in over Dong Ha at approximately 1340. Their call sign was Miss Muffet 516. I asked them to hold while Catkiller 41 controlled a strike east of my position. In the meantime, I flew over the target area and found NVA troops in a gulley covered by a hedgerow – located at YD132721. I saw 10 to 15 NVA troops moving inside the gulley. Catkiller 41 completed his mission just prior to 1400. I got Miss Muffet on station at 1400. The flight had eight D-2's. I pointed out Oldfield K's position to the fighters and told them all friendlies were located south of the road running from YD134719 to YD110710. I asked Oldfield K to mark the target. The target was marked, and I described the target to Miss Muffet. I directed a 270 degree run-in heading and a left break to keep the fighters south of North Vietnam and east of artillery firing west of the YD05 north-south grid line. The fighters made four passes. The first three drops hit in the target area. On the fourth pass, the wingman dropped short. I plotted the impact as YD140718 (or 800 meters short and 300 meters left of the target). After it impacted, I noted troops around the impact point. Very soon, I received a call from Lease Breaker C saying a bomb hit in the friendly lines of Lease Breaker C – a USMC Company. The fighter had expended their ordnance, and I had them hold while I tried to determine the damage. Lease Breaker C said the bomb hitting in the lines of Lease Breaker A was a dud and no damage was done. I told the fighters of the short round, gave them the coordinates of the impact, and relayed Lease Breaker C's report of negative damage. I advised the fighters that I would turn in a "short round report" and provide any additional information I could find.

After confirming the Lease Breaker position and receiving clearance from Oldfield 14K, I directed another set of fighters against the NVA position. I then turned over the control of the fighters to a Marine A. O., Sacred Mike.

Upon leaving the area, I tried to contact Lease Breaker 14 without success on FM 32.5. Later I was able to contact Lease Breaker 14 A. He said he was waiting for a med Evac for four WIA's. I was unable to determine the injuries of the four Marines or positively confirm that they were injured by the short round. I tried unsuccessfully to contact lease breaker B.

After landing, I filled out a "Short Round Report" I.A.W. 7th AF Reg 55-39. I tried to reach Landmark B by landlines, but all lines were out of commission. I then called the report into I DASC Duty officer.

Trail 61 talked to Lease Breaker A later and found that there were two bombs dropped. One was a dud. The other caused nine Marine WIA's.

LATER INFORMATION: Understand all survived but one Marine lost a leg. My boss went to the Hospital Ship to visit with the wounded.

DISTINGUISHED FLYING CROSS
(First Oak Leaf Cluster)
to Captain Hansford T, Johnson,
12 August 1967

NARRATIVE

At approximately 0220 on 12 August, Trail 64 was alerted at Hue to fly to Quang Tri. He was advised that a sub-sector near Quang Tri was under attack. Trail 64 arranged for maintenance personnel to accompany him to the airfield for the night launch of the O-1. The ride from the MACV compound to the field is approximately 4 miles over unsecured roads. After arrival at the field, Trail 64 secured his flight gear while the maintenance personnel pre-flighted the aircraft. Although it was an extremely dark night, Trail 64 felt the urgency of the mission would not allow time for putting temporary lights along the runway, He was off ground within twenty minutes after he was notified.

Immediately after takeoff, he was in complete darkness. He flew instruments while attempting to navigate using barely discernable objects on the ground. As he approached Quang Tri, he was advised that at least three ARVN compounds were under attack – Hai Lang sub-sector, 1st ARVN Regiment at La Vang Airfield, and Trieu Phong sub-sector. A Marine C-130 flare ship was on station and an AC-47 gun ship was enroute to Quang Tri. The Marine flare ship was directed to illuminate the Hai Lang sub-sector, but the crew was unable to locate Hai Lang. Through his familiarity with the area, Trail 64 was able to locate Hai Lang and direct the flare ship.

Trail 64 proceeded on to Quang Tri and found a confused situation. The command post was unsure of the ground situation and communications with the various compounds were either nonexistent or poor due the confusion of the attacks. Trail 64 decided to survey all the compounds under attack to determine the best use of the available airpower and the need for additional support. Despite intense fire – friendly outgoing and unfriendly incoming – he flew low enough over each area to get an accurate appraisal of the situations. He found that there were two combined mortar and ground attacks at La Vang -- one against 1st ARVN Regiment, and one against the 7th ARVN Cavalry. By this time, the AC-47 was on station. Trail 64 directed the AC-47 to keep the two La Vang compounds illuminated and watch for mortar flashes. The status at Thieu Phong was completely unknown since communications with the senior Australian advisor had been lost. Trail 64 proceeded to the area and found that the sub-sector and the PRU (Provincial Reconnaissance Unit) compound near shambles. He immediately directed the Marine flare ship to proceed from Hai Lang, where the attack had ceased, to Trieu Phong and illuminate the area. A more extensive survey of the Trieu Phong indicated that many of the bunkers had been blown up and several buildings were on fire. He was able to establish radio contact with an advisor in the sub-sector but was unable to determine the conditions of the compound since the advisor was pinned down in a bunker. Later a Vietnamese came up on the advisory radio in the PRU compound. Trail 64 was able to interpret his broken English and determine that the PRU compound had been overrun and demolished and that all American had been killed or were missing. The Vietnamese PRU men were able to regroup and push the enemy out of the compound. It was obvious that Trieu Phong needed air support quickly. Trail 64 directed the gunship to illuminate Trieu Phong and attempt to find enemy positions. The flare ship provided illumination for La Vang, and the 1st ARVN Regiment, and the 7th Cavalry were able to put out a large aggressive fire.

Trail 64 and the gunship began to receive intense automatic weapons fire from three positions around Thieu Phong. Trail 64 immediately cleared the gunship to return fire to an enemy position in an open field. He tried to get clearance to fire on the other two positions near hamlets. The situation on the ground was so unclear that no one could authorize the fire into these positions. Finally permission was received to return fire regardless of its point of origin. Trail 64 requested an immediate air strike against the center of enemy activity, but ARVN sources were unable to approve the target due to unknown location of friendlies.

While the gunship fired into the enemy positions, the mortar attack on Trieu Phong stopped, but the attack would begin again when the gunship ceased firing. At this time a new crisis developed. The gunship expended its last flares. There was still a hour of darkness, and no replacement gunship was available. The gunship was ready to leave station when Trail 64 decided to have the Marine flare ship drop flares over Trieu Phong while the gunship continued to fire into the enemy positions. This required a great deal of coordination but it was effective. [ADDED: Interestingly after the first firing, the gunship said, "Trail, are you still there?" After an affirmative response, the gunship said, "You were in my gun sights when I fired!" Apparently the Marine flares were above us and the Trail 64 shadow was in the gun sights!] Trail 64 kept the La Vang compounds under surveillance while it was illuminated with artillery flares. When the compounds were not illuminated, both sides would fire incessantly. Through judicious use of illumination flares, the compounds were kept lighted until first light.

Although Trail 64 was dangerously low on fuel, he remained over Trieu Phong to help coordinate medical evacuation of the wounded at day break.

After flying for more than four hours in an intense automatic weapon and artillery environment under illumination flares, Trail 64 was directed to land at La Vang if possible. The mortar attack had just ceased and the status of the runway was unknown. No advisor on the ground was able to inspect the runway. Trail 64 flew low over the field and inspected the runway. He determined that despite several small mortar craters on the runway he could land safely. He finally landed with almost no fuel remaining.

VIETNAMESE CROSS OF GALLANTRY WITH A SILVER STAR
to Captain Hansford T. Johnson,
20 October 1967
(Unfortunately, it was never presented or entered into my records)

CITATION (Prepared for a US Distinguished Flying Cross)
Captain Hansford T. Johnson distinguished himself by extraordinary achievement as a Forward Air Controller near Quang Tri, Republic of Vietnam on 20 October 1967. On that date, Captain Johnson responded to an urgent call from friendly troops engaged in heavy battle with hostile forces. Completely disregarding his own safety, he flew his unarmed O-2A aircraft at dangerously low altitudes through hostile mortar and antiaircraft fire to locate and direct tactical airpower against the heavily armed hostile forces allowing medical evacuation of friendly wounded and turning the tide of battle, which became a major victory. The professional competence, aerial skill, and devotion to duty displayed by Captain Johnson reflect great credit upon himself and the United States Air Force.

NARRATIVE
Captain Hansford T. Johnson distinguished himself by heroism while participating in aerial flight as a Forward Air Controller near Quang Tri, Republic of Vietnam on 20 October 1967. On that date, Capt. Johnson was flying a visual reconnaissance mission in the DMZ, when he responded to an urgent call from an ARVN advisor for air support. He quickly diverted to the area of the ARVN units. Two ARVN battalions and an armored cavalry unit had an enemy main force surrounded on three sides with the forth side being a natural barrier reinforced by ARVN artillery barrages. Being familiar with the battle plans, Capt. Johnson risked his life and flew low over the area to determine the friendly and enemy disposition of troops. To accomplish this, Capt Johnson had to fly through the incoming mortar barrage and expose himself to several anti-aircraft positions, which were now firing at him. The enemy forces were desperate and were furiously pounding the cavalry unit with mortars, recoilless rifles, and automatic weapons in an effort to break out of the cordon set up by the ARVN units. The cavalry unit was in an extremely vulnerable position, unable to maneuver into a more favorable position, and was receiving heavy casualties. The immediate problems were to silence the guns firing on the cavalry unit and to provide medical evacuation for the critically wounded. Despite marginal air support flying

conditions of 2,500 feet broken overcast, Capt Johnson called for medical evacuation helicopters, armed helicopter, and fighter support. When the medial evacuation helicopters arrived, the landing zone was not secure. In an effort to get the wounded out as quickly as possible, he elected to direct the fighters against the gun positions and have the medical evacuation of the wounded follow immediately. To successfully direct the fighters against the enemy, Capt Johnson had to stop the friendly artillery, clear all helicopters from the area, contend with low weather ceilings, fly through intense automatic weapons fire to mark, and direct the ordnance extremely close to the cavalry unit. After meticulous briefing of all units on two different radios, Capt. Johnson precisely directed the fighters against the enemy gun positions and held over the nearest friendly units to provide a visual foul line for the fighters, as the fighters pulled off of their last pass, he cleared the medical evacuation helicopter into the landing zone while directing the armed helicopters to make rocket and strafing passes on the known and suspected gun positions. The risks involved in sending the medical evacuation helicopters into a vulnerable, insecure landing zone were high, but Capt Johnson readily accepted the risk to himself and to his forces to get the critically wounded out so the cavalry unit could move and to save human life. To reduce the risk, he completely disregarded his own safety and held dangerously low over the landing zone to detect and ground fire, to correct the armed helicopter passes, and if need be, to stop the medical evacuation and bring in the fighters holding overhead. Through Capt Johnson's detailed planning, extremely close direction of the operation, and heroism and selfless devotion to duty in the face of intense ground fire, the medical evacuation was successful and the cavalry unit was able to redeploy to a less vulnerable position. By this time, the units on the flanks were receiving intensive automatic weapons fire. It was becoming more apparent that a large enemy force was trapped by the ARVN units and was desperately trying to fight their way out. Capt Johnson closely coordinated the ARVN artillery and armed helicopters to keep the enemy under continuous fire between air strikes which were extremely close to the ARVN forces. Capt Johnson had the fighter make dry passes under the clouds to, and by placing himself in a perilous position, he pointed out the friendly and enemy locations. When he was convinced that all units were briefed on the strikes, he again with complete disregard for his own safety, exposed himself to intense anti-aircraft fire by holding low over the friendlies, providing a visual reference point for the fighters. Knowing the key role played by the Forward Air Controller, the heavily armed hostile force desperately tried to shoot him down. Violent maneuvering his fragile O-2 aircraft, Capt Johnson evaded the intense ground fire and continued to coolly and precisely direct each pass of the fighters. The strikes were delivered with great precision and the enemy positions were devastated with resulting cessation of fire from these areas. By this time, Capt Johnson was dangerously low on fuel and was relieved by another Forward Air Controller, but through his outstanding direction of the battle, the tide of battle had turned giving the friendly forces the initiative which led to a large ARVN victory. When the battle was over, there were 195 enemy KIA by body count, versus 16 ARVN KIA, and an enemy main force unit was essentially wiped out as a fighting unit. This was a large one sided victory for the ARVN forces, but more importantly, it gave them renewed confidence as a fighting unit at a time when they were sorely in need of a victory. Capt Johnson's early decisive direction of the air battle and advise to the ground commanders played an extremely large part in this important victory and the low friendly KIAs. Following the battle, he was commended by the ARVN commanders through the US Army advisors for the heroism, skill, and selfless devotion to duty he displayed. By his outstanding heroism and selfless devotion to duty, Capt Johnson has reflected great credit upon himself and the United States Air Force."

FIGHTER REPORT
from Major Carl Wiedenhoeft

1. On 20 October 1967, Trail 64 was the Forward Air Controller that directed the air strikes in which I participated as Eagle 01. The strike was directed against a main force NVA unit, which had pinned down units of the 1st ARVN Division in a small hamlet near Quang Tri.

2. When I arrived in the area, Trail 64 contacted me and asked me to hold as he had troops in contact and the situation was very confused. Despite the hectic situation, he was able to clear the area of helicopters, artillery, and then proceeded to mark their position, assign us a precise run-in heading and then proceeded to mark the target all in a very short period of time. I am sure he was exposed to intense ground fire during the conduct of the missions and especially while marking the target, but he didn't hesitate and put his marker rocket precisely on the target. From that point on he was able to give us exact and timely corrections so that we were able to make the most efficient use of our armament.

3. The outstanding professional ability displayed by Trail 64 in conducting this strike was as much responsible as any other factor for the extra-ordinary results achieved by this air strike. The main force NVA unit was decimated and rendered non effective as fighting force as a result of this and a following air strike. The important role Trail 64 played in achieving this victory should be recognized and he should be suitably awarded.

Carl R. Wiedenhoeft
Major USAF
Eagle 01

THE VIETNAMESE ARMED FORCES HONOR MEDAL
to Captain Hansford Johnson, 25 October 1967

CITATION

Hansford Johnson – Captain – USAF. A brave pilot who fought with determination for the freedom of Vietnam. As an Air Liaison Officer to the 1st ARVN Infantry Regiment from 10 July 1967 to 25 October 1967, he assisted in gaining successful results for Operation Lam Son 138 by his sound advice on all aspects of the use of air power support.

THE DISTINGUISHED FLYING CROSS
(Second Oak Leaf Cluster)
to Captain Hansford T. Johnson
19 January 1968

CITATION

Captain Hansford T. Johnson distinguished himself by heroism while participating in aerial flight as a Forward Air Controller in an O-2A Aircraft in Southeast Asia on 19 January 1968. On that date, Captain Johnson found a large group of hostile trucks along a supply route, defended by antiaircraft weapons. Despite unfavorable conditions, Captain Johnson dove into the center of the guns to place a marking rocket on the target, and successfully directed fighter aircraft against the trucks and guns. The outstanding heroism and selfless devotion to duty displayed by Captain Johnson reflect credit upon himself and the United States Air Force.

NARRATIVE

Captains Hansford T. Johnson and Henry A. Salcido distinguished themselves by gallantry while participating in aerial flight as a Forward Air Controller in an O-2A aircraft in Southeast Asia on 19 January 1968. On that date, Capts Johnson and Salcido were flying as Forward Air Controllers on a night interdiction mission along a heavily defended supply route used by an opposing hostile force to transport vitally needed troops, supplies, and ammunition into the Republic of Vietnam. They were working as a team with Capt Salcido flying the aircraft and Capt Johnson using a starlight scope to reconnoiter the road. The night was extremely dark and because of a thick layer they could only see the road from directly above. Dragon 09 was flying with the FACs as the killer portion of the "hunter-killer" team. When no trucks were found, the FACs decided to expend Dragon 09 on a truck park. Capt Salcido marked the truck park and dropped an illumination flare. As Dragon 09 made his pass on the truck park, several anti-aircraft guns began firing. The hostile fire was much too accurate to continue the attack on the truck park. Capt Johnson had spotted the area where the majority of the anti-aircraft fire was coming. Despite the heavy concentration of guns firing at the fragile O-2 aircraft, Capt Johnson dove down the barrels of the actively firing guns to deliver a marking rocket for Dragon 09. Dragon 09 made one pass on the gun position, but by now there were at least five guns (including 23 mm and 37 mm guns) firing at the FACs and the fighters from all angles. The FACs became convinced that a large group of hostile guns had intentionally been set up to protect this section of the road. The FACs and Dragon 09 felt that a great deal of hostile traffic was being protected by the guns and decided it was imperative to attempt to silence the guns so other FACs and Dragons would be able to safely operate in the area later in the evening. They decided to wait until the second Dragon arrived in the area to continue the attack. When Dragon 10 arrived, the FACs briefed both fighters on the ant-aircraft situation and the plan of attack. Dragon 10 was to hold high while Dragon 09 made a pass on the gun positions. If the guns fired at Dragon 09, Dragon 10 would immediately roll in and bomb the active positions. The FACs marked the target and held near the area to direct the attack. The briefed procedure was used two times until Dragon 09 expended all of his ordnance. On the last pass, the haze had become so bad that Dragon 09 became completely disoriented and was able to recover only through superior pilot skill. The FACs were unable to determine if any of the guns were destroyed, but the bombs hit very near the guns and aircraft were able to operate in the area later in the evening without being fired upon. At this point Dragon 10 still had CBU, but the FACs had no more illuminating flares and should have returned to base, but they were determined to find what the guns were so eager to protect. The FACs held Dragon 10 high while they searched the road for traffic. A short time later, using the starlight scope, the FACs found seven trucks moving along the section of the road lined with the guns. With full knowledge that all of the guns were probably not destroyed, they held over the trucks until trucks move out of range of the guns. The FACs called for another aircraft to provide flare illumination, but no flares were immediately available. The FACs and Dragon 10 decided if flares were not available by the time Dragon 10 had to leave the area that Capt Johnson would use the starlight scope to direct the O-2 aircraft with lights on over the convoy. Using the O-2 lights as a reference, Dragon 10 would make a CBU pass down the road in a desperate effort to stop these vital supplies. As they were setting up for the run, a flare ship and another Dragon became available. By now the FACs had at least five of the trucks under surveillance at a ford. Dragon 10 was dangerously low on fuel, and the FACs had to get him on target as quickly as possible. Although they could only see the target with the starlight scope, Capts Johnson and Salcido displayed the ultimate in team coordination by placing a marking rocket on the target. The flare ship illuminated the target area and the two Dragons covered the entire area with CBU and bombs. Their accurate strike resulted in at least four trucks destroyed and three large secondary fires. Capts Johnson and Salcido had displayed complete disregard for their own safety, imaginative initiative, and fantastic determination in the face of seemingly insurmountable odds to successfully interdict this flow of hostile supplies. By their gallantry, superb airmanship, aggressiveness, and selfless devotion to duty, Captains Johnson and Salcido have reflected great credit upon themselves and the United States Air Force.

THE MERITORIOUS SERVICE MEDAL
to Major Hansford T. Johnson, 1 May 1968 to 16 July 1971

CITATION

Major Hansford T. Johnson distinguished himself in the performance of outstanding service to the United States as an Assistant Professor of Aeronautics, United States Air Force Academy, from 1 May 1968 to 16 July 1971. During this period, he was a prime contributor to the academic and military development of the cadets. By his leadership, inspiration, selfless devotion to duty, and dynamic example for the cadets and officers alike, Major Johnson has made a permanent contribution to the Air Force Academy that will be reflected in the Air Force leadership of the future. The singularly distinctive accomplishments of Major Johnson reflect great credit upon himself and the United States Air Force.

          Signed:
          General John Ryan
          Chief of Staff

NARRATIVE

Major Hansford T. Johnson distinguished himself in the performance of outstanding service to the United States as an Assistant Professor of the Department of Aeronautics, United States Air Force Academy, from 1 May 1968 to 16 July 1971. During this period, he has served as truly superb instructor in the fields of thermodynamics and aeronautics. His ability to present the difficult and comprehensive material in an interesting and understandable manner has stimulated even the most unresponsive cadet. He has related his own experiences in actual situations to the aeronautical problems discussed in class, adding tremendously to the meaning of these problems. He has always been exceptionally diligent in his preparation for class with the results that his lectures are always complete and concise. He is one of the most highly respected and admired classroom instructors that I have known.

  It is not only for his outstanding performance as a professor, however, that I recommend this award for Major Johnson. I have never known anyone so vitally involved in his profession. His professional skill, outstanding leadership, personable nature and very active involvement in a wide range of activities have made him a most laudable asset to my department as well as the Academy and the U.S. Air Force. In and out of class, he consistently displayed a genuine interest and concern for cadet development in all fields. He has provided many hours of extra instruction for his students and has served as primary source of advice and counsel for a large majority of the Cadet Wing. He has been besieged, both in his office and at home, by cadets seeking an officer who will listen and advise them on a wide range of problems. Although he is a strong disciplinarian, he is a good listener with such high personal integrity that he has been eagerly sought out by cadets. He spent many hours letting these young men solve their own problems as he stimulated their thought processes. His vital concern in every facet of the cadets' development has had a very profound effect on their inspiration and motivation for an Air Force career.

In keeping with his constant effort to prepare himself to meet the challenge of his profession, he has, through a combination of strong self-discipline and judicious management of his spare time, greatly enhanced his worth to the Air Force during the past three years. As a result of his regular attendance at night school, he has acquired a Masters Degree in Management Science. To further his engineering ability, he broadened his background in various technical disciplines and completed the requirements for registration as a Professional Engineer in the State of Colorado. To further his understanding of all facets of the military profession and to increase his involvement with the cadets, he accompanied them to Fort Benning, Georgia and completed the requirements for airborne training. In a desire to work on the latest "state-of-the-art" aircraft requirements and designs, he served with the atmospheric weapons branch of the Aerospace Defense Command during the summer of 1969. In this capacity, he worked on the requirements for an advanced manned interceptor and current efforts to modernize the air defense force. During the summer of 1970, he made a significant contribution to the Plans Directorate of the Air Staff by working three months in the Western Hemisphere Divisions. He quickly became fully qualified as an action officer.

The phenomenal aspect of Major Johnson's active participation in so many diverse activities and the enviable results he has achieved is the fact that those accomplishments have come at the same time he has carried more than his share of the load at the Academy. For example:

a. For the past two years, he has served as my Assistant Personnel Officer. This is an extremely time consuming task because we personally interview or actively correspond with over 200 Air Force officers as well as various civilian educators. He has displayed an uncanny ability to foresee pending problem areas, evaluate them, and take a competent corrective action prior to their materialization. He conceived and implemented an officer conference program which is serving to improve communications and develop a greater understanding between me as Department Head and my officers. This program continues to bear fruit and is significantly improving our department.

b. Throughout his assignment at the Academy, he has served as a member of the Association of Graduates. This, too, was a most time consuming duty at which Major Johnson is exceptionally adept. He has been called upon frequently to spend free time talking with the cadets about their future role as an Air Force officer. In addition, he has often been asked for advice and suggestions on the future development and changes required to insure that the Academy remains a viable institution for training future Air Force leaders.

c. Major Johnson has served as an academic advisor to a cadet squadron for his entire three years at the Academy. When he became the academic advisor, the squadron's academic performance was only average. Through his great understanding of cadet problems, compassion to assist struggling cadets, and the expenditure of tremendous personal effort, he has inspired them to absolutely superior performance. The squadron has consistently ranked first in academics among the 40 cadet squadrons for the past one and one half years.

It is not surprising that Major Johnson was officially recognized as an Outstanding Young Man of America by the Junior Chamber of Commerce in 1970. I know of no one who more richly deserves such recognition. He is undoubtedly one of the finest young men I have ever known.

The magnitude and breadth of Major Johnson's outstanding contributions to the accomplishment of the Academy mission are clearly evident to his associates as well as the members of the Cadet Wing. He is the kind of man who can easily make use of his personable nature, exceptional technical background, outstanding leadership and managerial competence to provide unique and laudatory service in almost any undertaking. I feel it is extremely fortunate, therefore, that Major Johnson has had an opportunity to serve at the Air Force Academy. I can think of no more important application for his exceptional performance than that it be directed toward the education and training of our future Air Force leaders. His efforts in behalf of the Academy and Professional Officers Corps of the Air Force have added great credence to the justification of the entire service academy system. By his consistently superior performance as an Air Force officer and member of the Academy faculty, he has made contributions of marked national significance.

In summary, it is the full application of his enormous capacity for meritorious service in numerous areas of responsibility that has produced a record which unquestionably entitles Major Johnson to the Award of the Meritorious Service Medal. In my many years of faculty service, I can cite no single faculty member whose quality of service makes him more deserving of this distinction. As a scholar, soldier, and teacher, he has engendered the genuine respect and loyalty of all. Further by his hard work and dedications, he has demonstrated a degree of excellence to the cadets that will be mirrored in the United States Air Force Corps for years to come. Few men have the opportunity to affect their nation's destiny. By his monumental impact on the Air Force leadership of the future, Major Johnson has had that opportunity. It is indeed fortunate that he personifies the kind of well rounded and dedicated officer that the Academy must produce if the Air Force is to continue to hold a position of leadership in the free world. The singularly distinctive accomplishments of Major Johnson reflect great credit upon himself and the United States Air Force.

Signed:
Daniel H. Daley, Colonel, USAF
Professor and Head,
Department of Aeronautics

THE LEGION OF MERIT
to Lt. Col. Hansford T. Johnson, 12 June 1972 to 31 July 1975

CITATION

Lieutenant Colonel Hansford T. Johnson distinguished himself by exceptional meritorious conduct in the performance of outstanding service to the United States while assigned to the Directorate of Plans, Headquarters United States Air Force, from 12 June 1972 to 31 July 1975. During this period, the leadership and initiative of Colonel Johnson led to the solution of multiple problems of major significance to the national security of the United States. Through his exceptional abilities to focus imagination and productive effort on the most complex of issues, Colonel Johnson significantly influenced United States military strategy and defense policy, as well as the system and procedures for implementing the strategy and policy. The singularly distinctive accomplishments of Colonel Johnson reflect great credit upon himself and the United States Air Force.

Signed:
General David C. Jones
Chief of Staff

NARRATIVE

Lieutenant Colonel Hansford T. Johnson distinguished himself by exceptional meritorious conduct in the performance of outstanding service to the United States while assigned to the Deputy Chief of Staff for Plans and Operations, Headquarters Unites States Air Force, from 12 June 1972 to 31 June 1975. During this period, LtCol Johnson's personal leadership of a team of strategy and policy specialists led directly to the solution of multiple problems of major significance to the national security of the United States. Through his extraordinary ability to grasp the essence of the most complex of issues and then to focus imagination, initiative, and productive efforts on that essence, he has led the following efforts to successful conclusions:

(a) Defense Policy and Planning Guidance (DPPG): During two complete cycles of the Planning, Programming and Budgeting System (PPBS), LtCol Johnson contributed substantially and meaningfully to this most important SECDEF policy document – so much so that the FY 76-80 and FY 77-81 DPPGs were literally "turned around" during their draft stages to closely parallel the USAF views. In both actions, LtCol Johnson's recommended courses of action were presented to, and received praise from, the highest levels of command within the Air Force. Lt Col Johnson's through understanding of national policy and objectives, key defense issues, advanced military planning, and the impact of austere budgeting on national security, lent his recommendations a unique authority and led to their rapid acceptance:

(b) <u>Planning and Programming Guidance Memorandum (PPGM)</u>: In recognizing the essential fact that the PPGM—although primarily a programming document – must also reflect the fruits of planning, LtCol Johnson took personal actions during the last two PPBS cycles to strongly influence the content of the PPGM, leading to OSD's accommodation of Air Force planning concerns to an unprecedented extent;

(c) <u>Program Objective Memorandum (POM) Strategy Assessment</u>: Creation of an analytical basis for the FY 77-81 POM Strategy Assessment was an initiative of LtCol Johnson which will ultimately lead to establishment of the POM as the Air Force's key single-source document for not only presenting the USAF program, as in the past, but also for explaining the rationale for the entire USAF force and support structure. Additionally, according to LtCol Johnson's game plan, the POM Strategy Assessment, as it continues to mature, will be used as the forum for systematically presenting the USAF force initiatives to the SECDEF. It is anticipated that this document will become the most critical document within the PPBS – combining initiatives with rationale, while directly coupling planning and programming:

(d) <u>Force Planning</u>: As the capstone of a brilliant tenure within the DCS/P&O, LtCol Johnson has laid the seed for revamping the entire force and development planning system within the Air Force, and effort of monumental proportion and consequence, which will culminate in a more visible and systematic process for the corporate development of future force and support structures. LtCol Johnson's contributions cannot be overestimated: they are of unique and long lasting significance to the United States. The singularly distinctive accomplishments of Lt Col Johnson reflect great credit upon himself and the United States Air Force.

Signed:
Major General Richard Lawson
Director of Plans

THE LEGION OF MERIT (First Oak Leaf Cluster)
to Brigadier General Hansford T. Johnson,
June 1976 to February 1981

CITATION

Brigadier General Hansford T. Johnson distinguished himself by exceptionally meritorious conduct in the performance of outstanding services to the United States as Assistant Deputy Commander for Operations, Assistant Deputy Commander for Maintenance, Deputy Commander for Operations, and Vice Wing Commander, 93rd Bombardment Wing, Castle Air Force Base, California and Wing Commander, 22nd Bombardment Wing, March Air Force Base, California, from 28 June 1976 to 23 February 1981. During this period, the exemplary ability, diligence, and devotion to duty of General Johnson were instrumental factors in the resolution of many complex problems in the United States Air Force. The achievements of units under his command contributed to a significant increase in the combat readiness of he Strategic Air Command and greatly enhanced the strategic deterrence posture of the unit. The singularly distinctive accomplishments of General Johnson reflect great credit upon himself and the United States Air Force.

NARRATIVES (March AF and Castle AFB)

Recommend Colonel Hansford T. Johnson for the award of the Legion of Merit, First Oak leaf Cluster. His superior performance and total devotion to duty – first as 93rd Bombardment Wing Assistant Deputy Commander for Operations, next as the Assistant Deputy Commander for Maintenance, then as Deputy Commander for Operations, and finally as the Wing's Vice Commander – contributed significantly to the effective accomplishment of the SAC mission. As the Assistant DCO, Col Johnson supervised the largest flying operation in SAC. Primary attention was devoted to maintaining maximum EWO readiness. In addition, he directed an effective training program that graduated over 1700 combat crew members annually for duty throughout the Command. During the 1977 ORI, the Operations Deputate received an excellent rating emphasizing the strong, effective support provided toward total mission accomplishment. With the closure of Kincheloe AFB, Col Johnson directed the tanker candidate realignment and tanker alert programs. Eleven KC-135 aircraft and 400 new personnel were added to the base as the two existing tanker training squadrons were combined and an air refueling squadron fulfilling a tactical mission was activated . The realignment action went virtually error free. As the Assistant Deputy Commander for Maintenance, he provided guidance and direction to the largest maintenance organization in SAC. Under his leadership, wing aircraft continued to fly three times as many sorties and hours as other SAC Wings while operating at relatively reduced manning authorizations. A significant maintenance problem identified during the 1977 ORI dealt with operations sortie requirements exceeding the maintenance capabilities. This caused disruptions in scheduled maintenance, excessive maintenance deviations, and numerous delayed discrepancies. Col Johnson immediately implemented procedures that resolved maintenance/operation scheduling differences. He created mutual cooperation to achieve the mission of the wing by establishing a delicate balance between maintenance resources available with operations requirements. The 1978 ORI report highlighted the effectiveness of his corrective actions and noted improved coordination and cooperation between operations/maintenance had eliminated the previously identified problem. Due to his improved maintenance scheduling techniques, preplanned maintenance accomplishments were increased significantly, while aircraft delayed discrepancies were sharply reduced , In addition, he initiated a waste fuel recovery program which resulted in an annual recovery of 117,000 gallons or a savings of $51,129. On 27 Mal~ 78 Col Johnson became the wing's Deputy Commander for Operations, supervising the largest B-52 squadron in SAC, two KC -135 squadrons, CFIC, a combat crew training squadron and eight divisions totaling over 1,200 people. Primary emphasis was again given to maintaining maximum EWO readiness in addition to conducting the daily CCTS training missions. Through skilful management of a $3.7 million budget, he was able to accomplish $150,000 worth of unfunded but necessary programs. Under his supervision, student crews participated in the HQ 15AF bombing competition to demonstrate the effectiveness of the 93rd training program. The high reliability in bombing, SRAM and ECM activities re-emphasized the quality of the CCTS product. He was also the guiding factor in the development of a night low level terrain avoidance training program. On 17 Aug 78, Col Johnson became the 93rd Bomb Wing Vice Commander. In this capacity he was actively engaged in both mission and personnel programs. As the Wing Inspector General, he was totally dedicated to making Castle a better place to work and live. His programs reflected the commitment to increased morale and greater recognition for base people while reemphasizing his firm support to maintaining Air Force standards. He developed and directed extremely innovative and realistic operational readiness and disaster exercises which fully tested and greatly enhanced the wing's ability to meet its mission under all situations. In the absence of the commander, Col Johnson led the wing to mission accomplishment. The 924 Air Refueling Squadron earned the Navigation and Top Tanker Crew trophies during the 1978 GIANT VOICE competition, and was selected as the Outstanding Air Refueling Unit in 15AF. Col Johnson's numerous contributions to the 93rd Bombardment Wing have been supported by the outstanding results of many higher headquarters inspections, evaluations: and staff assistance visits. A totally dedicated professional with impeccable bearing and complete devotion to duty, Col Johnson's absolutely superior performance in four of the most challenging assignments in the command makes him most deserving of the award of the Legion of Merit, First Oak Leaf Cluster.

                                      SIGNED:
                                      Colonel John A. Brashear
                                      Commander

THE DISTINGUISHED SERVICE MEDAL
to Brigadier General Hansford T. Johnson,
26 February 1981 to 2 December 1982

CITATION

The President of the United States of America, authorized by Act of Congress July 9, 1918, awards the Distinguished Service Medal to Brigadier General Hansford T. Johnson for exceptional meritorious service in duties of great responsibility. General Johnson distinguished himself as Assistant Deputy Chief of Staff, Plans, Headquarters Strategic Air Command, Offutt Air Force Base, Nebraska, from 26 February 1981 to 2 December 1982. During this period, General Johnson's outstanding achievements and his dynamic leadership and initiative resulted in the development of comprehensive command operational requirements for strategic weapon systems which will meet the vital national security objectives through the end of the century. The singularly distinctive accomplishments of General Johnson reflect the highest credit upon himself and the United States Air Force.

Signed:
General Charles Gabriel
Chief of Staff

NARRATIVE

I recommend Brigadier General Hansford T. Johnson for the award of the Distinguished Service Medal. General Johnson's inspirational leadership has been marked by innovative management, firm direction and uncompromising standards of excellence. This recommendation is based upon his vital contributions to the security of our nation while serving as the Assistant Deputy Chief of Staff, Plans for Operational Requirements, from 26 February 1981 to 31 July 1981, and as the Assistant Deputy Chief of Staff, Plans, Headquarters Strategic Air Command, from 1 August 1981 to 2 December 1982. General Johnson's favorable impact on the strategic capability of the United States will continue well into the next century. Most notable among his numerous accomplishments has been his deep involvement in leading and improving Strategic Air Command's effectiveness in the federal resource allocation arena. His insight into the Planning, Programming, and Budgeting System (PPBS) process and ready grasp of programmatic nuances allowed him to orchestrate the successful funding of all SAC's major requirements for Fiscal Year 1984. To do this, he forged a fledgling corporate process into a microcosm of the Air Force Board structure. Using this process to cut across parochial interests, strategic programs, once advocated by functional agencies with predictable fragmentation and inconsistency, are now melded into a single, credible product. The impact of his persuasive approach has been far-reaching and has redefined the relationship between field commanders and HQ USAF in resource allocation. This corporate review has been so successful that it has become a ready forum which can react in near-real time to the need for a Command position on complex issues not amenable to the normal functional staff response. This has resulted in Air Force-wide support for strategic modernization initiatives and planned force improvements in the annual Program Objective Memorandum. General Johnson's steadying influence during fast-paced negotiations has resulted in a clear, logical articulation of nuclear and conventional issues that are now receiving the high level funding emphasis they need to insure our forces can match the requirements of United States' military strategy. His successes in infusing credibility into SAC's PPBS process have caused the programming leadership of other Major Air Commands to emulate his techniques. Peacetime location of SAC forces is another area in which General Johnson's leadership and foresight were key to the success of an important program. He clearly defined requirements, developed a comprehensive policy for force management and provided planning guidance that optimized the deployment of forces. These plans provided increased survivability, maximum security and flexible force employment options for SAC's existing and future weapons systems. Further, he personally guided efforts to expand SAC's capability to provide air refueling support for theater commanders around the world. The ongoing KC-10 basing initiatives, which he spearheaded, enhanced the mobility of strategic airlift and general purpose forces. He focused the senior SAC staff's attention on the important defense issues associated with negotiations being conducted with the governments of Spain, Portugal, Australia, Greece, Egypt and the United Kingdom. The resulting inputs to the US negotiating team led to greatly increased availability of vital foreign operating rights. He further recognized that a coherent, consistent command involvement and interest in resource allocation does not end with the fiscal Defense Department review in the Planning, Programming and Budgeting System. Frequently, the Commander in Chief, Strategic Air Command, is called to give special testimony to the United States

Congress. General Johnson devised a unique organization concept and founded a posture team to develop supporting analysis and data for this Congressional testimony. General Johnson also directed development of the analysis that became the foundation for CINCSAC Congressional testimony. These efforts significantly influenced recent national decisions to modernize US strategic forces and to define conceptual requirements for future weapons systems. By a functional reorganization, he directed the formation of a policy division to focus on the full range of international agreements and negotiations which impact upon the Strategic Air Command. He incorporated a working group, with staff-wide representation, to address arms reduction issues and opened channels within the JCS and Air Staff for SAC participation in developing formal US government negotiating strategy. General Johnson recognized the potential impact of a nuclear freeze movement on US strategic force modernization and directed the development of an issues presentation to explain, with analysis and logic, the military consequences of a nuclear freeze. Also notable were his numerous achievements and his deep involvement in all phases of procurement of the B-1B aircraft. General Johnson has been directly involved in procuring this vitally needed $20 billion program into our inventory. He provided the SAC position to Congressional staffers during negotiations of the B-1B General Officer Steering Group which defined system requirements and program content. Under his leadership, several other vitally important aircraft programs were brought to completion. For example, he played a leading role in bringing the KC-10 to operational status. General Johnson also took the lead in the effort to re-engine the aging KC-135. This program, costing approximately $6.5 billion, is a major milestone toward improving USAF air refueling capability and will ultimately extend the life of KC-135 fleet well into the next century. He was involved in Strategic Air Command's acquisition of the $8 billion Air Launched Cruise Missile (ALCM) capability. The ALCM capability significantly enhances the SAC bomber force and contributes to the capability and deterrent value of the strategic nuclear forces. General Johnson has been directly responsible for the timely incorporation and problem solution of the many aspects of this complicated, state-of-the-art weapon system. General Johnson's oversight of SAC's requirements demanded that he also be a premier advocate for ICBM modernization. His intense concern for maintaining the ICBM leg of the TRIAD was reflected by his direct involvement in pursuing MINUTEMAN modernization programs and affirming SAC's absolute need for the advanced ICBM, the M-X. His efforts directly contributed to a new awareness of the command's problems in maintaining the current MINUTEMAN force and the development of corrective actions. He provided direction toward insuring that essential requirements are being satisfied in the M-X developmental process. Brigadier General Johnson was instrumental in the establishment of the SAC position advocating the Groundwave Emergency Network, a very LOW-frequency, highly-survivable one-way communications system for positive control launch of aircraft resources and emergency action message dissemination to both aircraft and missile resources. He has also been a strong advocate of the Worldwide Airborne Command Post replacement system. As a result of his personal efforts, a Joint Mission Element Needs Statement was issued in May 1981 that was supported by CINCPAC, CINCLANT, and CINCEUR. This system will replace current EC-135 aircraft with a new aircraft and command control and communications equipment capable of operating during a prolonged period of conflict. As dictated by evolving national policy, General Johnson seized the initiative for SAC and astutely directed an "Analysis of SAC's Capability to Fight a Protracted General War." The Office of the Secretary of Defense has praised the eight-month study, publicly acknowledging its timely, expansive utility to the OSD "Nuclear Weapons Master Plan" which was endorsed by the President. General Johnson structured the analysis to allow SAC to begin immediate implementation of readily achievable solutions to shortfalls in the operations concept, forces, force management and support areas. This includes development of a survivable, enduring force management system for trans/post-attack consisting of an airborne command post, a ground enduring battle management center and the survivable connectivity scheme. Under his incisive guidance, the FY 85-89 SAC POM was structured to accommodate the programmatic imperatives associated with study solutions. As a result, the future of SAC force structure has been positively altered to assure a survivable, enduring deterrent consistent with national policy. General Johnson established additional new initiatives to enhance aircrew and weapon system survivability in a trans/post-attack environment. Two are of particular note: The Nuclear Dust Filtration System will protect the aircrew and essential electronics from the debilitating effects of radiation. Also, the Passive Thermal Protection System will provide protection from nuclear thermal pulse and allow the additional safety an open cockpit provides. Under General Johnson's leadership, SAC took the lead in the emergency rocket communication system (ERCS) scintillation test. The first simulation ever done on a major communications system, the test defined ERCS performance in a nuclear scintillation-degraded environment. General Johnson has also been responsible for the management and direction of the Air Force's largest manpower account. He has established standards of performance by which other major command manpower functions are judged. His guidance and leadership were key to defining manpower requirements necessary for the planned acquisition, deployment and employment of the 8-18, M-X, ALCM, and KC-10 weapons systems. General Johnson seized the opportunity to develop an active interface with the Air Force Board Structure, especially during the FY 82 President's Budget Amendment deliberations. His foresight and support in developing Command requirements assured the acquisition of critical authorizations needed to continue essential weapon systems testing and bed-down. General Johnson's development and forceful advocacy of KC-135 contingency aircraft maintenance manpower resource needs succeeded in gaining the first Air Staff recognition of SAC's wartime manpower requirements. The 2000 authorizations funded in FY 83 provide a quantum improvement in the Command's maintenance posture. His initiatives continued through the development of the FY 83, FY 84, and FY 85 Program Objective Memorandums, where his personal intervention saved a large number of authorizations from deletion. General Johnson provided overall guidance to the Air Force's largest contract cost comparison program. Ninety-nine studies affecting nearly $30 million in manpower resources were conducted. The program was an unqualified success; savings from these studies are accruing at an annual rate of nearly $5 million. He led what is recognized as one of the three best Productivity Investment Programs in the Air Force. Currently approved Productivity Investment Fund projects have a life cycle savings of $170 million. Performing in a most demanding position, General Johnson's tremendous personality, innovative thinking and inspirational leadership have promoted harmonious relationships throughout the Senior SAC Staff. He has made a unique and crucial contribution to the vital national security interests of the United States through his own abilities and efforts, and through the emulation which he has consistently inspired among his fellow airmen. General Johnson's distinguished achievements reflect great credit upon himself, the Strategic Air Command and the United States Air Force.

SIGNED:
General B. L. DAVIS
Commander in Chief
AF/PRP

DEFENSE MERITORIOUS SERVICE MEDAL
to Hansford T. Johnson,
30 October 1985 to 18 December 1986

CITATION

Major General Hansford T. Johnson, United States Air Force, distinguished himself by his highly exceptional meritorious service as the Deputy Chief of Staff, Operations, Strategic Air Command Operations Staff, Strategic Air Command, from 30 October 1985 to 18 December 1986. In this position of great responsibility, General Johnson's dynamic and innovative leadership, managerial perception, and exemplary dedication to duty shaped the operational forces of the Strategic Air Command. His impact on strategic modernization in reflected in significant advances across the entire spectrum of our national deterrence capabilities and will contribute to the security of free world leadership well into the twenty-first century. The distinctive accomplishments of General Johnson reflect great credit upon himself, the United States Air Force, the Organization of the Joint Chiefs of Staff, and the Department of Defense.

Signed
Admiral William Crowe
Chairman, Joint Chiefs of Staff

NARRATIVE

Major General Hansford T. Johnson, United States Air Force, distinguished himself by exceptionally meritorious service to the nation from October 1985 to 18 December 1986 as Deputy Chief of Staff, Operations and Deputy Director Operations, Strategic Air Combat Operations Staff. Headquarters Strategic Air Command. In this position of great responsibility, General Johnson was a driving force in implementing the varied capabilities of our nation's strategic forces and integrating the President's Strategic Modernization Program into our operational forces. In the presence of an ever-expanding threat he has firmly committed our forces to an increased readiness and trained them to assure deterrence across the full spectrum of potential conflict.

General Johnson integrated key elements of this nation's strategic force into the operational inventory. Under his guidance the first B-1B assumed operational alert, three aerial refueling units reached operational status with the KC-135R, and the first Peacekeeper missiles were placed on SlOP alert as a result of the national Strategic Modernization Program. These significant events were instrumental to the command's capability to defend this nation's interests. Through his diligence and leadership this command shall possess a viable deterrent capability well into the next century.

General Johnson's leadership and foresight have contributed immeasurably to the readiness of the Strategic Air Command. His emphasis on training and preparedness during this period of strategic modernization has greatly expanded our nuclear and conventional warfighting posture. He demanded realistic training for all command aircraft. He reorganized the command's combat evaluation group (CEVG) to form a cadre of traveling tactics instructors to "teach" this command how to survive in a wartime environment. Senior officers and crew members alike are now believers, as they complete their respective training sessions. General Johnson also led in the formation of a tactics program for the Strategic Training Complex. This vast bomber training network located in the central U.S. provides an "electronic" war-like environment simulating up-to-date enemy threats. At General Johnson's urging, exercise participation increased significantly. He directed SAC's GLOBAL SHIELD, a JCS sponsored live fly exercise, involving over 100.000 personnel and 1,600 strategic weapons systems. In a 24-hour period over 350 SAC aircraft launched to demonstrate their EWQ mission. He supported other major conventional exercises such as Gallant Eagle, Team Spirit, and Sand Eagle to prove that SAC forces are prepared to fight in the joint arena.

Professionalism became the standard as he challenged the command to capture the warrior spirit, accepting nothing less than excellence in every area of the command's mission. Under his guiding hand, units with a secondary conventional mission are tested during their Operational Readiness Inspections, showing the capability to perform across the spectrum of war. In addition. General Johnson has been a driver in fully utilizing our weapon systems. He expanded the B-52's maritime capabilities, fully utilized the KC-10s vast air refueling and cargo potential, and successfully initiating the introduction of women into the Minuteman and reconnaissance crew force. His adoption of totally realistic training scenarios, complete revision of tactics, and the infusion of a war-winning spirit are examples of his tangible contribution to enhancing the command's capability.

An unsurpassed knowledge of complex technical issues involving ground and space-based warning elements, combined with his expert knowledge of command, control, and communications provided critical leadership to the national adoption of an integrated architecture. General Johnson was instrumental in creating a SAC Command Control Integration Board, serving as focal point for principles and policies for implementing and managing command control systems. He improved reliability, survivability and responsiveness of SAC forces to national guidance through the development on innovative procedures and increased emphasis on command training programs. This program was validated through subsequent exercises and received JCS accolades for the strong positive impact on current and future operations. Notable among numerous accomplishments are his deep involvement in identifying national warning system operational requirements for the 1990s and beyond and improving the network of primary command centers in the national command structure. His capability to marshal resources and achieve consensus across the DOD agencies resulted in achievement of the common goal of state-of-the art communications capability supporting the National Command Authority. The Worldwide Airborne Command Post aircraft entered the execution phase under General Johnson's leadership and is designed to ensure the NCA has the command's forces at their disposal throughout any crisis scenario. These and other communications advancements enhance SAC's effectiveness and improve the nation's capability to meet any aggressor.

General Johnson was the catalyst for many innovative concepts increasing SAC's and the nation's ability to deter, defend, and survive at any level of conflict. Expanding the role of the KC-I0 to enhance the execution of the SlOP is a prime example. The prodigious capabilities of the KC-IO are now available to augment the nuclear deterrent force. The development of tactical concepts for a small ICBM reflect his concern for improving and adopting a viable, affordable, and survivable nuclear asset . Among General Johnson's greatest contributions was his leadership in establishing the Strategic Air Command as a major weapons delivery adaptive to all warfighting arms of the DOD. The bombing, air refueling, and reconnaissance support provide by this command is the key element in this nation's ability to win any potential conflict. Through exercise participation he has proven the value of SAC's forces across the warfighting spectrum.

The capability of existing conventional warfighting forces to defend national interest is undoubtedly enhanced by General Johnson's guiding hand. He organized and directed the massive weapons delivery capability of this command to actively augment naval, theater air component, and allied forces worldwide. Selected Strategic Air Command B-52 units are now anti-ship capable, ready to deliver the Harpoon missile when required to protect vulnerable sea lines of communication.

General Johnson made interoperability and force projection cornerstones of SAC conventional planning strategy. Establishment of land based tanker support for carrier based aviation and planned modifications to tanker forces ensure sufficient support for future and allied tactical operations. SAC bomber and tanker forces now possess formidable long range conventional strike capability--no region of the world is beyond our reach. SAC's ability to carry out the wartime mission is being demonstrated through a new joint conventional operational readiness inspection program. General Johnson directed a realistic test of stateside and overseas multi-command operating locations to ensure SAC can successfully perform their mission in concert with other forces.

The Libya raid in April 1986 was an extraordinary example of SAC's capability while under General Johnson's guidance. He set the tone, refined the tactics, and assured all participants that SAC was ready to carry out the assigned mission. Using SAC tankers as a force multiplier, National Command Authorities successfully executed the largest long-range precision strike since the Southeast Asia conflict. This real-time deterrent demonstration now serves as an example for potential aggressors anywhere in the world.

General Johnson's vital contributions to this nation's full spectrum of deterrence warrant extraordinary recognition. His expertise and leadership has been of supreme value to the nation and its strategic military objectives. His foresight, innovation, and clear direction have produced exceptional growth in capability, readiness, and espirit de corps of our forces. In addition, he has been a stabilizing influence during this evolutionary period in strategic modernization and planning. The dynamic leadership of General Johnson in the development of current and future ICBM. Bomber, reconnaissance, tanker, command/control and communication systems, SIOP and conventional planning, and real world contingencies has assured effective deterrence, security, and the continuation of free world leadership well into the 21st century. He fully deserves the recognition inherent in this award and his accomplishments reflect great credit upon himself, the Strategic Air Command and the United States Air Force.

SIGNED:
General John T. Chain, Jr.
Commander in Chief

THE DEFENSE DISTINGUISHED SERVICE MEDAL
to Hansford T. Johnson, August 1987 to November 1988

CITATION

Lieutenant General Hansford T. Johnson, United States Air Force, distinguished himself by exceptional service as Deputy Commander in Chief, United State Central Command, MacDill Air Force Base, Florida, from August 1987 to November 1988. During this period, the United States Central Command faced its toughest challenges since inception as a Unified Command. The near wartime environment in the Persian Gulf tested the command leadership with situations directly affecting world peace. General Johnson's exceptional skills as a soldier-statesman, strategist and tactician, and persuasive leader provided crucial behind-the-scenes support to the Commander in Chief and the staff of the United States Central Command that guaranteed success. His constant presence, influence, and quiet assistance resulted in lasting and significant betterment of command organizational structure, policies and programs. The distinctive accomplishments of General Johnson reflect great credit upon himself, the United States Air Force and Department of Defense.

Signed
Frank C. Carlucci
Secretary of Defense

NARRATIVE

Lieutenant General Hansford T. Johnson, United States Air Force, is recommended for the award of the Defense Distinguished Service Medal for outstanding service during the period of 7 August 1987 through 23 November 1988. During this period General Johnson distinguished himself by unsurpassed and conspicuous superior performance of duty while serving as Deputy Commander in Chief, United States Central Command (USCENTCOM).

Under General Johnson's inspired leadership USCENTCOM continued to grow and develop as a unified command headquarters honed and fully capable of accomplishing its mission in support of national objectives. USCENTCOM emerged from relative obscurity to a command dominating the world news of the day. Under General Johnson's tutelage and quiet influence, Operation Earnest Will, the naval escort of American flagged ships in the Persian Gulf, was a profound success and had a positive, peaceful influence on world affairs. His behind the scenes leadership, vast experience, insights, and organizational talent touched every level of USCENTCOM. These qualities combined with his exceptional knowledge of the strategic and political implications of joint service activities and feel for the pulse of the organization were crucial in achieving the synergism necessary to enable the command to successfully plan, deploy, exercise, operate, and fight.

General Johnson grasped the significance of thoroughly understanding the AOR, its people, its characteristics and problems. He studied hard and travelled throughout many of the AOR countries to meet with their senior military leaders as well as our foreign service and military officers. Through these contact s and subsequent visits to USCENTCOM by many of the key personalities of these countries, General Johnson developed a rapport and "genuine feel" for the countries and their needs. This "sense" enabled him to focus considerable energies in assisting the CINC to find solutions that precisely addressed critical issues affecting the AOR, thereby furthering US Central Command's military goals as well as the United States' National policies.

His greatest contribution to the command was that of consummate team player and coach. No staff directorate escaped his watchful eye, his words of guidance, or his pat on the back for a tough job General Johnson took the extra time to care about officers, as well as the Generals and Heads of State policy decisions.

Across the spectrum of the day-to-day operations of US Central Command, General Johnson's interest and presence could be felt. Issues ranging from the color of carpet to be installed in the main entrance of the Headquarters building to designation of targets for the command's classified arsenal drew General Johnson's deep personal involvement. Joining the Command at the inception of the Joint Task Force Middle East, (JTFME) his vast experience and unequalled knowledge of air operations and the application of air power in the joint arena was critical to success. He guided planners and operators in finding the optimum solution to the use of a multiplicity of air assets in theater and a command and control apparatus to manage it. During the developmental stages of JTFME and its subsequent evolution and expansion of mission and tasks,

General Johnson adeptly blended the planning talents of all the services to achieve the optimum in warfighting capability.

A visionary, General Johnson applied his inspired brand of leadership to issues internal to the command as well as external. He played a prominent role developing a truly integrated command center capable of continuous operations involving all facets of the staff's functional areas. His quiet influence helped mature a good headquarters staff into a great headquarters capable of performing a myriad of tasks simultaneously with apparent ease. Logistics, operations, intelligence, security assistance - all of these critical elements and more were bettered under his purview as second in command.

As the Deputy Commander in Chief, General Johnson was truly the CINC's right hand. With the CINC half way around the world visiting countries in the AOR, it was business as usual at the headquarters. During the most critical phases of the past year and a half's activities in the Persian Gulf, the CINC relied heavily on General Johnson's sage impeccable advice and judgment.

A master in diplomacy, he routinely worked delicate issues both within DOD and State as well as with the nations in our AOR, always promoting and harmonizing U.S. national interest in the Middle East.

As on site Commander in Egypt for BRIGHT STAR 86 and for GALLANT EAGLE 88 in the California desert, General Johnson provided consistent, inspirational in directing the activities of the thousands of men and women of the United States Central Command and its subordinate commands. His vast operational knowledge and total grasp of joint doctrine ensured a smooth, uninterrupted continuum of command .as operational control passed from the CINC to the on-site Commander.

General Johnson was also responsible for extremely sensitive bilateral planning efforts in the AOR. His keen insights and understanding of the cultures and personalities involved enabled him to provide precisely the right guidance and leadership that ensured acceptance of this vital program.

In summary, General Johnson's USCENTCOM activities. From the formulation of JTFME, the planning and execution of Operation Nimble Archer and Praying Mantis, the responses to the Airbus shoot-down, the ammunition depot explosion in Pakistan, the permeated every aspect of crash of President Zia's aircraft, and most recently the support to the United Nation's sponsored cease-fire, no activity escaped his watchful gaze or subtle influence. His exceptional skills as a soldier-statesman, strategist and tactician and overall persuasiveness as a leader were the behind-the-scene forces responsible for his success in providing outstanding support to the CINC and US Central Command. His contributions over his tenure as Deputy Commander in Chief have served to further the achievements of not only US Central Command but the Nation. The distinctive accomplishments of Lieutenant General Johnson reflect the highest credit upon him, the United States Air Force, the Department of Defense, and the United States Government.

                                        SIGNED:
                                        General George Crist
                                        Commander-in-Chief

THE DEFENSE DISTINGUISHED SERVICE MEDAL (First Oak Leaf Cluster)
to Lieutenant General Hansford T. Johnson
December 1988 to September 1989

CITATION

Lieutenant General Hansford T. Johnson, United States Air Force, distinguished himself by exceptional service as Director, Joint Staff, The Joint Chiefs of Staff, from December 1988 to September 1989. In this extremely critical position, General Johnson was highly instrumental in developing insightful and sensitive military advice for use at the highest levels of the United States government. His ability to grasp and articulate a myriad of constantly changing complex issues enabled him to skillfully and efficiently guide and focus the efforts of the Joint Staff in support of the Chairman and Secretary of Defense. As a result of his extraordinary leadership, sound professional judgment, and personal effort, he substantially influenced the smooth transition of new Administration officials. Through his total dedication, technical expertise, and significant achievements, General Johnson earned the respect and admiration of senior officials and subordinates throughout the Department of Defense. The distinctive accomplishments of General Johnson reflect great credit upon himself, the United States Air Force and the Department of Defense.

Signed:
Dick Cheney
Secretary of Defense

THE DISTINGUISHED SERVICE MEDAL
(First Oak Leaf Cluster)
to General Hansford T. Johnson
21 September 1989 to 31 August 1992

CITATION

The President of the United States of America, authorized by Act of Congress July 9, 1918, awards the Distinguished Service Medal to General Hansford T. Johnson for exceptionally meritorious service in duties of great responsibility. General Johnson distinguished himself as Commander in Chief, Headquarters Military Airlift Command and Headquarters Air Mobility Command, Scott Air Force Base, Illinois, from 21 September 1989 to 31 August 1992. During this period, General Johnson played a key leadership role in the superb accomplishments of the United States Air Force in direct support of our nation's most important national security operations. His innovation in all areas of global air power postured the command to successfully accomplish the nation's largest airlift effort in support of Operation DESERT SHIELD/DESERT STROM. His tireless dedication and personal involvement in the implementation of Total Quality Management principles in the command have ensured Air Mobility Command's resource will continue to be an integral part of America's global reach capability. The singularly distinctive accomplishments of General Johnson culminate a long and distinguished career in the service of his country and reflect the highest credit upon himself and the United States Air Force

Signed:
Merrill McPeak, General
USAF Chief of Staff

THE DEFENSE DISTINGUISHED SERVICE MEDAL
(Second Oak Leaf Cluster)
to Hansford T. Johnson,
September 1989 to August 1992

CITATION

General Hansford T. Johnson, United States Air Force, distinguished himself by exceptional service as Commander in Chief, United States Transportation Command, from September 1989 to August 1992. During this period, General Johnson ensured America's defense transportation system was prepared to respond during any crisis or contingency. This was clearly demonstrated under fire during Operations JUST CAUSE, DESERT SHIELD, DESERT STORM, PROVIDE COMFORT, and PROVIDE HOPE. He led the Transportation Command and its components in meeting all transportation requirements levied by national command authorities. In preparing the Command for the challenges of the post-Cold War era, he was the principal advocate for numerous transportation programs including: modernization of America's airlift fleet, revitalization of the nation's sealift capacity, increased emphasis of intermodalism, continued development of automated logistical planning tools, Total Force integration, and a command-wide commitment to quality. The distinctive accomplishments of General Johnson culminate a long and distinguished career in the service of his country and reflect great credit upon himself, the United States Air Force, and the Department of Defense.

Signed:
Dick Cheney
Secretary of Defense

CERTIFICATE OF APPRECIATION
for Service in the Armed Forces of the United States

General Hansford T. Johnson, USAF

    I extend to you my personal thanks and sincere appreciation of a grateful nation for your contribution of honorable service to our country. You have helped maintain the security of the nation during a critical time in its history with devotion to duty and a spirit of sacrifice in keeping with the proud tradition of the military service.

    I trust that in the coming years you will maintain an active interest in the Armed Force and purposes for which you served.

    My best wishes to you for happiness and success in the future.

                                             Signed:
                                             George Bush
                                             Commander in Chief

THE DEPARTMENT OF THE NAVY
DISTINGUISHED PUBLIC SERVICE AWARD
to The Honorable Hansford T. Johnson
7 January 2003

CITATION

For exceptional service to the Department of the Navy as Assistant Secretary of the Navy (Installations and Environment) from August 2001 to January 2003. Using uncommon vision, astute judgment, and keen insight, Mr. Johnson handled extremely complex and sensitive issues facing the Department of the navy. An exceptionally dedicated and superlative leader, he was directly responsible for the replacement and upgrade of thousands of housing units for the Navy and Marine Corps. Mr. Johnson's knowledge and genuine concern for safety and survivability led to the establishment of the Safety Task Force and a Senior Executive Service position fully dedicated to safety. He continued to advance the environmental enhancement of naval vessels, and was instrumental in establishing additional environmental compliance agreements. In recognition and appreciation of his extraordinarily devoted service, dedication to excellence, and distinguished accomplishments, Mr. Hansford T. Johnson is awarded the Department of the Navy Distinguished Public Service Award.

Signed:
Gordon England
Secretary of the Navy

THE DEPARTMENT OF DEFENSE
MEDAL FOR DISTINGUISHED PUBLIC SERVICE
to Hansford T. Johnson
July 2004

CITATION

Mr. Hansford T. Johnson is recognized for distinguished service as Acting Secretary of the Navy from February 2003 to September 2003, and Assistant Secretary of the Navy for Installations and Environment, from August 2001 to July 2004. Mr. Johnson's visionary leadership, technical expertise, and unmatched professionalism let to significant improvement in the Department of Defense business practices and mission performance. His analytical skills and ability to forge consensus resulted in fundamental changes to the business processes of the Department of Defense installation management program, greatly reducing costs and enhancing mission accomplishment. As Acting Secretary, Mr. Johnson's thoughtful oversight guided Navy and Marine Corps preparedness for and support of major combat operations during Operation IRAQI FREEDOM. He ensured America's Sailors and Marines had the necessary materials for war and their families had what was needed on the home front. A driving force for the Department of Defense in the Base Realignment and Closure process, Mr. Johnson ensured the Department's effort remained on track. He worked with the other Military Department to develop policies and processes to commence Department-wide analysis of infrastructure, both in the United States and overseas. The distinctive accomplishments of Mr. Johnson reflect great credit upon himself, the Department of the Navy, and the Department of Defense.

Signed:
Donald H. Rumsfeld
Secretary of Defense

Made in the USA
Charleston, SC
28 August 2015